17395

Cave, Joy B
What became of Corporal Pittman?
Portugal Cove, Nfld., Breakwater Books,
1976.
xiv, 180, lxviii p. illus., maps.
Includes bibliography.

1. Somme, Battle of the, 1916. 2. Great
Britain. Army. Royal Newfoundland
Regiment. 3. European War, 1914-1918 -
Registers of dead. I. Title.

0919948227 pb   (018859X)
0919948235   0188581 *

What Became of Corporal Pittman?

WHAT BECAME OF
CORPORAL PITTMAN?

17395

MAY 5 '77

Joy B. Cave

BREAKWATER BOOKS LIMITED
NEWFOUNDLAND

Published by
BREAKWATER BOOKS LIMITED
P.O. Box 52, Site C,
Portugal Cove, Newfoundland.

Printed in Canada by
Robinson-Blackmore Printing & Publishing Co. Ltd.
18 O'Leary Avenue
St. John's, Newfoundland.

Cover designed and drawn by
Ian H. Stewart, M.S.I.A. (S.A.)

Canadian Cataloguing in Publication Data

Cave, Joy B
What became of Corporal Pittman?

Bibliography; p.
ISBM 0-919948-23-5 bd.
ISBN 0-919948-22-7 pa.

1. Somme, Battle of the, 1916.
2. Great Britain. Army. Royal Newfoundland Regiment.
3. European War, 1914-1918 — Registers of dead.
I. Title

D545.S7C38   940.4'272   C77-000100-9

Dedication

To the people of Newfoundland and their remarkable fighting men this book is affectionately dedicated.

It was written for P.L. who so nearly understood, and N.R. who always understands.

Permissions

The Regimental Association of the Royal Regiment of Wales for quotes from **The South Wales Borderers 1689-1937** by C.T. Atkinson.

B.T. Batsford Limited for **The Somme** by A.J. Farrar-Hockley.

Cassell and Company for **The Life of General Lord Rawlinson of Trent** by Major General Sir Frederick Maurice and for **History of the First World War** by Sir Basil Liddell-Hart.

G.T. Cheshire and Sons Limited for **The Worcestershire Regiment in the Great War** by Capt. H.F. Stacke, M.C.

Constable Publishers for **The Royal Inniskilling Fusiliers in the World War** by Sir Frank Fox and for **The Unending Vigil** by Philip Longworth.

Curtis Brown Ltd. on behalf of the author and the publishers for **The Battle of the Somme** by John Harris.

Peter Davies Limited for **Sagittarius Rising** by Cecil Lewis.

Gale and Polden Limited for **The History of the Lancashire Fusiliers 1914-1918** by Maj.-Gen. J.C. Latter, C.B.C., M.C.; **The Royal Dublin Fusiliers** by Col. H.C. Wylly, C.B.; **The Border Regiment in the Great War** by Col. H.C. Wylly, C.B.

William Heinemann for **The Royal Fusilliers in the Great War** by H.C. O'Neil.

Hutchinson Publishing Group Limited for **The Great War** by John Terraine.

Thomas Nelson & Sons Limited for **The King's Own Scottish Borderers in the Great War** by Captain Stair-Gillon and **Story of the 29th Division** by Captain Stair-Gillon.

Penguin Books Ltd. for **The First Day on the Somme** by Martin Meddlebrook.

The Times for "Newfoundland and the War" from **The Times History and Encyclopaedia of the War,** December 24, 1917.

The Newfoundland Government for **The Fighting Newfoundlander** (Cabinet Directive C219-76), by Col. G.W.L. Nicholson, C.D.

Mrs. Ollie L. Cramm for **The First Five Hundred** by Richard Cramm.

The Royal Canadian Legion for quotes from the **Veterans Magazine.**

John H. Burrows & Sons for **The Essex Regiment 1st Battalion** by John Wm. Burrows.

Associated Book Publishers Ltd. for **Private Papers of Douglas Haig,** Robert Blake, ed., published by Eyre and Spottiswoode Ltd.

The Hamlyn Publishing Group Ltd., for quotes from **War Memoirs of David Lloyd-George** by the Rt. Hon. D. Lloyd-George.

The Royal Hampshire Regiment for **The Royal Hampshire Regiment 1914-1918** by C.T. Atkinson.

Breakwater wishes to thank Ben Hansen for his work on many of the photographs.

Author's Notes

Very special thanks are offered to the District Director of Veterans' Affairs in St. John's, Mr. Vic Snow, and to his secretary, Miss Joan Wheeler. Without Mr. Snow's specialised knowledge and helpful encouragement, certain difficulties connected with the production of this book would have been well nigh insurmountable.

The author is also very grateful to Major C. Sydney Frost of Toronto, himself a "Blue Puttee" and an authority on the history of the Regiment, who kindly read the original rough draft and pointed out certain errors and omissions.

The author also wishes to thank most sincerely the friends who gave freely of their time and expertise to this project: Mrs. Barbara Broadhead-Williams of West Moors, near Bournemouth, for the prompt and efficient typing of the manuscript and for many invaluable suggestions for its improvement; Miss Olwen Lloyd-Jones of Shrewsbury, who read every hand-written chapter with a critical and helpful eye; Mr. G. Archer Parfitt for patient guidance with many technical problems; Mr. George Waters, A.R.I.B.A., of Shrewsbury, who drew the maps; Mr. Walter Day and Mr. J. Ryan of St. John's, who kindly allowed me to record their memories of the First World War; Mr. and Mrs. C. Parsons and Dr. W.D. Parsons and my many friends in St. John's who were so kind and hospitable on my visits to Newfoundland. I would include in my thanks Mr. Steve Austin, the Warden of the Beaumont Hamel Memorial Park, and his wife, and Mr. A.L. Disher of the Newfoundland Museum, and the staff of the Provincial Archives in Colonial Building, St. John's.

Thanks are due to the Director-General of the Commonwealth War Graves Commission in Maidenhead for the kind co-operation extended by that organisation; also to Miss R. Combes of the Imperial War Museum, to the National Army Museum in London, and to the Public Records Office in Chancery Lane.

Finally, my affectionate thanks to my husband and my daughter who, for five years, cheerfully accepted holidays on old battlefields instead of sunny beaches so that I could pursue my researches, and who gave a willing hand with the innumerable small (but essential) tasks that arise from such activity.

J.B.C.
August, 1976

Foreword I

Honorary Colonel of the
Royal Newfoundland Regiment

Beaumont Hamel, Gueudecourt, Masnieres, Monchy LePreux, Courtrai are rather obscure places in France that will forever mark the history of the former island colony of England in the Western Atlantic, Newfoundland, now the newest of the Canadian Provinces.

The Regiment from Newfoundland was one of many called upon in the Battle of the Somme in France in 1916. Few suffered more grievously. The Regiment's experience, so thoughtfully told by Joy Cave, reflects the many sacrifices made on all sides in that prolonged struggle, while depicting specifically the courage, discipline and loyalty of the men of the Royal Newfoundland Regiment during World War I. The effects of its tragic losses are still being felt in every Newfoundland community.

The Royal Newfoundland Regiment of today is proud of its history and traditions, and this book further enhances its name.

As Honorary Colonel I am pleased to express to Mrs. Cave on behalf of all ranks our sincere appreciation for her work and for her selection of the Regiment in this special way to represent the revered company of the fallen.

G.C. Eaton
Honorary Colonel

Foreword II

Beaumont Hamel is a name that will forever be remembered by all Newfoundlanders. Its story has been told and retold over the years but the detailed presentation of **What Became of Corporal Pittman?** stands out.

The story of the Regiment equals any work of fiction but unfortunately is true. There are so many "ifs" in its story that one would assume fate earmarked the Regiment for the Tragedies of Gallipoli, Beaumont Hamel, Gueudecourt and so many others.

The author has performed a remarkable task in assembling all the facts not only of our Regiment but of all the Divisions and Regiments with whom they fought side by side during World War I. Facts, generally unknown, are presented here.

If this work accomplishes nothing more than presenting the futility of war, it will have served its purpose.

I unreservedly recommend this history of the Royal Newfoundland Regiment to all veterans and their families and feel that it should be included in Memorial University's Library Collection.

Frank Wall
President
Newfoundland & Labrador Command
Royal Canadian Legion

TABLE OF CONTENTS

APPENDICES

Maps

CHAPTER ONE

INTROIT

"And everybody praised the Duke,
Who this great fight did win."
"But what good came of it at last?"
Quoth little Peterkin.
"Why that I cannot tell," said he,
"But 'twas a famous victory."
(Robert Southey - 'The Battle of Blenheim')

"What do you mean?" she demanded. "A whole battalion marched down that slope and just disappeared?"

"I didn't say they disappeared. I said they were annilhilated — inside twenty minutes or so."

Half-memories of other conversations about long ago, faraway things struggled to the surface. "Shelling?" she hazarded.

"Not altogether! Mainly well-placed machine guns."

"Who were they and what were they trying to do? What did they win?"

The sun shone brilliantly from a blue July sky. Overhead, behind the head of the Caribou Memorial, white clouds rushed past. There was little wind at ground level, just enough to set up a whisper in the coniferous trees round the edge of the park.

1

"They were the men of the First Battalion, the Newfoundland Regiment and they were trying to capture the village of Beaumont Hamel — down there, behind the trees. They didn't actually *win* anything. Beaumont Hamel wasn't captured till five months later."

Untroubled youthful eyes surveyed the green slope ahead, the grass-grown trenches and shell-holes. Then she glanced up at the bronze panels at the foot of the memorial with the long, long lists of names incised on them. "Wonder if there's anyone with our name," she mused. "Yes, there is — look, there's a Corporal Cave." She glanced down the lists, murmuring some of the names just out loud, "Ferguson, Galgay, Janes, Melee, Penney, Pike. I suppose they are all on the Roll of Honour in that book of yours?"

I opened the book at random, towards the back pages where the appendices are. The names stared up at us: "3511. Sgt. Pitt, Percy William: 3706. Pte. Pittman, Abel: 3404. Pte. Pittman, Arthur Henry: 2704. Cpl. Pittman, James Warren: 400. Cpl. Pittman, Richard." I closed the book again gently. "They won't all be up there. This is a memorial to those men who have no known graves."

"Poor souls," she said softly. "What a tragedy! What a pity! What a *waste!*"

Perhaps an impatient movement caught her attention, perhaps the silence seemed reproachful or there was some solemn echo. "All right," she demanded, "so tell me about it. What really happened?"

Tell me about it! Where does one begin to explain a situation that arose in a climate of thinking current over half a century ago now. It would be easier or at any rate more credible to her, to try and recreate the atmosphere surrounding the Roman legions that swung along the ruler-straight road that runs from Amiens, through Albert to Bapaume, and, beyond that, to Cambrai. History books deal adequately with the Battle of Waterloo. Dunant's reaction to the forty thousand wounded soldiers at Solferino in 1859 would find a sympathetic echo in her heart. But between this young

woman and her own grandfather is a vast gulf of incomprehension. And clamouring across that gulf are
many discordant voices. Out of the confusion the young
appear to have drawn the conclusion that not only is it
wrong to fight about anything, but there is nothing
worth fighting for any more. Sir Herbert Read, in his
introduction to *Promise of Greatness,* says:

> "War as we have experienced it in this
> century can hardly arouse exaltation. We
> have come to see the utter devastation and
> meaninglessness of war, those cruel
> realities that the blood-stained face of
> history has taken on....War has made us
> and our age harder and more cynical....It
> seems that we have learned war's lessons
> of illusion and disillusion."

Agreed. But there is no pose so easy to adopt as that
of cynicism and disillusion.

It does no service to the memory of these men to
sweep them under the historical carpet as a tragic
irrelevance. The cannon-fodder view is as dangerous
and mistaken as the brave and cheerful crusader view.
They certainly did not look upon themselves as cannon-
fodder or they could not have done what they did: and
what they did was, as far as they were concerned,
irrevocable. There is only the memory left.

Tell me about it! What tone of voice does one adopt
for such a story? Hushed reverence is inappropriate;
flippancy would be obscene; despair would be natural,
but pointless and destructive. It has become a modern
fashion to treat the First World War as a vehicle for
what the twentieth century calls satire. Neither Swift
nor Juvenal perhaps would recognise it as such. There
is a world of difference between ridicule born of
righteous anger barbed with wit, and snide com-
mercialised comment, aimed at making a profit out of
people's natural abhorrence of the horrors and
stupidities of war.

But the question still hangs, unanswered, in the air.
There is an easy way out: "How can I tell you about it?

I wasn't here then. I wasn't even born!'' But the blood-stained face of history is not veiled so easily. They deserve a more courageous effort than that; these simple, quiet men who came two thousand five hundred miles across the grey-green Atlantic to take part in a quarrel that was none of their making and from the outcome of which they could gain no possible advantage, deserve the meed of an answer, however stumbling and inconclusive it might be.

It is very quiet in Hell nowadays, and very peaceful. No one in their right senses, not even an historian, would want to climb into a time machine here, throw the lever into reverse and travel back fifty-eight years. This is the battle-field of the Somme.

It is a scene of decent agricultural economy now. There are no visible scars really and the cemeteries are tactfully placed so that their grim presence does not distress the passing traveller. Not that there are many of those. Few people seem to have pressing business between Albert and Bapaume now. It was different in 1916. There was a deal of traffic then. In the Imperial War Museum in London there is a picture called ''The Road to Bapaume''. The soldiers in that picture would find it difficult to recognise the road today. However, as most of them have tramped their way into eternity one way and another by now, the question does not arise.

The sunlit uplands with their tiny, quintessentially French villages carry on with the timeless business of producing food with purposeful determination. The four years of spoiling and wastage might never have been: except that the spring ploughing still, more than half a century later, turns up old shell-cases — especially those of gas shells. These are neatly stacked in rows in the ditches by the sides of the fields. Then they disappear. One assumes that some scrap-metal merchant removes them and they are processed into ploughshares (or car bodies). The one mineral in which the soil of Picardy cannot possibly be deficient is iron!

One of the more remarkable features of this countryside is the resolute way in which the French reconstituted it, as exactly as they could, as it was in 1914. A comparison between the maps (scale 1:40,000) used by Sir Douglas Haig in 1916 and the maps (scale 1: 50,000) printed by the Institut Geographique National, drawn in 1934 and revised in 1958 and 1970, show this very clearly. The population below ground must be one of the densest in the world, but above ground it is a quiet farming area again. Beaumont Hamel, a spot of brick rubble in a brown waste in 1917, is back on the map in exactly the same place in 1970, as a sleepy hamlet minding its own business. Delville Wood and High Wood have grown again. The spectral matchsticks and splintered remains are replaced by a tall green growth. Not that anyone seems minded to take a summer stroll in their shade, but they are back where they were.

There is a fine new motorway on the eastern edge of the battlefield, that streamlines the holiday traffic from the northern ports, past Arras and Bapaume, down to the sun in the south. But it is on another plane in time. The Somme takes no heed of the motorway, nor the motorway of the Somme. The name itself is misleading: the Somme marks the southern boundary of the great battles as far as the British are concerned. It is the Ancre stream, a slow brown tributary of the river Somme, that wound its way through the centre of the really important goings-on so long ago.

"So what really happened?" Perhaps that is the best place to begin answering the question.

CHAPTER TWO

OVERTURE AND BEGINNERS

"Man's inhumanity to man
Makes countless thousands mourn''.
('Man was made to Mourn' - Robert Burns)

The Newfoundland Battalion's story is but a paragraph in the bitter chapter of history known as the Battle of the Somme. The battle began on 1st July, 1916: it squelched to a halt in the winter rains on 19th November, 1916 — between those dates a number of actions were fought, but the whole series of engagements is known collectively as the Battle of the Somme.

However, the interest that this particular battalion had in the battle ceased in the first few hours of the first day because — like so many others — the battalion itself (as such) ceased to exist.

The description of a tremendous military operation like the Somme presents particular difficulties. The main problem is the sheer inchoate mass of the happenings to be described. But military activities were carefully planned on the basis of the units involved and the groupings of those units, so one might begin there.

In those days the British Army fought by battalions, not by regiments. A battalion consisted of 992 other ranks and 30 officers. The battalion was sub-divided into four companies and each company comprised four platoons, and there were four sections to each platoon.

There were four battalions to a brigade, three brigades to a division. The three infantry brigades were supported by artillery — normally 76 guns. Of these, 54 were 18-pounders, 18 were 4.5 howitzers and 4 were 60-pounders. There were 24 machine guns to each division.

The 29th Division consisted of the 86th, 87th and 88th Brigades. The Divisional emblem was a narrow red triangle — in reality half a diamond. It was designed by Major-General Sir Beauvoir de Lisle, the divisional commander, to remind all ranks of the importance of the diamond as a military formation in open fighting from a patrol to an Army.

The 86th Brigade consisted of the 2nd Battalion Royal Fusiliers, 1st Battalion Lancashire Fusiliers, 1st Battalion Royal Dublin Fusiliers and 16th Battalion Middlesex Regiment.

The 87th Brigade comprised 2nd South Wales Borderers, 1st Kings Own Scottish Borderers, 1st Royal Inniskilling Fusiliers and 1st Border Regiment.

The 88th Brigade was made up of 4th Worcestershire Regiment, 2nd Hampshire Regiment, 1st Essex Regiment and the 1st Battalion of the Newfoundland Regiment.

The 29th Division, together with 4th and 31st Divisions, made up VIII Army Corps under the command of Lieutenant-General Sir Aylmer Hunter-Weston. In Gallipoli the genial "Hunter-Bunter" had been the General Officer Commanding the Division until 23rd May, 1915, when he had been promoted to the command of VIII Corps. According to the 29th Divisional History,

> It was a happy reunion for both Commander and commanded, and even those who came to Gallipoli too late to serve under the corps commander, and those who had not been in Gallipoli at all, felt their backs straighten as they looked "eyes left" at him at Marieux on the route march to the French front.... [1]

One is reminded unhappily of Siegfried Sassoon's poem, "The General", concerning another high-ranking officer in a later battle.

He's a cheery old card
Grunted Harry to Jack
As they slogged up to Arras
With rifle and pack.
But he did for them both with his plan of attack.

In fairness to General Hunter-Weston, his VIII Corps undoubtedly had one of the most difficult tasks on the whole front that summer morning. His three divisions were required to attack over ground which lay over-whelmingly in the enemy's favour. Whatever plan of attack the General and his staff decided upon, geographically the cards were stacked against them.

The northern boundary of the sector in which VIII Corps' responsibilities lay, was four miles south of Gommecourt at the southern extremity of the ridge on which Gommecourt lies. Just north-east of the Corps boundary was the heavily-fortified village of Serre. In this area two ridges or spurs, Redan Ridge and Hawthorn Ridge, run out south-eastwards. About halfway up the re-entrant (or gully) between these two ridges lay the fortified village of Beaumont Hamel.

During the "quiet" months of 1915 on this front the Germans had been working efficiently and in-dustriously to strengthen their defences. ("Quiet" on the Western Front meant a steady drain of casualties day by day along the whole length of the line). However, during this period a formidable complex of trenches was dug, deep and well-revetted, with barbed wire entanglements in front. Dug-outs — deep, dry, comfortable and reasonably safe from artillery barrages — protected the German troops when they "stood down" from the trenches themselves. Cellars and ground-floor rooms in the villages were reinforced and strengthened. Redoubts, thick concrete forts bristling with guns, were built to guard particularly tender spots. The Heidenkopf, a square of reinforced and covered trenches, guarded the road between Beaumont Hamel and Serre. There was a redoubt on Redan Ridge and another on Hawthorn Ridge. There were natural strong points, such as the old chalk mine halfway back along Redan Ridge, that the German troops worked up into a formidable defensive position known as the Bergwerk. South of Beaumont Hamel, just behind the German front line of trenches, was a most useful defensive natural feature known to military history as Y Ravine. It was a very steep-sided cleft that ran up from just above the Ancre. It provided the Germans with a well-hidden sanctuary in which they sited a number of machine guns: these machine guns were to play an important part in the battle so far as the Newfoundlanders were concerned.

In addition to the professional activities of the German military engineers, the natural contours of the land were not favourable for attack from the western side. In front of the British trenches the ground sloped away across No Man's Land and then rose to the east, ridge upon ridge, so that banks of fire could be brought to bear upon the attackers.

Across this unpromising terrain lay the task allotted to VIII Corps. This was to squeeze open the left flank of the Fourth Army by pushing the enemy northward through the village of Serre. In order to achieve this it was necessary to capture both ridges on either side of Beaumont Hamel, and Beaumont Hamel itself.

There were four main options open to the Commander of VIII Corps. He could attack Serre directly, but a frontal attack could not hope to obtain a quick decisive result which was what was required by Fourth Army for the success of the overall battle plan.

A left-hand punch along the northern spur would have carried the troops round behind Beaumont Hamel, effectually isolating it. But the left flank would then have been open to attack from the grim fortifications of Serre.

Similarly, a right-handed approach over the southern spur, Hawthorn Ridge, would expose the battalions on a forward slope directly on to the village and the lower end of the re-entrant that there descends to the Ancre.

To move the bulk of VIII Corps down the valley between Redan Ridge and Hawthorn Ridge from Auchonvillers would merely have presented a compressed and concentrated target for every German heavy gun within range. Despite the Charge of the Light Brigade, this was an almost untenable proposition.

In the event, it was decided to compromise, to make the best of an obviously difficult job. Two main attacks were to be mounted simultaneously over both northern and southern spurs. To protect the left flank of the assault troops on Redan Ridge as the advance progressed, the 31st Division was to wheel north-east

9

and evict the defenders of Serre. In the centre a force advancing down the re-entrant would link operations of the attacking forces to north and south.

So the plan was made and approved and meshed-in with other larger plans because this was the way the military machine worked. An old soldier, a survivor of these campaigns of long ago and therefore entitled to a respectful hearing, once remarked that it was the easiest thing in the world to sit in a comfortable chair in an England at peace and spread out the maps and the battle dispositions and criticise the generals. "But", he remarked severely, "if you could transport those clever chaps back across the years to 1916, and set them the same problems with the conditions then obtaining, do you think they would have done any better? I don't think so!"

It was the southern spur, Hawthorn Ridge, that concerned the 29th Division.

The 88th Brigade was, in one sense, bringing up the rear in the battle. The Division was deployed over a front of about two thousand yards with three objectives, the furthest of which was about five thousand yards ahead - just under three miles! It was to the capture of this third objective, the Puisieux Trench just beyond the Grandcourt-Puisieux road, that the 88th Brigade was assigned.

Ahead of them the 86th and 87th Brigades would clear the way: the 86th on the left, in front of Beaumont Hamel: the 87th on the right, in front of Y Ravine. Their job was to capture the front line trench position, extending from the fortified village of Beaumont Hamel roughly along Station Road. Then they were to proceed to their second objective, the German Intermediate line on the Beaucourt to Beaumont Hamel road.

When all this had been accomplished, the 88th Brigade would pass through the other two brigades and advance beyond them to finish the job. It was envisaged that the final half mile surge towards Puisieux Trench would begin at three hours and ten minutes after zero hour.

In the event, the 88th Brigade covered scarcely the first half mile of their menacing three mile journey.

10

And by half past ten — three hours and ten minutes after zero — most of the Brigade had lost interest in Puisieux Trench or any trench or in anything at all in the living-world.

But during the night of June 30th all that was still in the future, and the 29th Division was assembling in its battle stations. In case the word assembling carries with it any association of ideas of a coming together of a body of persons in a normal manner of proceeding, it should perhaps be pointed out here that in 1916 a soldier in the British Army went into battle with a minimum load of 66 lbs distributed around his person. In "fighting order" he carried a haversack containing shaving gear and extra socks, the unconsumed portion of the day's ration allowance, special emergency rations, a gas helmet and goggles, field-dressings and iodine; in addition a rolled ground-sheet, a water-bottle, a steel helmet, an entrenching tool, wire-cutters, a mess-tin, two sandbags and 220 rounds of ammunition burdened him — and a rifle. Most of them carried items extra to this basic load: shovels, picks, wire, corkscrew stakes, extra bombs, flares and other items. Higher authority had considered every possible eventuality, but had missed one rather obvious point: a man, however strong, is not a mule. A man so burdened is physically incapable of moving at a pace speedier than a slow plod. They must have had a very high opinion of the strength and fitness of their rank and file, those Generals!

It is to be hoped that they did have a high opinion of these men: judging by their subsequent pronouncements, wherever the blame lay for the frustration of their "Big Push", it did not lie upon the fighting men. The generals were not quite sure at the time what had gone wrong; but, to do them justice, they did not blame the patient over-burdened khaki-clad masses who strove their utmost to carry out the plans so carefully made. There was one notable exception. The Commander-in-Chief recorded in his Diary:

North of the Ancre, VIII Corps (Hunter-Weston) said they began well, but as the day progressed, their troops were forced back.... I am inclined to believe from further reports, that few of VIII Corps left their trenches.[2]

Unfortunately, Generals, like other human beings, have prejudices. General Haig disapproved of Sir Aylmer Hunter-Weston and his 29th Division because they had been concerned in the Gallipoli campaign, which Haig had disliked intensely, as resources from the Western Front had been diverted to it. Illogically, he transferred this dislike from the campaign to the people involved in it: illogically, because doubtless if Sir Aylmer Hunter-Weston and the Twenty-Ninth had been consulted in the matter they would have admitted a distaste for the venture in that hideous peninsula — and with far more cogent reasons! It seems regrettable that Sir Douglas did not see fit to erase or to amend that entry in the light of later information. Perhaps he felt that it should stand, because that was what he honestly thought at the time, and that his later recorded statements would serve to put matters straight. Whatever his reasons, it seems a pity that this rather mean comment was left on record for history to observe.

The last day of June had brought beautiful summer weather. At nine o'clock that evening, the Newfoundland soldiers answered their names at roll-call in the village of Louvencourt where they had been billeted. A total of 776 N.C.O.s and men, together with 25 officers and their Commanding Officer, Colonel Hadow, marched off to keep their appointment with history.

They marched at attention for the first two hundred yards down the road to Acheux-en-Amienois. Then they marched at ease with their rifles slung, singing "Keep the Home Fires Burning". East of Acheux they halted for half an hour while the darkness thickened. The roads and tracks normally used to march towards Auchonvillers had been subjected to heavy German shelling, so the battalion, in single file, crossed the open fields south of Mailly-Maillet. It was a noisy night. The British field-guns were exceedingly busy hammering away at the German trenches and the German wire. The boom and crash and swish of the heavy calibre shells was interspersed with the clang, bang, clatter of the field batteries. The din, hideous as it was, must have been heartening to the soldiers stumbling across the dark fields. After such a prolonged and searching bombardment of white-hot steel and crushing explosion, surely the opposition facing them the next morning could not be insuperable? There had been confident predictions that the artillery would have cleared the way, that the men could walk over that three hundred odd yards of No Man's Land. In any case they had prepared for the morrow's task with many hours of exhaustive training. They knew exactly where they had to go and what they had to do. And yet — and yet there had been the trench raid led by Captain Butler on June 26th that had revealed the dismaying fact that, despite the incessant thundering of the artillery for several days previously, the thick belts of barbed wire in front of the German trenches were still more or less intact.

Whatever their private thoughts on the matter of barbed wire and the enemy to be faced on the dawning of the next day, the Newfoundlanders arrived at the entrance to Tipperary Avenue, the deep communication trench south of Auchonvillers. Here they spent a nerve-wracking period in the open waiting for another battalion of the Division to get clear of the trench. At 2 a.m. they had passed through Tipperary Avenue and settled down in their particular 750 yard section of the St. John's Road support trench directly opposite the Y Ravine.

To report that they settled down is misleading. Despite five hours of marching there was little sleep for anyone. There were heavier battle stores such as trench bridges and bangalore torpedoes to be issued to those detailed to carry them into action. In the early hours of that fateful Saturday morning carrying parties brought up hot food from the regimental cookers assembled in a wood near Englebelmer.

There was a period of waiting in the cool dampness of the night. Men dozed or smoked or talked to their neighbours. Officers made final inspections: at 6.25 a.m. an intensive bombardment began and battalion officers went to the Brigade Major to synchronise watches.

At 7.20 a.m. the great Hawthorn Mine went up. Forty thousand pounds of ammonal sixty-five feet below the German strong-point known as the Hawthorn Redoubt on the crest of the Ridge immediately opposite Beaumont Hamel was detonated. A thousand yards away the waiting Newfoundlanders felt the minor earthquake and saw the gigantic mushroom of earth, stones and debris climbing hundreds of feet into the air. In *Sagittarius Rising,* C. Lewis described a similar mine explosion at La Boiselle, seen from an aeroplane:

> ....the earth heaved and flashed, a tremendous and magnificent column rose up into the sky. There was an ear-splitting roar, drowning all the guns, flinging the machine sideways in the repercussing air. The earthy column rose, higher and higher to almost four thousand feet. There it hung, or seemed to hang, for a moment in the air, like the silhouette of some great cypress tree, then fell away in a widening cone of dust and debris.... [3]

The timing of this explosion had been the subject of much discussion in the planning conferences held before the attack. General Hunter-Weston, very wisely, had advised that the mine should be blown four hours before the attack commenced, i.e. at 3.30 a.m. in the hours of darkness: this would enable the resulting crater, an important new military feature on the German side of No Man's Land, to be occupied before the main attack began. Also a four hour interval supervening between explosion and attack might have lulled the Germans into a sense of false security. Such a tremendous explosion in their front line in the darkness would inevitably have caused much confusion. They would, quite properly, have been commanded to stand-to in anticipation of an imminent attack. When this did not materialise, either they would have had to stand down again or they would have remained in their trenches and been caught in the last hour of intense bombardment.

General Haig's Inspector of Mines pointed out that the Germans in the past had proved much quicker and more efficient at occupying disputed mine craters than the British. There was some reason in this point of view. So the British taste for compromise solutions again settled the question. The mine was to be blown at zero minus ten. Like many compromises it managed to combine the worst of two possible worlds. General Hunter-Weston must surely have regretted his agreement to the new timing. For one thing, in order to allow the British infantry time to rush and to occupy the crater, the barrage from the big guns and howitzers of the Corps onto the German front line would cease fire for the critical ten minutes before zero and concentrate on the German reserve trenches. So the Germans in the front line would not have their attention distracted from their khaki targets by a rain of high explosive shells. Secondly, the detonation of the mine answered a question with which the Germans had previously been troubled — the exact day and time of the attack.

That there was going to be an attack they were well aware. The tremendous artillery preparation, the lanes cut in the British wire, the bridging of the rear trenches and many other unmistakable portents signalled an offensive on the way. The German army of that time was one of the finest professional fighting machines the world has ever seen: it would have been difficult to hoodwink, even supposing anyone had tried to do so. In the event no one tried. The element of surprise, tactically so important in any battle, was completely absent from the preparations for the Somme. The British might just as well have printed large posters saying "Very soon now we are going to mount an attack": in Sheffield on 1st June, the Parliamentary Secretary to the Ministry of Munitions had appealed for a postponement of the Bank Holiday. On the 2nd June, the Labour Adviser to the Government, Arthur Henderson, made a speech in Leeds to munition workers; it contained these words:

> It should suffice that we ask for a post-
> ponement.... to the end of July. This fact
> should speak volumes. [4]

It did indeed, and it spoke volumes not only to the Leeds munition workers. The speech was reported in several leading London papers. Copies of these eventually made their way, via neutral Holland, to the desks of prominent German personages including Crown Prince Rupprecht of Bavaria. He was a most capable German Army commander, and this hint with hob-nailed boots on only served to confirm his own impressions. There were many obvious signs of impending trouble and German Intelligence carefully garnered and correlated them all. The only important question left for the Germans to answer was, "When exactly does it all begin?" The question of where the blow was going to fall they had worked out for themselves reasonably accurately although von Falkenhayn found it difficult to believe that the British would attack the strongest part of the German defences. In his opinion there would be an allied offensive in Alsace-Lorraine. Nevertheless, General Von Below, the commander of the German Second Army on the Somme, received reports of the feverish activity behind the British lines and quietly made plans to counter it. Falkenhayn made no effort to place adequate reserves behind either the Second Army or its neighbour farther north, Prince Rupprecht's Sixth Army.

When the mine went up on Hawthorn Ridge at 7:20 a.m. on Saturday, July 1st, the soldiers of the 119th Reserve Regiment opposite the 29th Division realised only too clearly that this was the signal for an infantry attack, and reacted as they had been trained to do.

Three sections and more of 9 Company had been blown into the air, but the remaining Wurttembergers got ready on the lower steps of their dug-outs, rifles in hand, waiting for the barrage to lift. Then they rushed up the steps to man their line and certain pre-selected shell craters. What they saw as they peered over No Man's Land is recorded in their regimental history:

"Ahead of us, wave after wave of British troops were crawling out of their trenches, and coming towards us at a walk, their bayonets glistening in the sun." [5]

CHAPTER THREE

THE FIRST WAVE

Oh, this is the song of the Twenty-ninth,
On every field you'll find it;
For wherever the Red Triangle went
It left its mark behind it.
(The Song of the 29th Division
by Lancelot Cayley Shadwell)

From left to right of 29th Division's front the soldiers that the Germans saw advancing towards them were the First Battalion Lancashire Fusiliers; the second Battalion Royal Fusiliers; the Second Battalion South Wales Borderers; the First Battalion King's Own Scottish Borderers. They did not walk very far in most cases.

Apart from the rifle and machine gun fire of the infantry, the German heavy guns added their screaming quota of white-hot metal fragments to the hail of bullets flying to meet the advancing British troops. It had been calculated that the German heavy artillery had been effectually silenced by the colossal bombardment laid down by the British guns during the previous weeks: but a number of the German guns had not fired during that period. It is the flash of a gun firing that gives away its position, alerting the opposing batteries to deal effectively with it by what is known as counter-battery fire. These previously mute monsters opened wide their mouths around half past seven on that bright Saturday morning, and they spoke of Death in unanswerable fury.

A man is a soft-bodied animal: he is a wonderfully complex amalgam of brain, nerves, blood, flesh and sinew mounted on an equally marvellous articulated framework; this skeletal framework, though hard, is brittle. Oppose to any man, however strong and fit and courageous he may be, a rain of white-hot steel and the steel will win. Oppose waves of men — thousands of them — to the walls of steel and the issue is still in no doubt. Steel has no morals, no aims, no feelings: it runs its appointed course and if it meets a soldier it makes a hole in him. Thereafter he ceases to be a soldier, a fighting man, either because he is dead and has ceased to function as a human being at all, or because his central nervous system is jangling the warning bell of pain. Put in such elementary terms why should any civilised society put its young, fit males into such a position vis-a-vis this all-conquering steel? It is a murderous nonsense (as, of course, it was).

But steel is aimless until someone aims it. Behind every bomb, every bullet, every shell is a man's eye and a man's hand. Militarily the argument runs thus: if matters can be so arranged that sufficient numbers of human beings on the opposing side — hereinafter called the enemy — have holes drilled in them or bits blown off them by steel and iron directed at them by the human beings on this side — hereinafter called our troops — then our troops can occupy that portion of land previously occupied by the enemy. This is known as a victory. Humanity has been settling disputes in this fashion since the beginning of recorded time. The odd thing about the whole situation is that, in cold fact, no dispute has ever been satisfactorily settled in this way. All that has ever happened is that the conclusion of any war merely breeds the start of another one some time in the future. Shakespeare puts into the mouth of the Norwegian captain in *Hamlet* words that describe the situation exactly:

> We go to gain a little patch of ground
> That hath in it no profit but the name.
> To pay five ducats five, I would not farm it;
> Nor will it yield to Norway or the Pole
> A ranker rate should it be sold in fee....

The First Battalion, the Lancashire Fusiliers and the Second Royal Fusiliers led the left of the Twenty-Ninth Division's line "to gain a little patch of ground" which included the most eastern thrust of the spur of Hawthorn Ridge and the village of Beaumont Hamel itself.

In the unemotional words of the Lancashire Fusiliers'
Regimental History:

To the north of the River Ancre, and just
to the left of the ground where the Salford
battalions fought on 1st July, lay another
important objective, the Grandcourt-Serre
ridge. This was the goal of the VIII Corps,
in which the 1st and 2nd Battalions were
serving, in the 29th and 4th Divisions
respectively. The distance from the British
front line to the ridge was about two
thousand yards, and the plan of attack
allowed the troops three hours and twenty
minutes to cross it. The Germans had
protected the ridge by a very formidable
series of defences, many of which lay in
valleys and out of sight of British artillery
observers and were consequently not
touched by the long preliminary bombardment. The most deadly of these was
the strongly fortified village of Beaumont
Hamel, lying in a salient of the front
system, which could cover with flanking
fire all the ground to be crossed by the 29th
and 4th Divisions. It stood right in the path
of the former, the 4th being immediately on
the left of the 29th. One of its outposts was
Hawthorn Redoubt, under which a large
mine had been prepared. After much
controversy, it was decided to explode this
mine at 7.20 a.m. on 1st July, ten minutes
before the attack was to be delivered. The
unfortunate effect of this decision was that
the Germans, who had been warned by the
seven days' bombardment that a big offensive was imminent and were uncertain
only as to the day and hour of its launching,
rightly interpreted the explosion as the
signal for the attack and thus had ten
minutes' grace in which to man their
trenches and make their final

preparations. These were helped by the fact that all the British heavy artillery had to stop firing on the front trenches when the mine blew up so as to avoid the risk of hitting the parties seizing the crater. When the troops of the 29th Division came to leave their own trenches, their only covering fire was a thin barrage of 18-pounder guns, Stokes mortars and machine guns.

The 1st Battalion (Lieutenant-Colonel M. Magniac, D.S.O.) had been in the Beaumont Hamel district since it came to France from Egypt in March, 1916. From 15th to 29th June, the majority of it was at Mailly Wood, practising the attack. "C" Company, however, and the ten per cent battle reserve, under Major A.T. Le M. Utterson, Leicestershire Regiment, took over a portion of the line on 23rd June and carried out a series of patrols and raids in order to discover the state of the German wire at various stages of the preliminary bombardment and whether the enemy was manning his front line. On 29th June the main body was addressed by the Divisional Commander, Major-General H.B. de Lisle, who said: "To you has been set the most difficult task — that of breaking the hardest part of the enemy's shell". That evening it went up into the line.

The Battalion's objective was the village of Beaumont Hamel itself. Between this and the British front line lay a sunken road, between ten and fifteen feet deep and running north and south, shallow at its northern end but overhung and lined with trees at the southern. Tunnels had been dug from the British front line to this natural trench, and one of these was opened up on the night before the attack, whereupon at 3.30 a.m. on 1st July, "B" and "D" Companies, with the Brigade Bombing Company and eight Stokes mortars, occupied the sunken road. Battalion headquarters moved thither at 7 a.m., at which time the Germans began shelling the road with field guns, having apparently noticed the communication trench made by the tunnels. Hot breakfasts were issued to all ranks; and several photographs were taken in the sunken road by Mr. Malins, the official photographer. Officers were dressed like the men. The latter each carried 120 rounds of ammunition, two days' rations and two bombs; the leading companies carried fifty shovels and ten picks each; each platoon carried two trench bridges; and men of the rear companies carried engineer stores. Few could get much sleep before the attack owing to the incessant roar of the bombardment.

At 7.20 a.m. the mine below Hawthorn Redoubt exploded, and "B" and "D" Companies lined up for the attack while the 86th Stokes Mortar Battery opened a hurricane bombardment. At 7.30 a.m. the leading sections of those companies moved forward and "A" Company began to leave the front line to support them. The first two lines of "B" and "D" Companies had not moved many yards when enemy machine guns opened fire. Their third and fourth lines were almost annihilated as they left the sunken road, and only a few wounded, including the two company commanders (Captains G.P. Nunneley and C.F. Wells), succeeded in crawling back into it. "A" Company also suffered heavily in its advance to the sunken road, but Captain E.G. Matthey managed to reach its northern end with a few men and to push on a short way before he fell mortally wounded. "C"

Company was caught by machine-gun fire as it left the front line, Captain E.M. Dawson and Company Sergeant-Major Nelson being hit as they stood up to give the order to advance. One platoon was blocked by wounded in the communication trench leading to the sunken road. But Second-Lieutenant W.R.B. Caseby and about sixty men reached the latter, though they were so encumbered with coils of wire and tools that many of them rolled down its steep banks and half an hour's delay resulted before the remnants of "A" and "C" Companies could be reorganized for a further advance.

Sergeant Caulfield, a Lewis gunner, spotted a German machine gun firing from behind some debris in the village and pointed it out to Lieutenant-Colonel Magniac, who ordered two Lewis guns to engage it. But no sooner had they opened fire than they were shelled by field guns, one gun being hit — a tribute to the quickness and accuracy of the German observation. The machine gun, however, did not again fire from the same position.

At 8.15 a.m. Lieutenant-Colonel Magniac ordered the Stokes mortars to open a rapid burst of fire, under cover of which Caseby was to lead forward some seventy-five men who had been collected, with a view to gaining a footing in the northern end of the village, where the ground was higher and promised a good field of fire. The party dashed forward with great bravery, but were caught by machine-gun fire as they topped the crest a few yards from the sunken road and were mown down, only Caseby, Lieutenant I. Gorgunkle and about ten men reaching the German wire.

It was by then evident that the battalion could not succeed in its task and, though the brigadier issued orders for a further attack at 12.30 p.m., with an artillery bombardment, he immediately countermanded them on hearing that Lieutenant-Colonel Magniac had by now only about seventy-five men and one officer in the sunken road and some fifty in the front line and elsewhere, while over one hundred wounded lay in the road. He ordered Lieutenant-Colonel Magniac to reorganize his battalion to make sure of holding the sunken road and watch his left flank. But before this fresh order arrived, an attempt was made to comply with the original message, Captain E.W. Sheppard doing very useful work in trying to collect unwounded men; and at 12.30 p.m. Major Utterson advanced with the only men he could collect, some twenty-five in all, with the intention of attaching to himself the unwounded men in the sunken road and pushing on to the German lines. Actually, he and four men alone survived to reach the road.

The afternoon was spent in trying to organize the road for defence. German shells caused more casualties; and snipers killed a good many of the wounded as they moved or tried to put on their field-dressings. At 6 p.m. the sunken road was evacuated except for a party of one officer and twenty-five men detailed to hold it during the night. After dark all available stretcher-bearers and other men searched for wounded. Throughout the night wounded men crawled in; and about midnight Second-Lieutenants G.R. Spender, I. Gorfunkle, G.R. Craig and Caseby came in with about twenty men, having spent the day in a small hollow just short of the German wire, too weak in numbers to force their way through, but able to make a useful contribution to the battle by keeping up a flanking fire towards Hawthorn Redoubt.

The day had cost the battalion many casualties: 7 officers had been killed and 14 wounded; of the other ranks, 156 were killed, 298 wounded and 11 missing. The brigadier in his report recorded his opinion that he did not think that any troops could have taken the German line as held that day. Indeed, it was not captured until 13th November, 1916, and then only by two brigades, with the help of special artillery preparation and a new method of using gas. [1]

So much for the Lancashire Fusiliers. What then of the Second Battalion, the Royal Fusiliers, on their right? Their regimental historian reports their story as follows:

From first to last no fewer than twenty battalions of Royal Fusiliers were engaged in the battle of the Somme. But no other Fusilier unit fought so unsatisfying an action with such heavy loss as did the Second Battalion. Its role was to hold the German reserves and occupy his artillery in order to assist the main attack south of the Ancre. But, as ill-fortune would have it, the enemy had expected the main attack on the front allocated to holding and subsidiary attacks, and the units engaged there suffered accordingly.

He goes on to describe the elaborate preparations for the Somme battle, including the great mine and the Battalion's efforts to occupy the ensuing crater.

Upon the battalion front the attack never had any chance of success. When "D" Company reached the mine crater they were only able to occupy the nearer lip as the other side was already held by the Germans. No advance could be made there, and on the rest of the front few of the men reached the enemy's wire. The British barrage was persistent in its attentions to the second and third lines of the German first defensive system, with the consequence that the battle was restricted to the first line where, armed with an ample supply of machine guns, the enemy was able to crush every attempt to rush it. At midday the few men remaining in No Man's Land had to give up the futile attempt and retire. The losses of the battalion had been very terrible. [2]

The extent of the casualties among senior officers is noted and then the historian tells a touching story about one of the wounded soldiers.

Captain Goodliffe, who was to have occupied the German front line when captured, examined the wounded in order to gain information. One poor fellow, whose jaw was shattered, could only mumble, but he insisted on telling his story. A guess was made at his meaning, "We are doing no good on the right". When this was repeated to him, he nodded and smiled, and went off to the dressing-station. Such was the spirit of the men in one of the worst experiences of the war.

The total casualties for the day amounted to 490, including 20 officers, 3 of them killed. This was in addition to the 8 officers who became casualties during the preliminary bombardment....

For forty-eight hours the wounded dribbled in, some of them mad. The Germans left their trenches under a Red Cross flag and collected some of the wounded.

They also removed Lewis guns on stretchers, a slight blot on otherwise unexceptional behaviour.

On the right of the Royals was the 87th Brigade. The Royals' nearest neighbours were the men of the Second Battalion, the South Wales Borderers. As the unfortunate soldier with the shattered jaw had insisted, they were "doing no good" either. Their regimental history records their plight:

Of the seven battalions of the Twenty-fourth on the Western Front only one actually "went over the top" on July 1st, 1916, when the great struggle of the Somme opened. Before July was out all but one were to have fighting enough and to spare in "the Somme", but on that day of desperate fighting, terrible losses and mixed success and failure, it fell to the 2nd Battalion only to sustain the Regiment's reputation for self-sacrifice, steadiness, determination and devotion to duty....

The 2nd. S.W.B. on the left of their brigade, faced the Southern side of the salient round the head of Y Ravine. It had A, C and D Companies in line from left to right with B in support; on its right the Inniskillings were attacking, the Borderers were to follow it, to go through it when the attack reached Station Road in the bottom of the valley 700 yards away, and to tackle the second objective....

During the night companies moved up to their assigned positions, to the accompaniment of considerable artillery activity. The men were heavily laden; indeed they could hardly be seen for the things they had to carry, and they spent a cold and cheerless night in the closely packed trenches. At 5 a.m. on July 1st hot tea was served out, at 6 a.m. our guns began a steady bombardment, which developed into an intense one an hour later. At 7.20 our big mine near the Hawthorn Redoubt on the 86th Brigade's frontage was exploded. It was the biggest yet fired, and sent a huge cloud of earth and stones 100 feet high, and the explosion shook the earth for a long way round. It seemed impossible that any Germans could have survived it, and hopes ran high as the companies began getting out of our trenches and filed through the gaps in our wire in readiness to assault. It was ominous that directly they reached the outer edge of our wire, not 100 yards from our trenches, machine guns opened a fire which increased rapidly in intensity. Indeed, before "Zero" (7.30 a.m.) casualties had already been serious. Nevertheless, the battalion went forward with admirable steadiness and deter-mination, though deluged with shrapnel as well as mown down wholesale by the devastating machine-guns. There were 600 yards to be covered on the right, and No Man's Land was pitted with shell-holes which, with the heavy loads the men were carrying, made the advance slow. The Germans manned their parapets in force before our men were half-way across, and though they gave targets to the rifles of the leading line it was only too clear that neither mine nor bombardment had done all that was hoped. A Company persevered till within 20 yards of the nose of the salient, where a shower of bombs brought the survivors to a standstill, a very few reaching the wire, only to be shot down in trying to get through it. A sunken road gave C some help to cross the hollow in its front, but C too was stopped, when about 60 yards from the wire, by machine guns from the right. D also pressed on, men dropping at every yard, till nearly 300 yards out from our line when scarcely any were left to go farther.

Meanwhile B had clambered out of the support trench at 7.30 and, undeterred by the fate of the leading companies, started to advance. Before its men were through our wire, the machine guns were bowling them over. They pushed on, gallantly led by Captain Hughes, who was last seen 50 yards from the enemy's wire, heading a handful of men, all of whom were shot down a minute later. Within twenty minutes of Zero the 2nd S.W.B. had been virtually wiped out.... Wounded and unhurt alike had to lie where they were among the killed, under intermittent machine-gun fire and shelling which swelled the already terrible casualty list. One of the few officers who survived narrates how after firing away all his ammunition and scoring several successes — he was sheltering in a hole made by a large trench-mortar bomb — he fell asleep from sheer exhaustion, and woke up later to watch our heavy artillery bombarding the hostile trenches with considerable accuracy. Rather after midnight, when there was a lull in the machine-gun fire, he managed to regain our lines.

In the meantime two attempts had been made to carry the line forward, the Borderers advancing as arranged at 8.15 a.m., the Newfoundland Regiment being put in an hour later. The Borderers suffered terribly from the machine-guns before they cleared the British trenches and none reached the forward line of survivors of the S.W.B. Of the Newfoundlanders, whose heroic but hopeless attempt was made because erroneous information had reached D.H.Q. that a lodgment had been

made in the German lines, a few worked
forward by the sunken road and joined the
survivors of C, the great majority went
down before they were half-way across No
Man's Land, and thereafter no further
advance was attempted. The long day
dragged on slowly, each hour adding to the
casualties and to the sufferings of the
wounded, till at last darkness enabled
survivors to creep back to safety and
allowed stretcher-bearers to go out on their
errand of mercy, though the Germans
started a heavy but intermittent machine
gun fire directly it became dark and kept
on sending up flares, as though expecting a
fresh attack. This greatly hampered the
work of rescue, and many of the wounded,
especially those lying in or near the German wire, could not be reached.

North of the Ancre indeed the British
attack had ended in unmistakable failure
and terrible losses. The Twenty-Ninth
Division had, as General Hunter-Weston
wrote: "shown itself capable of maintaining its high traditions". It had given "a
magnificent display of disciplined
courage", it had gone forward in the face of
a devastating machine-gun fire and heavy
shelling, without faltering or wavering, in
perfect order and undismayed by the odds
against it. But it had been shattered to
pieces and was incapable of further effort.
The 2nd S.W.B. had not been the heaviest
hit battalion in the Division, yet its
casualty list included 15 of the 21 officers
and 384 of the 578 men engaged in the attack, 235 of them killed and missing. There
was little chance that any "missing" might
later be reported as prisoners; scarce one
had reached the enemy's lines, and
"missing" merely meant that a man had
fallen too far out for his body to be

recovered.... The battalion was sadly changed from that which had been through the evacuation of Cape Helles and had landed in France full of hopes of achieving great things. Its gallantry and devotion had been conspicuous, but the task set it had been beyond even its capacity. [4]

No, indeed, they were doing no good on the right! On *their* right, the extreme right of the Division were the Royal Inniskilling Fusiliers. How were they faring? *The Royal Inniskilling Fusiliers in The World War* tells us that the capture of the German positions between Beaumont Hamel and the Ancre proved to be a hopeless task. It describes some of the difficulties involved in such an attack:

> The enemy's position rose in terrace after terrace of entrenchments, having a perfect field of fire across the glacis of nearly a quarter of a mile of bare slope, which the assaulting infantry had to cross... a system of ascending terraces in which machine-gunners and riflemen could sit as in the tiers of a stadium firing down upon the slope beneath.... [5]

Sir Frank Fox comments upon the disappointment of the high hopes associated with the springing of the great mine under Hawthorn Redoubt and the ineptitude of the timing of the explosion. He continues with the sad tale of the fortunes of the Battalion:

> So soon as the Platoons left the trenches they were met with a driving rain of machinegun and rifle bullets coming from the front and from each flank. The men faced the storm unflinchingly, moving as steadily as on the parade ground. Portable bridges which had been carried forward helped them to cross the deep enemy trenches on the right. A small remnant of

the Battalion reached the enemy's wire and were there held up. It had been hoped that an occupation of the crater of the mine under Hawthorn Redoubt by our troops on the left would have established a safe left flank; but the hope was vain, as the enemy took advantage of the ten minutes between the explosion of the mine and the infantry assault to occupy the crater effectively.

No reserves were brought up. In that field of fire nothing could live. The 87th Brigade fell back to the trench from which it had moved to the attack — or rather one third of it did: the rest were casualties....

So ended the Battle of Albert for the Inniskillings. It had been their hard fortune to be sent into action on the left sector of the great attack, and this sector proved to be impregnable. But on the right sector the British Army succeeded better, storming many German positions south of the Albert-Bapaume Road and making a beginning with that slow process of attrition which finally compelled the enemy to withdraw from the Somme area: and the attacks on the left sector if they had gained no ground had at least helped the attacks on the right. [6]

From left to right those are the various accounts of the four front-running battalions of the Division.

CHAPTER FOUR

THE SECOND AND THIRD WAVES

I sang as one
Who on a tilting deck sings
To keep men's courage up, though the wave hangs
That shall cut off their sun.

(*'The Conflict'* — C. Day Lewis)

Over on the left, behind the Lancashire Fusiliers and echeloned slightly to the right, was the 16th Battalion of the Middlesex Regiment. They covered the right flank of the Lancashire Fusiliers and the left flank of the Royals. Their history, *The Die-hards in the Great War — a History of the Duke of Cambridge's Own (The Middlesex Regiment)*, merely remarks tersely that "they were in support" in the battle.

On their right was the First Battalion, the Royal Dublin Fusiliers. They were directly behind the Royals. Their Regimental history, *The Royal Dublin Fusiliers (O'Neill's Blue-Caps)* is very slightly more communicative:

> Reached our allotted positions in the trenches via Broadway at 1 a.m. on July 1st. "W" Company on the right and "X" on the left in Essex Street, with "Y" Company on the right and "Z" on the left in the 88th's trench.... "W" with "Y" moved into support up F Street (Fethard Street?) and Broadway, and "X" with "Z" were in support up Bloomfield and Second Avenue ready to move out against the German second line system of trenches on Beaucourt Ridge, south-east of Beaumont Hamel. The battalion was supposed to move out behind the 2nd Royal Fusiliers by companies and reform at Station Road, also by companies, ready for the assault of the enemy second-line system; but this could only be done after the 2nd Royal

Fusiliers had gained their objective, the enemy front-line system, and this the 2nd Royal Fusiliers were unable to accomplish. [1]

It was certainly not for want of trying that the Royals had failed to gain their objective, as their own historian has already made abundantly clear.

On the right of the Royal Dublin Fusiliers and directly behind the South Wales Borderers was the 1st Battalion, the Border Regiment. Their history tells us:

The account in the Battalion Diary is unfortunately very meagre; it runs: the Battalion, less ten per cent, advanced just south of Beaumont Hamel, its objective being Beaucourt Redoubt. The 2nd South Wales Borderers, whose objective was the first two German lines, were wiped out by machine-gun fire in our own wire. The First Battalion the Border Regiment then went "over the top" from the support line and over the British front line, but the passage over the front trench having been ranged by the German machine-gunners the day previously, the 1st Border Regiment met with heavy loss while crossing the trench and passing through the gaps in the wire. The men were magnificently steady, forming up outside the wire according to orders, then, inclining to the right, advanced as directed at a slow walk into No Man's Land. The advance was continued until only little groups of some half-dozen men were left here and there, and at last these, seeing no reinforcements in sight, took cover in shell holes wherever they found them.

By 8 a.m. the advance had come to a stand-still, and the assault had definitely failed. An attempt was later made to renew it, but when it was found all the brigades of

the "Incomparable Twenty-ninth" were
equally reduced in numbers it was
recognised that only a defensive line could
now be held and on the morning of 2nd July
the 1st Border Regiment retired to just
north of the Ancre where they were busily
engaged in repairing the trenches and in
bringing in wounded and burying dead, all
under continued enemy sniping. [2]

The "attempt later made to renew the assault"
mentioned in the diary was, of course, the Newfoundlanders' entry on to the stage of battle. They were
directly behind the Borderers. But, before considering
the part played by the Newfoundland and Essex battalions, the story of the First Battalion of the King's
Own Scottish Borderers should be considered. They
were in the second wave of the 87th Brigade, behind the
Inniskillings, on the extreme right of the Corps'
boundary. Their regimental history was published in
1930: recollection in tranquillity revealed some spurts
of anger in the author, not observable elsewhere:

When the big mine at Hawthorn Redoubt
gave warning at 7.20 a.m. to the German
machine-gunners to be up and doing, they
lost no time in setting to work, and they had
ten minutes to spare for the preparation.
("The advertisement of the attack on our
front was absurd. Paths were cut and
marked through our wire days before.
Bridges over our trenches for the second
and third waves to cross by were put up
days in advance. Small wonder the
machine-gun fire was directed with such
fatal precision" — An officer present).
Confining ourselves to the right half of the
87th front, we find that when the Royal
Inniskilling Fusiliers went over the top at
7.30 a.m. on 1st July, 1916, they were
greeted with terrific bursts of machine-gun
fire, and those behind them felt the lash of

the barrage. If the G.O.C. could have flown
or rather hovered over the scene for ten
seconds the attack would have been
counter-manded. The carnage that so
swiftly destroyed the 87th was perfectly
useless. Dummies could have done as well.
The German Ancre garrison could not have
been hurried off at a moment's notice to
stop the leak astride the Somme. But the
terrible thing about war is that an attack
once launched can rarely be broken off.
Those in control don't and can't know what
is going on in front. So although the an-
swers presented themselves to the three
questions figured ran:

1. Counter-barrage? Yes, enough to
annihilate a division!

2. *M.G.? Yes, enough to sweep every
cubic foot of air.

3. Wire? Well, time enough if you ever
get there, to solve *that* problem!

The men on the spot had no alternative
but to go on and be killed or wounded, or
find cover. After the R.I.F. failed and after
the lapse of half an hour the battered
K.O.S.B. tried what they would do. But
without any discredit they did not succeed
in even reaching the few Fusiliers who
were lying out in No Man's Land.... By an
unfortunate coincidence the Germans put
up the precise signal — a white flare —
selected by us to mark the capture of the
first objective, just at the place and time
which made it seem imperative to launch,
in accordance with divisional orders, the
King's Own Scottish Borderers in the wake
of the Inniskillings. Fate was against the
Borderers. The fog of war was outspread
and they had to "dree their weird". They
were well aware of this. They knew the
first wave had broken to atoms yet they
never hesitated to start or wavered when

off until cut down in swathes... the Borderers handed over the impossible task to the 88th Brigade. Newfoundland Park calls to mind a superb effort on the part of the Newfoundland Regiment which, except as an example to future fighters, made no more impression on the Battle of Albert than the butt of a weddell seal against a torqual.... [3]

*Machine-guns.

The First Battalion, the Essex Regiment and the Newfoundlanders were originally scheduled to be the third wave of the attack. As the 86th and 87th Brigades had not reached even the first objective, their role in the battle was altered. The historian of the Essex Regiment takes up the sad tale: he records the impregnable nature of the position, and points out:

> The hill behind Beaumont Hamel, 135 ft. high, afforded admirable means of observation to the enemy, for practically the whole of the movements of the 29th Division could be watched therefrom and also the progress made by the divisions on the flanks. Had the assault been a surprise the chances of success of a frontal attack were remote, but on July 1st, 1916, the enemy were well-prepared and their line was strongly held. [4]

The burdened aspect of the soldiers is noted; each platoon had two trench bridges to carry, and every company distributed 50 shovels and 10 picks amongst its members. In addition to carrying this heavy equipment the men were on the move from their billets in the rear at 9 p.m. on the 30th and were not finally settled in their jumping-off trenches until 3.30 the next morning. They were very much fatigued even before the fighting commenced.

The Essex Regiment's historian records the explosion of the mine and the gallant but unsuccessful dash of a party of Royal Fusiliers to occupy the crater. There were three batteries of Stokes mortars which commenced firing as the mine blew up in order to cover the movement of the assaulting troops across No Man's Land. He says, "The mortars in front of the 86th Brigade could not be used as effectively as was desired owing to the shortage of ammunition, caused by the carriers having been killed." [5]

The history speaks of the tornado of machine-gun fire which met the leading battalions and then proceeds to the role of the Essex battalion:

> The confusion of the fighting was added to by reports which suggested the attack had been successful in some quarters and that the divisions on the flank were making progress.
>
> Believing that parties of the 87th Brigade were fighting in the enemy trenches, General de Lisle endeavoured to support them by ordering at 8.37 a.m. half the 88th Brigade to strengthen the right attack, two battalions being kept as divisional reserve and not to be utilised without express instructions. Accordingly, the Essex (on the right) and Newfoundlanders were ordered to attack independently. It was unfortunate for the first-named Battalion that a week before it had lost several of its bombing experts, including the bombing officer. They were wounded by the explosion of a hand-grenade due to a faulty fuse.
>
> The Newfoundlanders advanced from the support positions in St. John's Road and sustained heavy losses. Owing to the ground being under heavy fire the Essex moved up the communication trenches to the front line at 8.45 a.m. They found the former choked with wounded and damaged by shell-fire, and the men took two hours to reach the jumping-off point. At 10.50 a.m. the Battalion attacked on the right of the

divisional line, but as the companies leapt over the parapet heavy losses ensued from the enemy's artillery and machine-gun barrage, the advance being also held up by uncut wire.

At 1.50 p.m. instructions were given for the attack to be relinquished and the trenches cleared, the Royal Fusiliers having been forced to release their hold upon the Redoubt by trench mortar fire. The offensive, which had obtained such promising results farther south, had failed on the Beaumont Hamel sector, but not for lack of gallantry, for the G.O.C. 29th Division wrote: "No fault can be found with the behaviour of the troops, who did all that was possible. Their bravery and the severity of the engagement are best evinced by the casualities, which, I regret to state, were very severe, amounting to some 200 officers and 5,000 men. The spirit of the troops is good, but the physical fatigue among the young soldiers, who form three-fourths of the battalions, is marked compared with the stamina of the original troops of earlier days."

The casualities in the Brigade were 40 officers and 995 other ranks, no fewer than 766 being reported missing. Essex went into action with 26 officers and 840 other ranks, 14 officers and 91 men being held in reserve. Their casualties were nine officers and 209 other ranks. [6]

Behind the Essex battalion the 2nd Battalion the Royal Hampshire Regiment waited in reserve. Their history reports:

Of the Twenty-ninth Division, not only had both attacking brigades been engaged without avail, the 88th's leading battalions, the Essex and the Newfoundland

Regiment, had also gone forward with equally disastrous results. However, their fate had caused the Divisional commander to stop the 2nd Hants and the Worcesters from advancing beyond our own lines, where they came under artillery fire but escaped serious exposure to the machine-guns. To support the Fourth Division it was now proposed to utilise these two battalions in a fresh attack upon Beaumont Hamel, while such of the 10th Brigade as was still in hand advanced on their left. Terribly congested trenches prevented this attack from being started at the time ordered, 12.30 p.m.; indeed the orders never reached the 2nd Hampshire till long after that hour, and eventually the plan was abandoned and further fruitless sacrifice avoided. The 2nd Hampshires therefore remained in our own lines.... [7]

The Worcester's regimental history tersely reports: "At 11.30 a.m. ordered to advance" (from their reserve position).

At 1 p.m. the 4th Worcesters and the 2nd Hampshires were the only battalions of 29th Division still in the fighting to hold the line against counter-attacks. [8]

But the counter-attacks did not materialise. Like the battered pugilist in the old story, Kitchener's New Army (what was left of it) could say, "But you should see the other feller!" "The other feller" in fact was not quite so badly mauled, but — whatever the reason — no counter-attack broke over the heads of the Worcesters and the Hampshires.

All the regimental histories agree on the salient points: the Hawthorn mine went spectacularly up on time: the crater was not decisively occupied by the British: the preliminary bombardment had by no means annihilated the opposition: the barbed wire defences were largely intact. The first and second assault waves ran into a wall of steel that stopped them literally dead. Most of the histories mention with soldierly respect the gallant and hopeless effort of the Newfoundlanders.

Out of the undecorated military prose one or two jagged phrases emerge like a half-suppressed cry of pain: "For forty-eight hours the wounded dribbled in, some of them mad"; "The long day dragged on slowly, each hour adding to the casualties and to the sufferings of the wounded"; "mown down wholesale by the devastating machine-guns"; "a driving rain of machine gun and rifle bullets"; "The carnage that so swiftly destroyed the 87th was perfectly useless. Dummies could have done as well"; "shortage of ammunition, caused by the carriers having been killed"; "decimated by enemy fire"; "Terribly congested trenches".

But even the 1st July, 1916, ran a course of only twenty-four hours. Eventually the sun went down. The day was over. But it was not a day like other days. Afterwards a number of things changed.

CHAPTER FIVE

CARIBOU ATTACK

"I have fought a good fight, I have finished my course, I have kept the faith."

(II Timothy 4.7)

She brushed the chalk-dust off her sandals. We had walked through Auchonvillers towards Beaumont Hamel and seen the sunken road that was such a fateful feature in the history of the Lancashire Fusiliers; we had peered into the crater left by the mine under the Hawthorn Redoubt. Now it is choked with undergrowth, and tall trees rear their heads from its grim floor: it does not seem sixty feet deep, as the vegetation masks its full depth. It is still surrounded with wire — perhaps the original wire has been utilised — in order, it may be assumed, to keep the unwary animal or human from plunging into it. We had plodded along the two thousand yards of the front so far as it was possible to ascertain its course from observation of the contours of the land, and without trespassing upon the ploughed fields with their springing crops. We had returned to the Memorial Park and were sitting in the grass at the northern end of Y Ravine, near the place marked on the trench maps as Point 89. Clad in summer frocks and burdened only with a sense of history, we were hot and tired and the afternoon quiet of the July sunshine was somewhat oppressive.

"Lancashire Fusiliers, Royals, South Wales Borderers, Inniskillings and Royal Dublins from Ireland, the Middlesex, the Border Regiment from Cumberland, King's Own Scottish, men from Essex and Hampshire: it sounds like one of those funny stories that begins, 'There was an Englishmen, an Irishman and a Scotsman and a Welshman.' Except," she added hastily, "it wasn't a funny story. And there was a Newfoundlander too."

Indeed there was. Up and down the front there were also Canadians, Australians, New Zealanders, Indians,

42

men from all over the world. But the 29th Division was, in itself, very representative.

"And there was a Newfoundlander," she repeated, "I haven't really heard about him yet."

In one sense there is so pitifully little to tell. The whole story hinges on a coincidence, a tragic mistake involving a signalling flare. The pre-arranged signal that the first objective had been reached by the 87th Brigade was that a white Very light would be fired. It was reported to the Divisional Commander, Major-General Beauvoir de Lisle, that white flares had been observed going up on the right front of the 87th Brigade. He, therefore, not unnaturally, assumed that the Brigade's leading troops had gone through and were in need of support. In his official report of the battle he wrote:

> I therefore decided to make another effort to capture the front line, and thus support the parties of the 87th Brigade who were, I believed, fighting in the enemy's trenches. At 8.37 a.m. consequently I ordered the 88th Brigade to attack the enemy's front between Points 03 and 89, but to keep two battalions in hand as Divisional Reserve, and not to utilize them without my express instructions.... [1]

Actually the white flares were also used by German signallers, in this case to indicate to their artillery that the guns were dropping their rounds short.

Brigadier-General Cayley, in command of the 88th Brigade, duly issued orders on the telephone at 8.45 to the Newfoundland and Essex Regiments to advance as soon as possible and support the attack on the divisional right.

So the story passed down the chain of command and finally reached the Newfoundlanders.

Hidden away in a dark recess somewhere in the Public Records Office in Chancery Lane is a stout cardboard box. It has a number — 2308 — and is marked "Closed until 1965". In it are the flimsy sheets

43

of the Regimental Diary. They tell the bare bones of the story.

Trenches
St. John's Road   1st July 1916
Clonmel Avenue

0600 - 0730   Intense bombardment.
0730   86th and 87th Brigades attacked 1st system of enemy trenches. 88th Brigade, under pre-arranged orders, were to move forward at 0840 to attack 3rd line system of trenches. About 0820 received orders not to move until further orders. Presumably the first attack not having been successful.

0845 Received orders on telephone to move forward in conjunction with 1st Essex Regiment and occupy enemy's first trench — our objective being point (89) to just north of point (60) and work forward to Station Road clearing the enemy trenches — and move as soon as possible. Asked Brigade if enemies (sic) 1st trench had been taken and received reply to the effect that the situation was not cleared up. Asked Brigade if we were to move off to attack independently of Essex Regiment and received reply in the affirmative.
0915 Reported to Brigade that New-foundland Regt was moving off. It was subsequently found that the Essex Regiment did not attack until 0955 i.e. after our attack had failed. The Regiment moved off in previously arranged for-mation i.e. A and B Companies (A on left) in 1st line in lines of platoons in file or single file at 40 paces interval and 25 paces between sections — followed by C and D Coys. (C on left) in similar formation at 100 yards distance. C Coy had been specially detailed as consolidating company and

44

therefore carried additional equipment. The advance was made direct over the open from the rear trenches known as St. John's Road and Clonmel Avenue. As soon as the signal for advance was given the regiment left the trenches and moved steadily forward. Machine gun fire from our right front was at once opened on us and then artillery fire also. The distance to our objective varied from 650 to 900 yards. The enemy's fire was effective from the outset but the heaviest casualties occurred on passing through the gaps in our front wire where the men were mown down in heaps. Many more gaps in the wire were required than had been cut. In spite of losses the survivors steadily advanced until close to the enemies (sic) wire by which time very few remained. A few men are believed to have actually succeeded in throwing bombs into the enemy's trench.
0945 The C.O. reported personally at Brigade Battle H.Q. 100 yards behind our firing line that the attack had failed. Shortly afterwards enemy opened an intense bombardment of our trenches with heavy artillery which was kept up for some time.

During the night and evening unwounded survivors managed to crawl back to our own lines and by next morning some 68 had answered their names in addition to stretcher bearers and H.Q. runners. During the afternoon the 10% reinforcements under Capt. Forbes-Robertson arrived in the trenches and orders were received to occupy the support trench in the right sub-sector known as St. James Street, where we remained on July 2nd.

(A report by Capt. G.E. Malcolm commanding D Co. 1st K.O.S.B. which formed part of the first attack carried out by the 87th Brigade is attached).[2]

The diary entry is signed in Colonel Hadow's small, precise hand-writing. He was not a Newfoundlander. He was a regular soldier from the Norfolk Regiment, and was appointed C.O. of the Battalion on December 6th, 1915, about a month before they were evacuated from Suvla. He was in command for two years, and was invalided home on December 21st, 1917.

The report by Captain Malcolm, mentioned in the diary, reads as follows:—

> Copy of Report from Capt. G.E. Malcolm 1st K.O.S.B.
> To: Adjutant 1st K.O.S.B. July 5/16
> From: O.C. D. Coy 1st K.O.S.B.
>
> Sir, I have the honour to make the following report.
> On the morning of "Z" day at 0.20 D Coy received the whistle signal to advance.
> On leaving the trenches they came under very heavy machine gun fire. The Company moved forward in line of Platoons in column of sections in single file, No. 13 Platoon on the left and No. 16 on the right. At 60 yards from our own trenches I gave the signal to lie down as I intended to make the right wheel on to our objective at that point and "C" Coy and the Border Regt. were not yet in position. Owing to casualties I had 3 men of No. 13 (2 wounded) and 1 of No. 14 left. I could see no one of the other platoons.
> At 0.35 I sent a message to the Adjutant 1st K.O.S.B. by Private Douglas stating estimated casualties.
> At 1.00 a company of Newfoundland Regt. 40 strong came up without officers. I gave the signal to my company to advance and took command. I hoped to get a footing

in the enemy trenches and so hinder the machine-gun fire.

I was wounded 60 yards from the enemy trenches. The advance ceased 20 yards further on.

I should like to congratulate the Newfoundland Regiment on their extreme steadiness under trying conditions.... [3]

Another comment on the behaviour of the Newfoundland Battalion was made by an officer of much higher rank than poor Captain Malcolm. Major-General Sir Beauvoir de Lisle, the Divisional Commander, wrote in his report on the operations of 1st July, 1916:

> It was noticeable that in spite of two attacks having failed on the right, the two Battalions detailed for the third attack behaved with exemplary bravery. The Newfoundland Battalion on the left, for example, attacked 750 strong. Forty odd unwounded returned in the course of the day, and the remaining 710 were casualties. This example of discipline and valour was equalled by others but cannot be surpassed.
>
> No fault can be found with the behaviour of the troops who did all that was possible. Their bravery and the severity of the engagement are best evidenced by the casualties, which I regret to state were very severe, amount to some 200 officers and 5,000 men. [4]

The official history of the 29th Division, first published in 1925, does not dwell too long on the activities of 1st July, 1916. Captain Stair-Gillon reports the doings of the 86th and 87th Brigades, and then continues:

> The attack had failed. What would the fate of the 88th be? If they went forward

they went to certain death, but when the
military machine gets in motion it is hard
to divert or stop. Those in command had
imperfect and rather encouraging reports.
If our men were really fighting in the
Station Road on the right — i.e. well behind
the enemy's front line — they must be
supported, and a determined effort made
to prevent them from being cut off and
undone through the very brilliance of their
success. Accordingly the G.O.C. ordered a
fresh attack to be carried out by the Essex
and Newfoundlanders. The latter were
ready first, and launched a determined
attack at 9.15 a.m. Many eye-witnesses
have testified to the superb steadiness of
that astonishing infantry. Undaunted by a
hail of machine-gun fire, they went forward till out of 700 men a mere handful
remained.

These men from a far land spent their
blood like water for their distant kindred,
their love of justice, and the Pax Britan-
nica. The site of their glory is a little bit of
extra-territorial Newfoundland dedicated
for ever as a consecrated memorial to
valour. No one should neglect to read the
chapter on Newfoundland's contribution to
the war in the *Times History of the
War* . [5]

This chapter, Part 175, Vol. 14, Dec. 24th, 1917, has
this to say of the opening day of the Somme:

The distance to be crossed at this point
varied from 650 to 900 yards. Despite our
tremendous artillery bombardment, the
way over this long distance was by no
means clear. Lines had been cut through
our own wires through which the troops
might move, but those gaps were not
nearly sufficient in number. The enemy

knew all of these lanes and had their machine guns playing directly over them. There was a slight dip in the ground shortly after leaving our trenches, about three or four feet deep. The German machine guns had thus an admirable line of sight towards which they could sweep their fire, making the passage impossible. Immediately our artillery barrage slackened, the German machine gunners poured from their dug-outs.

Our men moved off at 9.15. They were the very pick of the population of the Island Colony. They had been thoroughly trained. Many of them were skilled sharp-shooters, men who, living for years in the open hunting and trapping, had all the keenness of vision of the born forester. Some were picked lumbermen. Most had been accustomed to open-air life, and were magnificent specimens of humanity. For months they had trained, day after day, for this hour.

They knew before they started that they were undertaking an almost impossible task. The Colonel called his Company Commanders together and briefly addressed them telling them what was ahead. The men in the ranks exchanged words together with tight-set lips. 'If I go down,' said the corporal to the private at his side, 'you take charge and go straight ahead.'

The Newfoundlanders advanced as steadily as though on parade. The ranks kept perfect line. They moved forward with two companies in the first line in platoons in file at 40 paces interval and 25 paces between sections, followed by two other companies in similar formation at 100 paces distance. Their line of advance was over the open from the near trenches known as St. John's Road and Clonmel

Avenue. The German machine guns played right on them. As the men passed through the gaps in our own front wire they were mown down in heaps. The survivors kept on. 'Push on with it,' said the sergeant to the man under him as he himself fell, struck by a bullet in the chest. 'Push on with it.' Some survivors got as far as the German wires. It is told of one officer that, finding all his men were shot down, he himself ran forward straight at the Germans, to be shot before he reached them. One man, Regt.-Sergt.-Major W. Clare, kept on alone, and was one of the very few who succeeded in reaching the enemy wire.

The blow was so sudden and so overwhelming that it seemed almost impossible that it could be true. A number of wounded dropped down in shell-holes where they remained, some of them, for days before they could creep in. But for the time nothing could be seen of them. The officers and men left behind did their utmost to rescue the wounded in No Man's Land....

Every officer had been hit except the Colonel and a Captain. Newfoundlanders suffered more heavily in the advance of July 1st in proportion to numbers than any other branch of the British Army.

Sir Douglas Haig sent a message to the Government of Newfoundland which well voiced the general feeling. 'The heroism and devotion to duty they displayed on 1st July has never been surpassed.' The Lieutenant-General now in command of the Corps,'' (presumably Sir Aylmer Hunter-Weston, though he is not mentioned directly by name), ''expressed, both to the Premier and to the survivors themselves, his appreciation of their splendid courage and determination. He declared that the charge would live in history, and that the

Newfoundlanders had added another deed
to that glorious chronology of valiant deeds
on which our Empire was built. In a letter
to Sir Edward Morris the Lieut.-General
said: 'That battalion covered itself with
glory on July 1 by the magnificent way in
which it carried out the attack entrusted to
it. It went forward to the attack when two
other attacks on that same part of the line
had failed, and by its behaviour on that
occasion it showed itself worthy of the
highest traditions of the British race, and
proved itself to be a fit representative of
the population of the oldest British colony.
When the order to attack was given every
man moved forward to his appointed objective in his appointed place as if on
parade. There were no waverers, no
stragglers, and not a man looked back. It
was a magnificent display of trained and
disciplined valour, and its assault only
failed of success because dead men can
advance no farther. They were shot down
by machine-guns brought up by a very
gallant foe under our intense artillery fire.
Against any foe less well-entrenched, less
well-organised, and above all, less gallant,
their attack must have succeeded. As it
was the action of the Newfoundland Battalion and the other units of the British left
contributed largely to the victory achieved
by the British and French farther south by
pinning to their ground the best of the
German troops and by occupying the
majority of their artillery, both heavy and
field. The gallantry and devotion of this
battalion, therefore, was not in vain, and
the credit of victory belongs to them as
much as to those troops farther south who
actually succeeded in breaking the German line. An attacking army is like a
football team; there is but one who kicks

the goal, yet the credit of success belongs not alone to that individual but to the whole team, whose concerted action led to the desired result.

I should like you to let my fellow citizens of the Empire in the oldest Overseas portion of the British Realm know how well their lads have done, both officers, non-commissioned officers and men, and how proud I, as their Corps Commander, am to have had such a battalion under my command, and to be a comrade in arms of each and all of them.' [6]

"Which is all very fine," commented my seventeen-year-old bitterly, "all this talk of gallantry and valour and courage: all very masculine. But they might just as well have been sent out to face a firing squad: in effect, that's what happened to them. Think of all the black holes left in the lives of the people they belonged to, back in Newfoundland!" She glanced over the German lines, up the grassy slope towards the Caribou Memorial about a quarter of a mile away. "No," she continued with a sort of pleading urgency, "there's just got to be more to it than that!"

More to it than what? They were given orders and they obeyed them. The middle of a battle is no time to stand around arguing. What alternatives were there? Perhaps their own records throw some light on the subject. *The First Five Hundred*, under the heading 'Impossible Frontal Advance' has this to say:

The ground over which they had to advance could scarcely be more difficult. It formed a gradual descent which rendered our troops completely exposed. It contained enormous quarries and excavations in which large numbers of the enemy could remain concealed, almost immune from shell-fire, and ready to rush out and attack our men in the rear. Although the bombardment from the British guns was terrific it had comparatively little effect in lessening this danger. There was another condition which tended to minimize the success of the Twenty-Ninth Division. It was found that the artillery fire had thoroughly cut the Germany wire, but our own wire had not been cut to the same extent and proved a serious menace to the advance of the troops. Some gaps were cut, but they were not sufficient and they were quickly discovered by the Germans who played their guns on them with terrible results.

At 7.30 on the morning of July 1st the whistles blew, and the men, determined to force the lines of Beaumont Hamel or show the absolute impossibility of the task, sprang from their trenches and advanced in successive waves of assault against the enemy trenches. The entire 86th and 87th Brigades were drawn into the fight and suffered tremendous losses, and about 8.40, scarcely more than an hour after the opening of the "Battle of the Somme" the Newfoundland Regiment and the 1st Essex were ordered forward to take the first line of the enemy trenches. Like the other battalions, our Regiment and the Essex were held up by the murderous machine-gun fire in front of Beaumont Hamel. They were also subject to the fire of flanking machine-guns. The whole action was so rapid, the positions occupied by the enemy machine-guns so advantageous and commanding, and the fire from those guns so destructive that by 10.20 the assault had to be given up, and only a defensive line could be held.

The Regiment suffered very heavily, but only in proportion to the indomitable courage and fortitude displayed under most adverse conditions, and even in the face of death itself. It is said that no other unit suffered so heavily in proportion to the number of men engaged. One hundred men were reported killed, 210 missing and 374 wounded. No action could be more fitting than that this field should be bought by the voluntary subscriptions of the people of Newfoundland and forever held in memory of the men who sacrificed their lives that day. July 1, 1916, will be remembered in the history of our country as at once glorious and tragic." (Then follows the text of Sir Douglas Haig's telegram and General Hunter-Weston's letter.) "It would be an injustice to the whole Regiment to single out any one man or half a dozen men because of conspicuous gallantry on this occasion. On other occasions if two or three men were to perform deeds of fearless gallantry such as were performed by every man that day, they would receive the highest distinction of the British Army. Every man distinguished himself. Sergeant Thomas Carroll is credited with having got farther than any other man before he was detected by the enemy and killed. There is abundant evidence that the heavy casualties suffered by their comrades did not shake the courage of those who remained. [7]

No, there is little there to help her; even one or two slight discrepancies: the artillery fire had *not* cut the German wire, and it is difficult to see how men burdened as they were "sprang from their trenches"! Perhaps Colonel Nicholson's *Fighting Newfoundlander*, the official history of the Regiment, published in 1964, will help to assure her that there was "more to it than that". The book is admirably objective, written by a soldier; written, moreover, fifty years after the event, with all the advantage of hindsight. Certainly the

Colonel had not overlooked a point that was not so obvious to the writer of *The First Five Hundred*!

....The resolve and determination of each man remained firm. His chief concern seemed to be *how could a man burdened with sixty pounds of baggage hoist himself up on to the parapet* when the order came.

In spite of all, cheerfulness abounded, and the traditional sense of humour went unchecked, particularly when it was recalled that the awards awaiting them were not confined to the honours of battle. For had not a prominent St. John's society maiden let it be known by confiding to her friends, and they to all who would listen, that she intended to marry the first V.C. in the regiment. Thus it was then, that on the lips of many a single man as he went over the top was the battle cry, "Buxom Bessie" (not her real name) "or a wooden leg!"

Quickly Hadow summoned his Company Commanders for a brief conference. There was no time to work out new tactics. The assault would be made using the same formation that had so often been rehearsed at Louvencourt — "A" and "B" Companies abreast followed by "C" and "D", each company advancing in lines of platoons in columns of sections. Quickly the orders were relayed to subordinates, and at 9.15 the message went to Brigade Headquarters: "The Newfoundlanders are moving".

An eye-witness has described the beginning of the Battalion's advance.

'As in all rehearsals the C.O. was the first to move, carrying, as always, his thick ash stick. When he had advanced about twenty yards he gave the same signal to the O.Cs Companies and immediately the parapet swarmed with men. From each corner of every traverse men came pouring. With remarkable precision they took up their correct positions in their sections; not a single section, so far as can be ascertained, went in the wrong direction, that is to say, tried to crowd through a gap that was cut for a neighbouring section. The rear sections stood on the parapet waiting for the leading ones to gain their proper distance (40 paces). Steadily they advanced to the first line of wire under a heavy machine-gun fire, first from the right and then from the whole front. Men began to drop, but not in large numbers, as the enemy had their guns trained on the gaps. The first gaps were reached and men fell in each of them. Those who could not go on did their best to clear the gaps of wounded, killed and equipment'.

From their starting position in St. John's Road the Newfoundlanders had to cross 250 yards of fire-swept ground before they reached even their own front line. Then there were four belts of their own wire through which they had to pass, and the zig-zag gaps had been purposely made few and narrow to conceal them from the enemy. As officers and men of "A" and "B" Companies, led respectively by Captains Jim Ledingham and Joe Nunns, struggled through the second and then the third belt — many of them over-burdened by the battle stores which they had picked up from dead or wounded comrades — casualties came with increasing frequency. But there was no hint of wavering. Steadily they pushed forward through the hail of bullets. "The only visible sign that the men knew they were under this terrific fire", wrote one observer, "was that they all instinctively tucked their chins into an advanced shoulder as they had so often done when fighting their way home against a blizzard in some little outpost in far off Newfoundland." The remaining two Companies followed at an interval of 100 yards, Captain Rex Rowsell's "C" Company had been specially detailed to act as consolidating company: thus when one of its men fell, he had to endure the additional torture inflicted by a pick or shovel strapped on his back.

When the remnants of "A" and "B" Companies finally emerged from their own front wire, they could look down the incline and see for the first time the barrier of the German wire, until now hidden from view by the convexity of the slope. It appeared to be alarmingly intact. The long grass which covered No Man's Land was beaten down, and the ground was becoming churned into a mass of shell-holes. Ahead the Newfoundlanders could see the burnt and blackened hillside rising behind the German trenches. To reach that hill-side was becoming every minute a more and more impossible goal.

The advance went on. The Newfoundlanders were still alone, receiving the full force of the enemy's fire; for on the right the Essex attack had been delayed by the complete congestion of their forward trenches with the bodies of dead and dying from the 87th Brigade. "B" Company had not got far before its Commander, Captain Nunns, fell shot in the leg. He called to one of his subalterns, Lieutenant Hubert Herder, to take charge of the Company, and to carry on. Snatching up rifle and bayonet from his Platoon Sergeant, who had just been hit, Herder shouted to his men, "Come on boys!" and led them forward — only to fall mortally wounded shortly afterwards. Half-way down the slope the little clump of trees used as a rallying-point by Captain Butler's raiders four nights before were now blasted bare of their leaves, with most of their branches shattered. One of these stricken trunks, standing gauntly isolated from the rest, was to mark an area where the enemy's shrapnel was particularly deadly. Before the dreadful day ended the bodies of many gallant Newfoundlanders lay near its base. In after years returning veterans, treading once again the course of that doomed advance, would pause silently with poignant memories before the twisted skeleton of "The Danger Tree".

Here fell Frank "Mayo" Lind, whose cheerful letters to the *Daily News* written from camp and shipboard, billets and trenches, had brought so much comfort and confidence to relatives and friends of the lads in the Regiment. His last letter, written from Louvencourt on June 29, had closed with a message that was indeed to prove prophetic: "Tell everybody that they may feel proud of the Newfoundland Regiment".

It was said afterwards that the wonder was that any men could remain unhit more than a minute in the inferno of fire that swept over No Man's Land. Yet still a few defiant figures could be seen moving doggedly down the slope. "C" and "D" Companies had a higher proportion than the other companies of young soldiers who were going into action for the first time, but no distinction was discernible between their conduct and that of the veterans of the Gallipoli Campaign.

Where two men had been advancing side by side, suddenly there is only one — and a few paces farther on he too pitches forward on his face. A young subaltern looks around him in vain for men to lead. Defiantly he brandishes his field telephone at the German trenches; then putting down his head he charges to his death. The leading man of a pair carrying a ten-foot bridge is hit, and as he falls he brings down with him bridge and partner. Without hesitation the latter gets up, hoists the bridge on to his head, and plods grimly forward until machine-gun bullets cut him down. A very few reach the German wire, and are shot down as they try to cut a passage with their clippers.

All this had taken place in less than thirty minutes. At 9.45 Colonel Hadow, who from a spot in front of the support trench had observed the destruction of his Regiment, made his way to Brigade Battle Headquarters, where he reported to Brigadier-General Cayley that the attack had failed. The Brigadier was shocked at the extent of the Regiment's losses, but after some discussion he directed that the C.O. should gather together any un-wounded Newfoundlanders that he could find and make a renewed attempt to reach the German trenches. On leaving Brigade Headquarters Hadow worked his way forward to the firing line in the hope of collecting even a handful of men fit to continue the attack. The trenches were packed with the dead and wounded of all regiments, but not a single sound Newfoundlander could he find. For-tunately, however, before the order for the forlorn, suicidal effort could be put into effect it was countermanded by a senior officer from Corps. From an advanced observation post on the high ground north of Hamel he had witnessed the Newfoun-dlanders' advance, and he could find no words to express his admiration of the magnificent way they had pressed forward to the last man.

... The German shelling continued, and several of the Newfoundland reinforcements (who now formed the Battalion) were hit. During the afternoon many wounded tried to crawl back to their own line. But in the blazing July sun the tin triangle on each man's back flashed like a heliograph, signalling his position to German snipers and machine-gunners. To move was to invite fire. The only hope of survival was to lie with wounds unattended through the heat of the long day until darkness brought cover from enemy eyes. The Regiment's twenty stretcher bearers worked magnificently all day bringing wounded back to the Aid Post in St. John's Road, where Ambulance Sergeant Art Hammond and his staff dressed their wounds and did what they could to alleviate their suffering before turning them over to the men of the Royal Army Medical Corps from the Advanced Dressing Station. As the stricken Newfoundlanders lay on their stretchers awaiting treatment, there was one thing that left a deep impression on anyone who was nearby at the time. Captain Raley has reported that the almost universal question asked by each of the wounded was, "Is the Colonel satisfied?" "Is the Colonel pleased?" In that revealing moment, while suffering the agony of bullet-torn flesh or shattered limb and the bitter realisation of defeat, these Newfoundlanders had one thought above all others — whether they had come up to the expectation of the Commanding Officer whom they had come to admire and respect. [8]

Perhaps there lies the answer to her question about what "there was to it". The relationship between a Colonel and the battalion he commands is a very special one. The battalion is the working unit of military life and its Commanding Officer is the real pinnacle of authority so far as the ordinary soldier is concerned. Beyond his visible figure lie the shadowy heights of Brigade, beyond that is Corps Headquarters. The General commanding the army is so far distant from the ordinary soldier that it is doubtful whether the Newfoundlanders ever even saw General Rawlinson or would have recognised him if they had. As for the Commander-in-Chief, General Haig, he was as remote as Mount Olympus. It was the Colonel who mattered to the battalion.

Colonel Hadow, the regimental history records

> was a strict disciplinarian — many would say a martinet and a driver.... He was extremely conscious of the fact that the Battalion of which he had been given command lacked the training and experience of the regular regiments of the 29th Division.... His role was clear to him. He was determined to do everything possible to bring the Newfoundland Regiment to a standard of military efficiency that would make it second to none. To attribute to him anything but the best motives in his handling of the troops under his command is to be blind to the virtues of the man as a soldier.
>
> Colonel Hadow hid under a stern exterior an admiration of the Newfoundlanders that was very real. But in the early days he had yet to understand fully the free and easy spirit of independence which characterised these men from the island Colony. He would sternly condemn anything that appeared to him to be slackness on parade, or neglect of duty, or insubordination... but after a time came a better understanding

on both sides, and as time passed veterans of the Mediterranean days would find themselves reciting without any feeling of rancour the ditty that had greeted the Colonel on his first appearance with the Regiment: (presumably it was sung to the tune of "Gilbert the Filbert, the Kernel of the Nuts"!)

> I'm Hadow, some lad-o,
> Just off the Staff,
> I command the Newfoundlanders
> And they know it — not half;
> I'll make them or break them,
> I'll make the blighters sweat,
> For I'm Hadow, some lad-o,
> I'll be a General yet.

Commanding Officers who came after Colonel Hadow may have enjoyed a greater measure of popularity, but not one of them would ever merit the tribute that in later years thoughtful, fair-minded Newfoundland veterans would come to give as their considered opinion: 'Colonel Hadow made the Regiment'.... [9]

My daughter gazed disbelievingly at me, and sadly shook her head. "You're not trying to tell me that they went into that inferno just to please the Colonel, surely. He wasn't even very popular, apparently."

Popularity, as a quality of authority, rates very highly nowadays: certainly above admiration and respect. Authority itself, in every aspect, is questioned. Whether the chaos resultant upon "doing your own thing" produces happier human beings is very doubtful. War is a kind of chaos, and armies deal with it by imposing upon it the necessary evil of discipline. Under few other circumstances can blind obedience be described as a virtue, but in war it is the element that transmutes a fighting man from a confused and terrified human being into a soldier. A soldier is not, under battle conditions, an individual in the terms understood by peaceful, civilised society. He is a part of a gigantic machine and, as such, must perform as smoothly as the bolt in his own rifle: the human oil that slides him efficiently into his place in battle is discipline. Part of this is imposed upon him from outside, but a great deal of it lies within himself and arises, paradoxically, from his acceptance of the necessity for the external discipline.

The Newfoundlanders, a collection of highly individualistic and independent men, had volunteered for a complex of reasons to be soldiers. They wanted to be good at the job of being fighting men: if they were better at it than their opponents, then they would win a victory and could go home again to follow their own normal pursuits. The man fate assigned to instruct them in the business of soldiering was a Regular Army officer, a professional soldier. He had studied war, so presumably he knew more about it than they did. The methods he adopted they found irksome — drilling, marching, detailed attention to apparently unimportant minutiae. But gradually, probably almost imperceptibly, they disciplined themselves into acceptance and, in the process, turned into soldiers. They gained confidence. If they did something of which the Colonel, with his impossibly high standards, approved — then it must have been absolutely right. It seems he was more prodigal with criticism than with praise. So, in the final analysis, the survivors of that dreadful half-hour turned to him. With defeat and disaster and despair at their shoulders, they appealed to this stern arbiter of their fighting efficiency. If the Colonel were satisfied, then they had done it right. Whatever had gone wrong, *they* could do no more.

What the Colonel thought, as he watched the battalion he had so painstakingly prepared for battle, cut to pieces before his eyes, history does not precisely record. To say that he was pleased is probably to use entirely the wrong word. General Hunter-Weston, addressing what was left of the Battalion in Englebelmar six days later, told them: "You have done better than the best". The Divisional Commander,

General de Lisle, wrote to the Prime Minister of Newfoundland: "It was a magnificent display of trained and disciplined valour, and its assault only failed of success because dead men can advance no farther". These raw troops from a far-distant colony, these amateur soldiers, civilians in uniform, had gone into a battle line which included the great Guards regiments and the formations of Regulars, stiff with tradition and experience, and had emerged labelled "better than the best". Dead men can advance no farther. Surely the Battalion had no need to ask whether the Colonel were satisfied?

She shifted her gaze, which had been riveted for some time on the Y Ravine cemetery, less than four hundred yards away to the south where the land dips to its lowest point. "They may have emerged 'better than the best', but most of them emerged dead. Truly I don't see the point of it all. But at least Newfoundland was finished with the war. Their Battalion had gone, so that was the end of that I suppose. What happened to the few who lived through it?"

Indeed that was not the end of the story, not by a long way.

General Sir Douglas Haig
Commander-in-Chief

General Sir Henry Rawlinson
Forth Army Commander

General Sir Aylmer Hunter-Weston
VIII Corps Commander

General Sir Beauvoir de Lisle
Commander 29th Division

Major-General Douglas Cayley
88th Brigade Commander

Lieut.-Colonel A.L. Hadow
Newfoundland
Battalion Commander

Officers of the Newfoundland Regiment

and men.

Four members of one family who died on 1st July. (l. to r.) Capt. Eric S. Ayre, Capt. Bernard Ayre, Lieut. Wilfrid Ayre and Lieut. Gerald Ayre.

Corporal Richard Pittman
Lamaline, Newfoundland

CHAPTER SIX

THERE ARE FOUR MORE OF THEM

There is a road that turning always
Cuts off the country of Again.
Archers stand there on every side
And as it runs Time's deer is slain .
             ('The Road' — Edwin Muir)

Prime Minister Lloyd-George in his *War Memoirs* says:

> Newfoundland sent over a regiment, which took part so unyieldingly in the conflict that it used up reinforcements far quicker than they could be sent along to it. It fought at Suvla Bay in 1915, on the Somme in 1916, at Monchy and Cambrai in 1917; and by the end of 1917 its death-roll alone was more than a quarter of all the men sent from Newfoundland. Casualties had wiped out the regiment twice over.[1]

There are three other Caribou Memorials in France, besides the one at Beaumont Hamel, and one in Belgium. Each bronze caribou marks a place where the Newfoundlanders had fought with the same dogged determination as they had walked towards the machine-guns at Beaumont Hamel. The first Battalion was all but wiped out there, but on 11th July, 127 reinforcements arrived from the base at Ayr, and others followed until the Battalion was brought up to strength again. It is a grievous comment on the casualties they suffered throughout the war that they never got around to forming a Second Active Service Battalion.

The regimental structure of the British Army is not easy to explain. The Regiment enshrines spirit and tradition, it is not a quantitive entity: the home depot is a focal point for several battalions; the number varies with each regiment. Each infantry regiment bears a number which denotes its seniority: in the Twenty-Ninth Division the oldest regiment represented was the Royal Fusiliers — the 7th of Foot: the youngest, apart from the Newfoundland Regiment, was the Royal Dublin Fusiliers — the 102nd of Foot. They often had nick-names dating back to battles fought two centuries and more before: the Middlesex were known as the "Diehards", the Royal Dublins were "Neill's Blue Caps". The Newfoundlanders had no number. They were Colonial troops, supernumerary to the battle line of the British Army. But after Beaumont Hamel, number or no number, the Newfoundland Battalion could stand proudly with any British army unit. They had made their tradition. They made it in the only way possible — the hard way.

At the end of July the Battalion went up to Ypres. For ten weeks they slogged away in that unsavoury Salient. They did two ten-day tours in the front trenches north of Hooge; otherwise they built and fortified and repaired trenches — they dug and baled and riveted and wired. Inevitably some were wounded and some died.

On October 12th the Newfoundlanders found themselves again engaged in an attack in the Somme area. Whilst they had been up north in the Salient the Fourth Army had inched its way forward four and a half miles. At the end of September General Haig planned a further attack designed to push the whole line forward an average of two miles from Le Transloy and Beaulencourt (on the Peronne-Bapaume road), across the valley of the upper Ancre to Gommecourt. This was the tenth of that dreadful dozen that make up the Battle of the Somme, and it was named the Battle of the Transloy Ridge from a spur of that name that covers the villages of Le Transloy and Beaulencourt. It was to this battle that the 88th Brigade, temporarily attached to the 12th Division, was committed.

The Brigade was given two successive objectives labelled the Green Line and the Brown Line. The Green Line involved the capture of a portion of the German defences known as Hilt Trench, about 400 yards from the British position on the northern outskirts of Gueudecourt. The Brown Line was about 400 yards further on than that. Military Intelligence could supply little information about the German defences that far back, although two features named Grease Trench and Bacon Trench were surmised.

A new form of tactics had been devised for this operation, which involved unusually close co-operation between advancing infantry and supporting artillery. Briefly, the artillery put down a curtain of shrapnel fire just ahead of the attacking lines: the guns shifted their fire forward at a rate of about fifty yards each minute and the infantry were ordered to keep not more than fifty yards behind it. The obvious advantage of this manoeuvre was that the Germans were compelled by the shelling to remain under cover and had no time, as at Beaumont Hamel, to bring their machine-guns into action before the attackers were on top of them. The disadvantage was that any divergence from the strict time-table or any premature bursts and the artillery are killing their own infantry. This was what happened. *The Fighting Newfoundlander* comments:

> The innovation of the creeping barrage eventually proved to be of tremendous value; but why in this instance the barrage was first concentrated on a line 200 yards from the German front-line trenches, nobody ever understood. None of the enemy was in No Man's Land, and to try to gauge exactly where the shrapnel was falling was an impossible task .... It was estimated that thirty per cent of the attackers were put out of action before reaching the first objective, and that fully half of these fell victim to their own shell-fire. [2]

Despite this, the Newfoundlanders did capture Hilt Trench and two platoons pressed onward towards the Brown Line. Caught in the open by heavy fire and under fire in enfilade from the right by German machine guns with still three hundred yards to go, they began digging in. An already difficult position was rendered untenable by the fact that the Essex on their left, who had originally got as far as Grease Trench, were forced to retire because of the failure of the 35th Brigade on *their* left. German counter-attacks developed and the Essex Battalion was ordered back to the starting-line on the outskirts of Gueudecourt. Still the Newfoundlanders hung grimly on to their hard-won section of Hilt Trench and even extended their thin line to cover 350 yards to include part of Hilt Trench vacated by the Essex. At 3 a.m. on the 13th the Hampshires relieved the Newfoundland Battalion.

They were one of the few units in action that day who captured and retained an objective successfully; but it cost them 239 casualties, of which 120 were fatal. They collected an impressive array of medals — 1 Military Cross, a bar to an existing M.C. for Captain Butler, 3 Distinguished Conduct Medals, 8 Military Medals and 2 Croix de Guerre. The farthest point reached by men of the Regiment on 12th October, 1916, is marked by a caribou, bronze brother to the one on Hawthorn Ridge. It stands on a low mound in a small copse north of Gueudecourt, on the road to Beaulencourt, staring challengingly eastwards.

The third bronze caribou is to be found in the little village of Monchy-le-Preux, a few miles south-east of Arras. It stands above the ruins of a German strong-point in the middle of the village in front of the church: it looks towards Infantry Hill and the Bois du Sart. It commemorates the part played by the Battalion in the British offensive astride the River Scarpe in April 1917: these various battles came to be known collectively as the Battles of Arras. It was to the latter part of the First Battle of the Scarpe that the 29th Division was committed. In their part of the fighting on 14th April, the Newfoundland Battalion suffered losses only exceeded by the fatal casualties at Beaumont Hamel the previous year. Between April 12th and 15th, 7 officers and 159 other ranks were either killed or died of their wounds: 3 officers and 150 men were captured, and during their captivity 28 of them died from wounds or other causes: 7 officers and 134 other ranks were wounded. A staggering total of 17 officers and 443 other ranks were out of action, the greater percentage of them permanently. What went wrong at Monchy?

The tactics that doomed both the Newfoundland and the Essex Battalions in that ill-fated action were, to put it mildly, questionable. The Third Army, commanded by General Sir Edmund Allenby, aimed to break through the German defences between a point two and a half miles north of the Scarpe to Croiselles, a village eight miles southeast of Arras, thus turning the northern flank of the Hindenburg Line. A swift advance of five miles in the first twelve hours would open the way for the cavalry to gallop through to Cambrai. It was this vision of static warfare converted into a war of movement that guided the generals who planned the offensives. It was illusory.

On Easter Monday, April 9th, General Byng's Canadian Corps had won a brilliant victory on Vimy Ridge. The Third Army's left flank advanced three and a half miles on that day north of the Scarpe — exhilarating progress. But in the centre the advance by Sixth Corps was slowed to a halt by a defence line about two miles west of Monchy-le-Preux known as the Monchy Riegel. On the right little progress was made against the northern end of the Hindenburg Line.

On April 11th the village of Monchy was stormed by two battalions of 37th Division assisted by mounted squadrons from the 3rd Cavalry Division. This created a salient, and the village was pounded to ruins by a devastating German bombardment. Twelfth Division relieved the exhausted troops of Thirty-Seventh Division in a blinding snow-storm after dark on the night of April 11th.

The Army Commander transferred to his forward corps four divisions from his reserves; among them was the Twenty-Ninth, ordered to relieve the 12th Division at Monchy.

The 86th Brigade were in reserve in Arras. The 87th were on the right of the 88th, and their front extended southward to the Cojeul river.

The key to the battle was really the village of Guemappe, to the south of the Arras-Cambrai road. But with the 29th Division now extended over a front

previously held by two divisions — the 12th and the 3rd
— General de Lisle reported to Corps Headquarters
that the 87th Brigade had not enough time to organise
its attack on the strongly fortified Guemappe before the
proposed zero hour — dawn (5:30 a.m.) on April 14th. It
was, therefore, directed that the 87th should stand firm
whilst Guemappe was kept under bombardment and
the 88th should attack Infantry Hill at zero hour as
planned.

("I've got a nasty suspicion," said my seventeen-
year-old sternly, "that I'm going to hear a repeat
performance of Beaumont Hamel and Gueudecourt all
rolled into one!" She swept a hand across the map with
trench names that played a fleeting, tragic part in the
Battalion's history — Strong Trench, Pick Trench,
Shovel Trench, Shrapnel Trench, Arrow Trench — and
the sinister snout of Guemappe poking in from the
south. "I don't know much about tactics, but even I can
see that isn't very clever. Why couldn't they wait until
the 87th were ready? What was so urgent about Infantry Hill?")

Infantry Hill was important: it rose almost to the
height of Monchy Hill, thus blocking effectual observation eastward. But precisely why it could not wait
for twenty-four hours until the 88th could be supported
on the right flank is not clear. The battle was in its sixth
day, its initial momentum lost. The Regiment's War
Diary comments grimly: "The result of this operation,
if successful, would be a balloon-shaped position blown
from Monchy-le-Preux, which was already the apex of
a salient". (3) Such a position would obviously be the
target for German counter-attacks. Moreover, the
Twenty-Ninth Division's History reports, "A strange
thing had happened: attacks had been planned by both
sides for the same morning, and we had only forestalled
the Germans by an hour". (4)

Why the idea of a German attack upon Monchy
should be so strange is hard to understand. The Germans had been driven off Monchy Hill; it was an important stronghold: surely they would attempt to get it
back at the earliest opportunity? Be that as it may, the
hard fact remains that the Newfoundland and Essex

Battalions were going to walk head-on into trouble of awe-inspiring magnitude. The obverse side of this grisly coin is that had they not done so the massed German attack by the 3rd Bavarians would not have been broken up and would, very likely, have swept back into Monchy as planned. As it was, it was a close-run thing; in the end it was a tiny party of ten Newfoundlanders from the Headquarters staff who just saved Monchy: but more of that anon.

The assaulting companies were "D", commanded by Captain Herbert Rendell on the left, and "C" under Captain Rex Rowsell on the right. "B" Company was in support. "A" Company, under Lieutenant J. G. Bemister, was given the job of securing the right flank of the attack: as already noted, this wing was unsupported owing to the inability of the 87th to deploy in time.

Over the top they went at 5:30 a.m. They attained their objectives on Infantry Hill: after that, nothing more was seen or heard of them. On the southern flank most of "A" Company, having captured the Windmill, pushed forward to Machine Gun Wood and were likewise silenced. From later reports it appears that by nine o'clock, the pitiful remnants of the 88th Brigade's attacking companies were counter-attacked from three sides, and there was no hope of reinforcements.

At 7:30 a.m. the Essex reported that they had captured their objective and were consolidating. At 7:30 a.m. they reported an enemy mass on their left front in the vicinity of the Bois du Sart. There were no messages from the Newfoundland Regiment: snipers and machine gunners in the valley to the south (where Guemappe lay) had dealt very effectively with runners and wounded men trying to struggle back to Battalion Headquarters in Monchy.

At H.Q. Colonel Forbes-Robertson, in temporary command of the Newfoundland Battalion, had only the confused reports of the wounded as information. At ten o'clock a wounded survivor of the Essex Regiment came in saying that he was the only one of his Battalion neither killed nor captured. Lieutenant Keegan, the Signals Officer, was sent forward to reconnoitre the situation. He returned in twenty minutes with the dismaying news that there was not a single unwounded Newfoundlander east of Monchy, and further there were several hundreds of advancing Germans not a quarter of a mile away.

The Colonel reacted promptly. He sent the Adjutant back to Brigade Headquarters to report (the telephone line had been destroyed by shell-fire). He then collected about twenty men of Headquarters staff and some stragglers of the Essex Battalion and set off towards the edge of Monchy-le-Preux with the laudable intention of winning the battle by himself. The bizarre fact is that he did just that. It would, of course, be invidious to forget the deadly rifle-fire of the 4th Worcesters, the barrage put down by the Divisional Artillery and the eventual relief of the Colonel's tiny force by the 2nd Hampshires. But if Colonel Forbes-Robertson had not acted as and when he did, the German tide would have flooded into Monchy, and General de Lisle afterwards estimated that, had this happened, it would have taken 40,000 troops to recapture it.

The small force reached the last big house on the south-east corner of the village and made a dash across one hundred yards of open ground, in full view of the enemy, to a well-banked hedge that offered them protection. Inevitably they did not all reach this cover: it turned out to be the parapet of a short section of disused trench. The time was 10:50 a.m. Into the tactically fortunate ditch tumbled Lieutenant-Colonel Forbes-Robertson, Lieutenant Kevin Keegan and seven other ranks. They immediately began bursts of rapid fire which, as at Mons, misled the Germans into believing that they were opposed by a large force: so they went to ground. Ninety minutes after the beginning of the engagement, the Battalion Orderly Room Corporal crawled in from a shell-hole; his tardy arrival was caused by a bursting shell in the initial rush which had temporarily knocked him unconscious. For the next four hours these ten men coolly and professionally set about convincing the Bavarians that further advance was impossible. Their ammunition was limited, so every bullet had to count. They, therefore, reserved their fire to catch small parties attempting to reinforce Assembly Trench and Shrapnel Trench, and to pick off scouts sent forward to ascertain the size of this troublesome defence. Had not the C.O. in particular been a very good marksman (it was estimated that he personally accounted for thirty Germans in the first two hours) the enemy might not have remained in ignorance of the small numbers opposing them, and the story would have had a different ending.

On the other side the Bavarians had their troubles: heavy shelling had destroyed their telephone wires, so their urgent need for reinforcement could not be communicated to the rear. The heavy guns of Sixth Corps' artillery plastered their assembly areas in the Bois du Vert and the Bois du Sart, and a most effective curtain of fire was laid down in front of the village. They had ammunition problems too. So their attack faded out. At the end of the day everyone was "back to square one". The Newfoundland and Essex Battalions had been cut to pieces, but the Germans had not re-taken Monchy and their losses were heavy.

After dark a platoon from the Hampshires relieved the handful of Newfoundlanders. Lieutenant-Colonel Forbes-Robertson received the Distinguished Service Order, and Lieutenant Keegan the Military Cross for their part in the defence of Monchy-le-Preux. The other ranks were each awarded the Military Medal. It is sad, when recording their names to note also that at least three of them wore their M.Ms less than twelve months — the dates of their deaths, where applicable, are in brackets after the name.

Sgt. J. Ross Waterfield, Provost Sergeant, St. John's. (9th October, 1917)

Cpl. John H. Hillier, Orderly Room Corporal, St. John's.

Cpl. Charles Parsons, Signals, St. John's.

L/Cpl. Walter Pitcher, Provost Corporal, Old Bonaventure. (20th November, 1917)

Pte. Frederick Curran, Signaller, St. John's.

Pte. Japheth Hounsell, Signaller, Wesleyville. (13th April, 1918)

Pte. Albert S. Rose, Battalion Runner, Flowers Cove, St. Barbe.

Pte. V. M. Parsons, 1st Battalion, Essex Regiment.

It has to be imagination, because all five Caribou Memorials were cast from the same mould, but the one at Monchy-le-Preux does seem to have a more defiant stance than the others.

("That's three," she said, "two to come. Where are they?")

The next caribou, the one that follows in time that is, stands outside the cemetery on the Masnieres-Cambrai road. As the crow flies it is roughly fifteen miles southeast of Monchy-le-Preux. This is a proud caribou: two weeks after the Battle of Cambrai, in which the Newfoundland Battalion lived up to its already high reputation, the King approved the grant of the title 'Royal' to the Regiment. No other regiment was to have such a distinction awarded during the First World War while fighting was still in progress.

Briefly, the aim of the operation was to capture the city of Cambrai, the commanding height of Bourlon Wood on the left and the crossings of the Sensee River north of Cambrai. New tactics, involving the massed use of tanks to protect the advancing infantry, were employed: when the planned break-through had occurred, five divisions of the Cavalry Corps would pass through to exploit it.

("I've heard that one before," she said wearily.)

But this was a new approach and it began with a great victory on November 20th, 1917. Precisely why on 4th December the British line settled down for the winter only two and a half miles in front of its November starting-point (at the most advantageous: some ground to the south-east had been lost) is a matter best left to military historians. The reasons for the failure to capture Cambrai are very complex; but one thing is certain — the tanks proved their worth; the patient, suffering infantry did all that was asked of them, and more; and it was no fault of the cavalry divisions that they did not cover themselves with glory.

They had a glamour but that protects neither man nor horse from a traversing machine-gun or a shell-burst. By 1917 they were as out-dated as the bow and arrow. At Cambrai they were in action with their technological supplanters — the tanks, steel's logical answer to steel. But still the High Command could not see the obvious! The mounted man had been supreme on the battlefield since the days of chivalry: it took an unimaginable slaughter of noble chargers — and a new generation of generals — before the myth of the cavalry galloping to victory was finally laid to rest.

However, at the beginning of the battle the 6th, 20th and 12th Divisions were to capture 10,000 yards of the main Hindenburg Line and Support Line north-westward from Banteux. This accomplished, the 29th Division was to pass through: the 86th to capture Nine Wood (1000 yards north of Marcoing), the 87th to capture Marcoing itself and the objective of the 88th Brigade was Masnieres. The three Brigades were then to cross the St. Quentin Canal and seize the Masnieres-Beaurevoir Line on a three-mile front. The success of the whole operation depended upon the Division's ability to establish strongly-held positions on the far side of the canal.

Without going into too much agonising detail, a great deal of the above had been achieved by night-fall on the 20th. But the reserves of fresh infantry so necessary to maintain the momentum of a battle of this kind were not available: the nearest reinforcements were eight miles behind the front, in Havrincourt. To the north, despite bitter fighting, the British had not succeeded in dislodging the Germans from Bourlon Wood. However, the 29th Division had captured its objectives — Nine Wood, Noyelles, Marcoing, Masnieres: they had a foothold on the eastern side of the St. Quentin Canal. Unfortunately a tank, attempting to cross the main bridge from les Rues Vertes to Masnieres, crashed down into the Canal and took most of the structure with it. The bridge had already been weakened by German mining and partially destroyed, but this complete destruction meant that there was no hope of getting further armour and artillery over to the bridgehead on the farther bank.

For a week, whilst the struggle for Bourlon Wood went on, the Third Corps dug themselves in. Meantime Prince Rupprecht of Bavaria gathered together nine divisions to launch a counter-attack against the four British divisions holding the front between Marcoing and Epehy (three miles south of Gouzeaucourt): these were the 29th, 20th, 12th and 55th Divisions. On November 30th the German counter-stroke was delivered: its main thrust came from Crevecoeur and les Rues des Vignes in the south-east against the thinly-held base of the salient created by the capture of Masnieres. As at Monchy-le-Preux, had it not been for the determined resistance offered by the 88th Brigade in particular around Marcoing, alarming developments would have occurred: the Germans had succeeded in pushing in the right flank of Third Corps and would have rolled up the salient towards the north with catastrophic consequences.

November 30th was a day of "fire and movement" fighting with bayonet, rifle and bomb that cost the Newfoundland Regiment one officer and 130 other ranks. They had lost most of the ground captured earlier on the eastern bank of the canal, but the German tide was stemmed. At the left of the line beside a lock just north of les Rues Vertes the Newfoundlanders dug in. On December 3rd the Germans bombarded the Canal bank with appalling quantities of shells and mortars. Towards the end of the morning the Brigade Commander reported to Divisional Headquarters that the South Wales Borderers and the Newfoundland Regiment were "almost wiped out by shell-fire". But somehow or other the Germans were denied entry to Marcoing.

Brigadier-General Nelson said of the units of the 88th Brigade: "I have commanded the most wonderful troops in the world, who have fought the best fight any man can see and live". [5]   In 1924 Sir Douglas Haig went to St. John's to unveil Newfoundland's National War Memorial. He spoke of "the high courage and unfailing resolution'' of the Newfoundland Regiment, and particularly mentioned the important part they had played in the Battle of Cambrai. He said, ''The story of the defence of Masnieres and of the part which the Newfoundland Battalion played in it is one which, I trust, will never be forgotten on our side of the Atlantic''.

''But it has been forgotten, hasn't it?'' said my daughter gently. ''I suppose it's all in the history books with Balaclava and the Battle of Waterloo''. She climbed out of the tiny copse on to the road where the great lorries thunder along to Cambrai. ''Where is the last one — the one in Belgium?''

We had to do some travelling to find that one. Over the Belgian border to Ypres, then westward to Menin we went: beyond Menin is Courtrai and the main road to Ghent. It is a busy, ugly route with unremarkable ribbon development on either side. For an hour we drove up and down in the general area of Harlebeke and had almost given up hope of finding our last caribou; then, momentarily halted by a traffic-light, we saw it. It is on the left of the road from Courtrai in a tiny copse, sandwiched between two high garden-walls. The River Lys flows sluggishly in the valley behind the houses.

The site is close to the area of the Battalion's final engagements at Vichte and Ingoyhem, and is not far from the point where the Royal Newfoundland Regiment crossed the river at 4:00 a.m. on October 20th, 1918. This caribou commemorates those of the Regiment who lost their lives in various phases of the battles in Belgium over a period of more than two years, of which the last forty days were the toughest. The fighting at Keiberg Ridge, Ledeghem and Drie Masten exacted a heavy toll of casualties.

It was during the advance from Ledeghem to Drie Masten on 14th. October, 1918, that Private Thomas Ricketts from Middle Arm, White Bay, won the Victoria Cross. At seventeen he was the youngest holder of this highest honour for bravery in the British Army. He had joined up in 1916, falsely declaring his age to be 18.

On November 11th., 1918, the great war-machine

ground exhaustedly to a halt. The Unit War-diary briefly records: "No parade owing to Germans signing Armistice." Our caribou trail ends here.

So we turned the car southward again, back to where we had started — on the Somme.

CHAPTER SEVEN

BATTLE PLANS

"Nothing except a battle lost can be half so melancholy
as a battle won....."
(Duke of Wellington — Dispatch from
the field of Waterloo)

We climbed out of the car outside the Thiepval
Memorial, high on its windy hill. The sunlit silence was
broken only by a little breeze moaning gently through
the great arches.

She looked up and down the seemingly endless lists of
names carved on every side of every pillar of the
structure. Then she looked northwards across the
valley to Hawthorn Ridge where we had seen the first
caribou and talked together about that other July day,
the first day of the Somme.

"We lost then," she said, "but I remember hearing
somewhere once that the British tend to lose all their
battles in a war except the last one."

Stunned silence followed. A complex of misunderstandings encapsulated in so few words takes some
dealing with: one thing at a time then.

Firstly, the stretch of ground we had reviewed
together is just over half a mile wide. The total frontage
of the Twenty-Ninth Division was only 2,000 yards. The
whole battle on that day was raging up and down over
approximately 20,000 yards of the front, about 18 miles.
Therefore what happened there was not necessarily the
whole story. There were successes further south.

Secondly, the battle was, in a way, neither won nor
lost on its first day. Historically the period from 1st
July to 18th November, 1916, is designated as the Battle
of the Somme. Actually, after the initial surge on July
the first, the action developed into a slogging match:
there were a number of battles, some of them on a
major scale, interspersed by a series of trench actions.
These "minor" trench actions were of ferocious intensity and resulted, almost without exception, in
dreadful loss. Almost yard by bloody yard, however,
the British army pushed back the German army until in

November the troops were more or less in the position that the British High Command had hoped they would be in during the early days of July.

The various phases of the Somme Battle were given separate titles after the war: the phase beginning on 1st July was the First Battle of Albert. There followed:

Battle of Bazentin Ridge - July 14th to 17th
Battle of Delville Wood - July 15th to September 3rd
Battle of Pozieres Ridge - July 23rd to September 3rd
Battle of Guillemont - September 3rd to 6th
Battle of Ginchy - September 9th
Battle of Flers-Courcelette - September 15th to 22nd
Battle of Morval - September 25th to 28th
Battle of Thiepval Ridge - September 26th to 28th
Battle of Transloy Ridges - October 1st to 18th
Battle of the Ancre Heights - October 1st to
     November 11th
Battle of the Ancre (1916) - November 13th to 18th

Death is sometimes depicted as an old man with a scythe: he garnered a bumper harvest in 1916. Approximately one million two hundred thousand British, French and German individuals were casualties.

Thirdly, that old arrogant assertion that the British win only their last battles is a canard, and, in this context, a peculiarly stupid one. In 1914 Kaiser Wilhelm II instructed General von Kluck to "concentrate your energies for the immediate present upon one single purpose...to exterminate the treacherous English and walk over General French's contemptible little army". The contemptible little army referred to was the British Expeditionary Force of four infantry divisions and a cavalry division, grouped into two Army Corps under Generals Haig and Smith-Dorrien. There were approximately 90,000 men, 15,000 horses and 400 guns. They were Britain's minute standing army, the regular soldiers who fought for a shilling a day. They gleefully adopted the Kaiser's contemptuous reference as a specially honourable title: the survivors — although there were pitifully few of them after the end of 1914 — proudly called themselves "Old Contemptibles". They were followed by the Territorial units and the Yeomanry and the Indian Corps. Their quality was undeniable, but quantitatively their numbers were no match for the mighty German army.

Lord Kitchener, the Secretary for War, foresaw that the war was likely to be a prolonged business. Historically the British have an intense dislike of, and distrust for, large standing armies and for conscript service. They relied upon their navy and their small professional army for the policing and rebellion-quashing that arose in the imperial possessions they had acquired over the centuries. Kitchener saw, as few others did, the necessity for raising armies on a scale previously unthought of. He relied upon the voluntary principle, however. The famous poster with Kitchener's martial image and inescapable pointing finger with the caption "Your country needs you" was the way chosen to produce the armies. It succeeded. By the end of 1914 one million one hundred and eighty-six thousand men had volunteered. This was a splendid response; but a volunteer, however enthusiastic, cannot be metamorphosed from civilian into soldier overnight. That takes time. It was these "Kitchener's men" (as they called themselves) or the "New Armies" (as they were more officially known) that swarmed on to the Somme in the middle of 1916.

That date was just under two years ahead: meantime, the job of holding back the German armies fell upon the French and, on the left of their line of battle, the regular British Army battalions hastily called home from garrison duties all round the globe. They fought and died, retreated and died, advanced and died. The names of the battle honours on their flags are sufficient testimonial to their success in the expensive business of buying time until Kitchener's enthusiastic civilians could turn into real soldiers - Mons, Le Cateau, Landrecies, the Marne, the Aisne, First Ypres. The cost was enormous; by the end of November 1914 one-third of the original Expeditionary Force lay under the soil of France and Flanders; the average strength of these original battalions at the end of that time was one officer and thirty men.

But, whatever lost or won may mean, the B.E.F. did not lose those first battles. They certainly retreated when ordered to do so. The ordinary foot-soldier was often confused and annoyed by such orders. So far as he could see, he was standing up to his opponents well enough. Why all these rear-guard actions and retreats then? The reasons were complex and hidden from him in the fog of war. Hot and exhausted in that broiling August weather he retreated all right, but beaten he certainly was not.

After the Battle of the Marne the Allied troops began to move eastward again and then began that series of attempts at out-flanking movements that is known as "the Race to the Sea". But that is another story; and the story had no ending, happy or otherwise: it ended in stalemate. Both sides dug themselves down into the ground in deep ditches: this was the real start of trench warfare. A man standing upright is a target for bullets: a man lying prone is vulnerable to shell-splinters. Fundamental instincts of prudence and self-preservation send him literally to earth. A man in that position is much more difficult to kill. So the balance of warfare swung over in favour of the defensive position. Senior officers, trained and experienced in older ideas about movement in warfare, cavalry charges and out-flanking movements were sadly puzzled by the new situation. They mustered their martial skills and theories to overcome the problems.

In 1915 the Germans made a curious experiment on the Ypres Salient on 22nd April. The experiment was the release of a cloud of poison gas: the curious aspect of the situation was that, although it was hideously successful, Falkenhayn had supplied no reserves and no extra ammunition to exploit the four mile gap that the gas had cleared in front of the German troops — a lane that led directly to Ypres. Errors of military judgement were not confined to the British and French High Command!

In March the British attacked at Neuve Chapelle and in May at Aubers Ridge and Festubert. In September they attacked at Loos. The main results were merely to provide material for the Commonwealth War Graves

Commission cemeteries that lie so thickly clustered together in those areas.

The French undertook offensives in Artois around Arras, particularly Vimy Ridge, at a cost of a hundred thousand men. In Champagne in September the story was the same, a tragic tale of brave onward rushes checked in heaps of dead.

In Gallipoli the British attempted a bold and imaginative stroke. It was thought that an attempt to force the "back door" into Germany by defeating their allies, the Turks, might succeed where battering at the closed door of the Western Front was obviously failing.

Gallipoli is the point where the 29th Division — and ultimately the Newfoundlanders — enter. The 29th was the last of the British Regulars, formed of overseas garrisons with very few reservists. They came back to England from Calcutta, Karachi, Rangoon, Madras, Tientsin, Lucknow, Trimulgherry, Maymyo, Burma, Mhow and Mauritius. There were eleven fine regular battalions back in England by the beginning of 1915: 2nd Battalion Royal Fusiliers, 1st Battalion Lancashire Fusiliers, 1st Battalion Royal Dublin Fusiliers, 1st Battalion Royal Munster Fusiliers; these four battalions formed the 86th Brigade: the 87th Brigade consisted of 2nd South Wales Borderers, 1st Battalion King's Own Scottish Borderers, 1st Royal Inniskilling Fusiliers and the 1st Border Regiment: the 88th Brigade had the 4th Battalion Worcestershire Regiment, the 2nd Battalion Hampshire Regiment, the 1st Battalion Essex Regiment. One more battalion was required to make up 88th Brigade, and an Edinburgh Territorial unit, the 5th Royal Scots, was ordered to fill the gap.

The heavy losses sustained by the Royal Scots in the Gallipoli campaign were not made up by replacements and they lasted only till September 1915. The Newfoundlanders were assigned to take their place, thus becoming the only non-regular battalion in a division of veteran troops.

It is interesting to speculate whether the Quintishill railway disaster indirectly affected the fate of the Newfoundland Battalion. The date and the troops involved are significant, but I have never been able to establish a documentary link between the losses involved in the railway accident and the despatch of the Newfoundlanders to Gallipoli. At 6.48 on 22nd May, 1915, a troop train carrying 4th and 7th Battalions the Royal Scots from Larbert to Liverpool ran into a local train standing at Quintishill Station. Quintishill is ten miles north of Carlisle, near Gretna Junction just over the Scottish border. One minute after the first impact, which had scattered wreckage over both up and down lines, the Scottish express going north ploughed at high speed into the whole sorry mess and set it on fire. The precise number of soldiers lost was not established because the muster roll of the Royal Scots was lost in the accident: but there were only seven officers and fifty-seven other ranks who survived. Leith and Edinburgh mourned their dead. The Newfoundland Regiment was moved south to Aldershot, the place of assembly for regiments selected to go to the front, on 2nd August. On August 12th Lord Kitchener inspected them and said, "I am sending you to the Dardanelles shortly, so be prepared, and sharpen those bayonets for the Turks, for when the order comes, it will come sharply". There was an air of haste about the whole proceeding: on August 20th they were on their way to the Mediterranean in the "Megantic". If the Royal Scots were on their way to Gallipoli, via Liverpool, as regimental replacements when they were tragically and accidentally wiped off the balance sheets of war at Quintishill, then it seems reasonable to conjecture that the Newfoundland Battalion, which replaced the 5th Royal Scots in Gallipoli, was affected very nearly by the railway disaster. If the signalman at Quintishill had not made a mistake, then the Newfoundlanders might not have joined the Twenty-Ninth Division and would not have been on Hawthorn Ridge on 1st July, 1916. However, the odds are that they would have been on the Somme anyway.

Be that as it may, to Gallipoli the Newfoundlanders went. For their share in the closing months of that ill-fated campaign they earned a Military Cross and two Distinguished Conduct Medals. They survived the terrible November storm and were involved in the final successful evacuation of the peninsula from Cape Helles during the night of 8th/9th January, 1916. So the Gallipoli campaign closed in failure and withdrawal. Although the idea was a good one and there were times when it came within aching inches of being successful, although the troops involved (particularly the Australians and New Zealanders) fought and endured with unbelievable courage and did all that was asked of them and more - despite this, the planning and execution of the whole affair were devilled by conflicting plans and mismanaged muddle.

So at the end of 1915 the Allies were left with appalling casualty lists, a healthy respect for their opponents — particularly "Johnny Turk", and a few military lessons learned the hard way. Most military lessons are so learned: generals, like doctors, bury their mistakes and military education tends to proceed by enlarging cemeteries. One self-evident proposition of 1915 was that a man who stayed in his trench and used machine-gun, rifle and bomb and called in great cannon to his aid was at a distinct advantage compared with the man who climbed out of his ditch with the intention of occupying the opposition ditch. The intervening strip of ground, appropriately entitled No Man's Land, appeared to be habitable only by the dead. The opposing generals pondered over this proposition and made plans for the following year that they hoped would overcome the problem.

Out of the Allied deliberations came the Somme Offensive. Originally this was the brain-child of General Joffre. On December 5th, 1915, the Allied commanders met at Chantilly to discuss their future strategy and the French Commander-in-Chief put forward his plan. As originally envisaged, the French would attack on a twenty-five mile front from Lassigny to the Somme with forty divisions. The British would attack on a fourteen mile front from the Somme north to Hebuterne with twenty-five divisions. General Joffre's reasons for choosing as the sector for attack one which could be considered the most strongly defended on the whole Western front, the most difficult terrain and, in any case, a strategic dead-end, are not absolutely clear. The British Official History suggests that Joffre's decision "seems to have been arrived at solely because the British would be bound to take part in it." Joffre's own inappropriately cosy phrase was that the combined offensive by French and British armies should be "bras dessus bras dessus". The idea of going into battle shoulder to shoulder and with arms linked conjures up a comradely picture, but there must be a better reason for fighting a battle than merely to prove that friendly allies can fight side by side.

General Haig, militarily more realistic in approach in this instance than Joffre, favoured an attack in Flanders assisted by a landing on the Belgian coast in the rear of the Germans. To adopt one of those useful metaphors so dear to the military historians, Haig wanted to smash at the northward hinge of the front. Joffre was proposing to charge at the middle of it like a bull at a gate. But Haig was in no position to push his ideas to the point of open dissension with the French: the reasons for this were partly political. The British had started the war in the role of junior partners to the French: the small British contingent under Sir John French was insignificant beside the huge armies of France: as the British army grew in size the commander's position became stronger, but in December 1915, Sir Douglas Haig, newly appointed to be Commander-in-Chief, felt obliged to be guided in his strategy by Joffre. The British Expeditionary Force was in a foreign country — in order to get back home again it had to be shipped across the Channel. Any attempt to act independently could have led to its isolation and destruction. Kitchener's instructions to Sir John French in late 1914 were very clear: "...to co-operate closely with our Allies and render them continuous support. They (the Government) expect that you will, as far as possible, conform to the plans of General Joffre for the conduct of the campaign." Sir John had disappeared from the scene late in 1915, but Joffre was still very much there.

Whatever complex strands of thought composed Sir Douglas Haig's final attitude, he did agree to the main part of Joffre's plans for an offensive in the Somme area. Agreement was reached at a conference on February 14th, 1916. The attack was to begin in June of that year.

Astonishingly no one at that conference appears to have mentioned the possibility that the Germans might have been making plans too. It was only a week after the conference mentioned that the steel fist of an unprecedentedly massive bombardment fell upon the unfortunate French troops in the area of the Bois des Carres and the Bois de Ville in the Verdun salient. The ultimate result of this blow, which heralded the beginning of the Battle of Verdun, was to knock the Allied plan of campaign for 1916 completely out of shape.

Almost immediately Joffre asked Haig for help, which was promptly given. The French Tenth Army round Arras was replaced by Allenby's Third Army which had been holding the front between Maricourt and Hebuterne. This front was taken over by Rawlinson's newly formed Fourth Army. The front from Ypres, south almost to the River Somme, eighty or so miles of it, was now held by the British.

French soldiers referred to the Battle of Verdun as "the mincing machine". It minced the heart out of the French army and ground down its contribution to the Somme offensive from forty divisions to sixteen, of which only five attacked on 1st July. Their share of the front of attack came down from twenty-five miles to eight. Obviously with so much of their resources devoted to Verdun they could not take the part originally envisaged in the "Big Push." Joffre's men and guns could not be in two places at once, and his losses in both were horrifying.

It would seem logical that the unhappy fact of Verdun should alter the Somme plans, that the unavoidable reduction in men and material available should force Sir Douglas Haig to adjust his aims. This he did not do. He had adopted Joffre's original plan and loyally set about carrying out his part of it.

If the element of surprise could have been introduced, if the sector chosen had not been so well-defended, if Sir Douglas had examined more critically and suspiciously the information laid before him by subordinate commanders (or even lent a heeding ear to dissenting voices), if Rawlinson had not insisted upon the Fourth Army attacking in successive waves, if the French had been able to contribute more — then, perhaps, the "Big Push" would have lived up to its name and toppled the wall of the German defences. But even that long list of qualifications is not exhaustive: from the beginning the Somme Battle was dogged by far too many "ifs".

To be just, that is the hindsight of history. It has become fashionable to condemn Sir Douglas Haig on grounds varying from callousness to incompetence. There is a great deal of evidence to show that he was neither callous nor incompetent. Errors of judgement there undoubtedly were, but no one had ever had to fight such a battle before. The generals, from Sir Douglas Haig downward, made some palpable mistakes and that is understandable. What is not so easily comprehended is why they kept on making the same mistakes. R.C. Sherriff, the famous playwright and novelist, joined the Army on leaving school in 1914 and served as an infantry officer on the western front. He has this to say about the generals:

> For the most part they were men in their middle fifties, some around sixty, all near retirement age, and they had spent their best years in an army that had mainly been at peace. Their whole training had been for a type of open warfare that served well in years gone by: the Boer War and the Afghan War, campaigns against hostile tribes around the frontiers of the Empire. Many of these campaigns had needed skill and courage, and they had acquitted themselves well.
>
> Now suddenly, as elderly men, they were confronted with a totally different sort of war. The Army had fought valiantly at Mons and in the retreating engagements

that followed. It played a decisive part in stemming the German hordes and to its honour well-nigh destroyed itself in the process.

To that point the generals had fought a war of tactics and manoeuvre that they understood. In a bigger way it was like the wars they had fought in the past and were competent to manage.

But when the stale-mate came, when the armies entrenched themselves in a line of impenetrable fortifications from the sea to Switzerland, the old sort of war was over, and a new and totally different one began. It needed men with resilient, imaginative minds who could discard all the old out-dated methods and adapt themselves to new ones.

But you can't teach an old dog new tricks, and that went for the generals.

...The Germans had been bent on quick victory by attack. The Allies' main purpose was defence. They had won the first and vital round. If they had then thrown all their resources into building a line of fortifications and had garrisoned it with their ample supplies of men, they could obviously have denied the enemy all hope of victory, and the end would eventually have come, as it did in fact come, through the starvation of the German homeland through blockade. By that means victory would have come with a negligible loss of men instead of through the slaughter and maiming of a generation.

But the generals saw things in a different way. It wasn't war to dig oneself in behind a line of impregnable fortifications. It was demoralising, humiliating, a confession that you had sacrificed the initiative and lost your fighting spirit.

Most of them had won medals for open warfare in campaigns gone by, and they wanted to get back to the sort of fighting they were good at. Trench warfare, in fact, gave them nothing to do, no opportunity to display their prowess. The trenches, they admitted, were a tiresome necessity until they had mobilised enough men to break through into the open country behind the enemy lines. Once that was achieved, they could show their mettle. By bold manoeuvre, brilliant strategy and tactics they could soon have the Germans beaten. In that they were probably right. They all had experience of active warfare abroad, and the German generals had none. They had not fought a war since 1870, nearly fifty years before.

The British generals had every justification in believing that once they had broken through those German trenches, a brilliant and decisive victory lay ahead.[1]

So the generals were ageing, out-moded, old dogs to whom new tricks could not be taught. But they were the only ones we had. "Men with resilient, imaginative minds who could discard all the old out-dated methods and adapt themselves to new ones" would have made splendid generals doubtless, but where did you look for them in 1914 and 1915? Soldiering is a trade: it is learned by experience. It is difficult to select a general by competitive examination. These men had climbed the ladder of their soldierly careers by the normal method of promotion by seniority. Many of them were brave and honourable: some of them were obstinate, short-sighted and hide-bound. They all strove for success, planned and worked hard for that break-through they so desperately required. Equally, all of them seemed to suffer from that limited vision of which R.C. Sherriff speaks. History has dealt harshly with them on that account.

"I think I should like to hear about the battle itself, please," interrupted my seventeen-year-old with patient politeness. "Let's take it as read that the generals weren't all they might have been, but they probably weren't as bad as has been made out since. They made plans and the plans didn't succeed as they'd hoped. So, what really happened?"

. CHAPTER EIGHT

"IF YOU WANT TO FIND THE
CORPORAL, I KNOW WHERE HE IS!"
(Old song: "Hanging On the Old Barbed Wire")

There is no escape from the answer given on July 1st to the question of the human race. War had been "found out", overwhelmingly found out. War is an ancient impostor, but none of his masks and smiles and gallant trumpets can any longer delude us; he leads the way through the corn-fields to the cemetery of all that is best. The best is, indeed, his special prey....

('The Mind's Eye' — Edmund Blunden)

"So what really happened?" That difficult question again! I looked away from Pozieres Ridge, palely green on the sky-line in the south, and glanced somewhat distractedly north towards the village of Serre on its high ridge. There are many accounts of the Somme: some are detailed and particular, some treat it in general terms as a tragic catastrophe. But how does one encapsulate simply this tremendous and confused happening? Perhaps the best way is to take it sector by sector and, although it is militarily incorrect to describe a battle from right to left of the line, to begin in the south where there was some success.

Before we leave the generals behind in their headquarters and move out into the battle line, it is necessary to mention General Rawlinson, the commander of the Fourth Army. This great battle was, after all, mainly his responsibility. At the very beginning of March he made a complete personal reconnaissance of his twenty-mile front and on March 6th called together his corps commanders at Querrieu for detailed planning work.

Apart from the actual fighting, an enormous administrative effort was required beforehand, and to this conference came the heads of the specialist branches who would have to cope with the multifarious problems involved in supplying and maintaining a force of 17 divisions, plus three G.H.Q. divisions in reserve. Around Amiens and Albert would be thronging five hundred thousand men and one hundred thousand horses. They needed food, water, ammunition and some kind of shelter. All-important communications must be organised — roads repaired, some new ones built: railways extended; telephone cables buried under six feet of earth. Medical services had to be made ready: First Aid Posts, Advanced Dressing Stations and Casualty Clearing Stations had to be stocked with dressings, drugs and surgical instruments. Ambulances were only one of the many types of vehicles that had to be serviced with fuel and spare parts and workshops. Bore-holes had to be sunk for much-needed extra water.

Into the area in the spring of 1916 poured thousands of specialists — butchers, bakers, farriers, blacksmiths, signallers, gunners, sappers, clerks, storemen, cobblers, mechanics, medical orderlies and many more. Of course the war did not stop whilst all this was going on: the infantryman, the spearhead of all this effort, still had to man the trenches and repair them. He also dug new assembly trenches and saps. Mines were burrowed into the chalk. In addition, the divisions trained for the battle ahead and sent out night patrols to gather information for the Intelligence services.

Looking back at the scale and complexity of the detailed problems besetting that human ant-heap, it is amazing that when the day came, the whole complicated organisation meshed into gear and worked reasonably competently. One most unfortunate delay was in the matter of ambulance trains to be held in readiness for Fourth Army. On 1st. July only five trains altogether arrived in the area. But in the main the administrative organisation stood up well to the strains imposed upon it.

The original date for the beginning of the battle was June 29th. On 24th June the bombardment, the overture for Satan's Symphony of the Somme, began. This massive demonstration of fire-power cost the British tax-payer about six million pounds sterling; it involved 1,437 guns firing 1,508,652 shells. There was a gun, howitzer or mortar for every seventeen yards of enemy front line. The noise was as impressive as the figures involved, and could be clearly heard across the Channel in Southern England. The extent of the bombardment was so tremendous that some battalions were told by senior officers, "You will meet nothing but dead and wounded Germans"; "You will find the Germans all dead, not even a rat will have survived"; "Success is assured"; "You can march all the way to Pozieres before meeting any live Germans". This reassuring optimism appeared to be justified by the weight of explosive that was being hurled on to the German front-line, almost without pause. Each morning every available gun fired a concentrated barrage for eighty minutes: for the remainder of the day a continuous, but not so concentrated, barrage was employed. At night half the guns rested, but heavy machine-guns added their insolent chatter to the noise quota, harassing the rear areas in order to dislocate enemy traffic of supplies and reinforcements. Less encouraging for morale was the weather. The gunners depended on the Royal Flying Corps for information as to the effect of the bombardment on trenches and wire and to correct their fire. Because the pilots and observers were hampered by low cloud on Saturday, June 24th, Monday the 26th, Tuesday the 27th and again on June 28th, the gunners' firing programme was in arrears. It was, therefore, decided to postpone "Z" day, as it was called, to Saturday, 1st. July. (The weather on that day, as it happened, was very fine indeed).

Unfortunately, for the optimists on the Staff, the bombardment, despite its weight and duration, had certain imperfections. Some of these deficiencies were not immediately obvious, but they eventually produced conditions which swelled the casualty lists.

Firstly, shells had been mass-produced and there had been a lowering of quality. The hazard of a premature burst either just out of the gun-muzzle or in the barrel itself was an every-present nightmare to the artillerymen. Also, the delicate fuses that detonated the shells were often inferior, and produced much too high a proportion of "duds", that is shells that do not explode. There are several grimly amusing stories about "duds": even the efficient Krupps factories occasionally produced one of these useless objects. (To this very day there is a historic dud in the underground tunnels preserved on Vimy Ridge; it burrowed its way down through the chalk in 1917 and nowadays, with its ugle snout painted yellow, it is respectfully pointed out to the curious tourist).

Secondly, there were not enough guns of heavy calibre: it required a monster of 9.2" or larger to hurl a projectile that would effectually deal with the deep German dug-outs. There were only thirty-four such pieces on the British front: the French had four times as many heavy guns for each mile of their front.

Thirdly, the vital task of cutting the barbed wire was entrusted to the eighteen pounders, and their ammunition consisted mainly of shrapnel shells. These were sophisticated descendants of the old grape-shot: they exploded in the air, scattering small steel balls, resembling ball-bearings, on to the ground. They were effective against the flesh of human beings: in the first year of the war they plunged lethally into many British skulls that were protected only by the soft Service cap. When the authorities finally introduced the shrapnel helmet, or tin hat as it was popularly known, in early 1916, the number of casualties from head-wounds was dramatically reduced. (The Germans, of course, had been issued with metal helmets almost from the beginning!) But against barbed wire shrapnel had its limitations: it was the setting of the fuse that was so critical. If the shell exploded too high, the balls missed the wire. If the fuse were too long delayed, the balls were buried harmlessly in the ground. This critical timing of the fuse demanded a high degree of skill — and a certain amount of luck — in the artillery officer responsible. Optimum fusing did produce the desired result; but there was far too much uncut wire in front of the German trenches on 1st July.

General Haig does not seem to have been adequately informed about that wire; his diary entry for 30th June reads:

The weather report is favourable for

tomorrow. With God's help, I feel hopeful. The men are in splendid spirits. Several have said that they have never been so instructed and informed of the nature of the operations before them. *The wire has never been so well cut,* nor the Artillery preparation so thorough. I have seen personally all the Corps Commanders and one and all are full of confidence. The only doubt I have is regarding VIII Corps (Hunter-Weston) which has had no experience in fighting in France and has not carried out one successful raid. [2]

General Rawlinson, in his diary on the same day, records: "The artillery work during the bombardment, and the wire-cutting has been done well except in the VIII Corps, which is somewhat behindhand."[3] It seems a pity that neither senior General had the time to enquire more fully into poor "Hunter-Bunter's" predicament. (Sir Douglas disapproved of the Gallipoli venture — for a number of very good reasons; but unfortunately and illogically his displeasure extended to everyone who had been concerned in it.) Repetitions.

The day following those diary entries duly dawned. The miners of the Royal Engineers stood by the plungers that would activate the explosion of 11 mines up and down the front: between 6:25 and 7:00 a.m. the final tasks of the artillery programme were completed: the assault, support and reserve waves of the infantry waited in the crowded trenches. There was a white mist along the valleys of the Somme and the Ancre, but the rising sun soon began to disperse it. It was a beautiful summer morning.

At 7:30 the men went "over the top", that is to say they climbed out of the shelter of the trenches and walked over open ground towards the enemy. Many of them had never been "over the top" before. Far too many were never to repeat the experience. Before the war was ended the business of going "over the top" recurred hundreds of times. But it was never like this again: so many high hopes, so much enthusiasm and

optimism and so many valuable human beings — all
died that day.

South of the Somme and north of it as far as
Maricourt, the French gained all their objectives with
minimal losses. The reasons for their success were,
firstly, the overwhelming weight of their barrage — 85
heavy batteries had been pounding 8,000 yards of
German front for almost eight days with pulverising
effect; secondly, the Germans were surprised that the
French were attacking at all, because the German
Intelligence officers had deduced that the Battle of
Verdun had exhausted the French Army sufficiently to
preclude any attempt at an attack astride the Somme;
thirdly, the French tactics were more flexible — they
drew into groups crossing No Man's Land, for one
thing, and the loose spacing denied the German infantry the massed targets for their rifle-fire that were
presented by the British wave-formation. The French
had experience of mass attacks in battles such as Arras
and in the Champagne and they had learned from their
experience. Also, some formations were assisted by the
morning mist which persisted later into the morning in
the Somme valley and helped to cloak their
movements. But few of their advantages were for-
tuitous: the 12 French battalions had been set an infantry task which, although it did not present quite all
the problems facing their British allies farther north,
was quite difficult enough. They quit themselves of
their task bravely and in a business-like, soldierly sort
of way.

On their left, General Congreve's XIII Corps was
attacking up the spurs of Montauban between
Maricourt and Fricourt. The 30th and 18th Divisions
reached their objectives and by 11:30 the reserve
brigade of 30th Division had passed through Montauban
and was looking down into Caterpillar Valley and
across the Bernafay Wood. Reliable reports indicated
that Bernafay and Trones Woods and Trones Alley, the
trench connecting the two, were empty; as also was
Marlboro Wood to the north, across Caterpillar Valley.
Here was success. Here, surely, was the point where
the cavalry would ride through and gallop to victory?

Precisely why no attempt was made to exploit the success on the right wing seems a matter of some debate. One source suggests that General Rawlinson received a telephone call from XIII Corps Headquarters and had refused General Congreve permission to advance beyond his original objectives, despite the urging of the French commander on Congreve's right who was anxious to push on and exploit their joint successes. Another suggestion is that it was General Congreve himself who was disinclined to move, that he was cautiously abiding by General Rawlinson's Operation Order of 14th June which clearly stated

> ...the success of the operations as a whole largely depends on the consolidation of the definite objectives which have been allotted to each corps. Beyond these objectives no serious advance is to be made until preparations have been completed for entering on the next phase of the operation.[4]

Sir Douglas Haig had clearly expressed to General Rawlinson his view that any opportunity for a breakthrough should be seized. He was a cavalryman: he saw the Fourth Army as a gigantic knife that was to rip a hole in the enemy defences through which General Gough's cavalry could ride. General Rawlinson was an infantryman (King's Royal Rifle Corps and the Guards) with a distinguished record in Burma, the Sudan and the Boer War. He saw the army under his control as a massive battering ram, flattening the opposing trenchlines one by one, and then careful defensive preparations made before another step was taken. He was no facile optimist: his diary entry, made at 7:30 p.m. on 1st July, gave a realistic resumé of the battle — realistic save in one particular. His estimate of his battle casualties was 16,000: the cold fact was that his Army had suffered over 50,000 casualties.

Certainly General Congreve was aware that XV Corps on his left was not entirely up with him. Certainly he was careful and meticulous in his detailed planning and training and this contributed to the success achieved by XIII Corps: but he was a V.C. and people who wear that particular medal can seldom be described as cautious! On balance it would seem most likely that he, quite properly, applied to his Army Commander for approval of an advance and that this was withheld.

Lieutenant-General Horne commanded XV Corps (21st and 7th Divisions in line, 17th Division in reserve) charged with the task of capturing Fricourt and Mametz. After a bitter fight 7th Division duly captured Mametz by mid-afternoon. Like their neighbours to the south they gazed across an unscarred valley towards the village of Longueval and wondered why they were not moving forward again, and particularly they were wondering when the cavalry would come galloping through. To the north of them the 21st Division was having trouble around Fricourt. It had been planned that 21st Division should circle north of that village aiming to meet up with 7th Division, after they had completed their task of capturing Mametz, on the line of the Willow Stream. At 7:28 the Tambour mine in the German lines north-west of Fricourt was exploded; a single machine-gun crew survived the blast. It was sufficient to riddle the line of the 10th West Yorkshires on the left flank. Four machine-guns in the village itself tacked across the advancing lines of the 4th Middlesex, the 8th Somerset, the 9th and 10th King's Own Yorkshire Light Infantry with similar devastating effect.

The 50th Brigade of the 17th Division had been removed from reserve at the beginning of the battle and were in the trenches directly in front of Fricourt. They were designed initially as a holding force. By some tragic misunderstanding one company of 7th Green Howards joined the assault at zero hour. The rest of their battalion watched the horrifying spectacle of machine-gun fire knocking out all but 16 of "A" Company before they had covered scarcely forty yards. At 2:30 the remaining three companies of this unfortunate battalion went into frontal assault upon Fricourt. Brigadier-General Glasgow, in command of 50th

Brigade, upon receipt of the order, pointed out that a senior officer in command of 64th Brigade had reported to 21st Division Headquarters at 11 a.m. that there could be no link-up with 7th Division behind Fricourt in the foreseeable future; that the excessive casualties suffered by the 10th West Yorkshires in the primary assault meant that the enemy outposts were still uncrushed; that the wire in front of Fricourt was still untouched; that Fricourt itself was an enormously strong position. In reply he was told "to press home the attack as planned". At 2:00 a barrage containing a high proportion of "duds" was laid down for the prescribed thirty minutes, and then "over the top" went the Green Howards. In three minutes 15 officers and 336 men fell.

The III Corps was attacking astride the Albert-Bapaume road. The 34th Division under the command of Major-General Ingouville-Williams had the unenviable job of capturing La Boisselle, a small village to the south of the road. They were then to push forward to Contalmaison.

The composition of this Division was interesting in that it contained the Tyneside Scottish (102nd) Brigade and the Tyneside Irish Brigade (103rd). "Geordies" are generally regarded as tough and hardy, and those Brigades certainly lived up to that reputation this day.

("Died up to it is more to the mark, if this part of the front was like the others," interrupted my Young Idea gloomily.)

"Inky Bill" as the Divisional Commander was nicknamed, had no illusion about the problem facing his division and his plan was straightforward. At zero hour all the battalions in his command were to climb out of their trenches and advance. Part of the Tyneside Scottish Brigade would proceed from the front trenches up Mash Valley on the north of the main road and move in on La Boisselle, whilst the other battalions of these Northumberland Fusiliers moved in on the south. The 101st Brigade — 10th Lincolns, 11th Suffolks and two battalions of the Royal Scots — were scheduled for a march up Sausage Valley, south of La Boisselle, towards Contalmaison. One whole mile behind the British front line across a stretch of open ground named the Avoca Valley was the Tyneside Irish Brigade: their job was to follow the leading brigades, pass through them when they had captured the German trenches and the village, and then go forward towards Contalmaison to create that much-hoped for gap which the Reserve Division (19th Western, waiting behind Albert) and the cavalry could exploit. As an exercise in saturation tactics it had much to commend it: it was, at least, bold and uncomplicated.

Unfortunately, four and threequarter hours before zero on 1st July, a German listening-post just south of La Boisselle picked up the tail-end of General Rawlinson's message to all ranks before the attack. In plain language they heard

> .... impress on all infantry units the supreme importance of helping one another and holding on tight to every yard of ground gained. The accurate and sustained fire of the artillery during the bombardment should greatly assist the infantry. [5]

This resulted in a German general alert against a morning assault. Moreover "the accurate and sustained" bombardment had not destroyed the defenders of La Boisselle. Add to that the fact that the German machine-gun posts were in dominating positions relative to the surrounding ground and .... ("Here we go again!" she said wearily.)

At 7:28, right on time, up went the mines — Y Sap on the left, Lochnagar on the right and several smaller ones in front of the "Glory Hole," a British outpost opposite La Boisselle. Y Sap mine was of little help, as the Germans had evacuated these trenches because of the preliminary bombardment. So the two Tyneside Scottish battalions were caught in enfilade fire from La Boisselle and from Ovillers in the north as they advanced up Mash Valley. Few of them reached La Boisselle.

The Lochnagar mine, 90 yards across and with a rim raised fifteen feet above the trenches, was a comparative success. The left hand companies of 22nd Northumberland Fusiliers arrived at the German reserve trenches 500 yards further on, but the right-hand companies were harassed by machine-gun fire from Sausage Valley. Resistance, in the form of rifle grenades, grew ferocious as these troops neared the village fortress. Their right flank was unprotected as the Suffolks and Lincolns who should have come up Sausage Valley were not to be seen.

Their journey of 500 yards up Sausage Valley had run into enfilade fire from a German strong-point called Heligoland Redoubt, half right. In addition to that they were running into a hail of bullets from Bloater Trench, straight ahead. The unlucky Suffolks had been heavily shelled as they left their trenches. Nevertheless a handful, some 80 men, reached the Heligoland Redoubt and vanished from existence under German flame-throwers. Some detachments reached Peake Wood, 500 yards from German Brigade Headquarters in Con-talmaison. Repeated counter-attacks eventually drove them back to Wood Alley, a German support trench captured earlier.

Meantime, the Tyneside Irish battalions, 3,000 strong, began their mile-long journey across Avoca Valley promptly at zero hour. The German machine-gunners raised their sights and opened fire, belt after belt, at this extraordinary target. Very few of the two left-hand battalions reached the British front line. The 1st and 4th on the right were on slightly less exposed ground. Their journey might fairly be described as epic: twenty minutes after the start the survivors reached the British front line. Here they might have been forgiven had they taken shelter from the terrible fire, but they had been ordered to pass through the leading battalions of the 101st Brigade so on they went, across 500 yards of shell-bursts and more machine gun fire in Sausage Valley's No Man's Land, losing men every yard of the way. Two small groups of survivors joined the remnants of troops from the leading brigades in the German front line. Ahead they could see their objective — Contalmaison. There were about fifty of them. They had covered 3,000 yards of fire-swept ground since they started. There were several more trenches held by the Germans ahead, but they had been ordered to take Contalmaison so on they went again. Fragments of the unit actually did penetrate to the village but were driven back. They might have been a bit short on military experience and skills, those "Geordies", but they were very long on courage.

When night fell, "Inky Bill" went out with the stretcher-bearers into Sausage Valley to look for the remains of his Division. Three weeks later he joined the greater proportion of his Division: on 22nd July he went up to Mametz Wood and was killed by a shell-burst.

General Ingouville-Williams' northern neighbour in III Corps on 1st July was the 8th Division, a Regular Army formation commanded by Major-General Hudson. Their job was to climb the main ridge up Ovillers Spur and to capture the village of Pozieres, 2000 yards further on. General Hudson and his staff made detailed personal reconnaissance of their front prior to the battle. They concluded that their excessive frontage, the enfilade fire from the Thiepval ridge to the north and from La Boisselle across the notorious Mash Valley to the south rendered the task well-nigh impossible. The Divisional Commander suggested that it might be more advisable to delay his assault until La Boisselle and the Thiepval Spur positions were pre-occupied by the projected attacks by 34th Division and 32nd Division respectively. General Rawlinson did not agree.

Subsequent events on 1st July proved General Hudson right. The wave formations of 8th Division beat against the cliffs of the defensive positions around Ovillers practically in vain. Of the total of 4,908 casualties in the division 1,927 were killed outright.

To the north of them was General Morland's X Corps, consisting of the 32nd and 36th (Ulster) Divisions in line and the 49th (West Riding) Division in reserve. Like the 8th Division, the 32nd beat against Thiepval in vain. "Only bullet-proof soldiers could have taken Thiepval this day". [6]

From Thiepval the land falls in a sharp contour to the floor of the Ancre valley. Here road, railway and river run side by side, jammed together. Looking down to the Ancre from Thiepval one can see on the left towards Albert a large wood the French call Bois d'Authuille — the British in 1916 named it Thiepval Wood. Down in the trees by the river is the village of St. Pierre Divion. To the west of it is Grandcourt. Just below the summit of the Thiepval Ridge nowadays there is a stone tower, seventy feet high, with an avenue of flowering trees leading to it. The architecture is faintly alien to these French hills, north-east of Albert. That is not surprising as it is a replica of Helen's Tower at Clandeboye in County Down. This is the memorial, financed by public subscription in Ulster, unveiled in 1921, to the Ulstermen who died in the Great War. Inside is a handsome memorial room, on the wall of which are inscribed the words that Tennyson wrote for the Marquis of Dufferin who erected the original tower in memory of his mother:

> Helen's Tower here I stand,
> Dominant over sea and land;
> Son's love built me, and I hold
> Ulster's love in letter'd gold.

Just as the South African memorial to all their dead is in Delville Wood because that hideous place just outside Longueval is especially significant to the people of South Africa, so this Ulster Tower occupies this position because it is an especially significant place for Ulstermen.

It was around here on 1st July that the 36th (Ulster) Division won a great victory. Sadly it must be recorded that circumstances, mismanagement and misunderstandings snatched it from them — but, nevertheless, it was a high achievement.

In an hour they advanced a mile to the top of the ridge. They had stormed through the German front-line and into Schwaben Redoubt. The 9th Inniskillings consolidated at an intersection of trenches called the Crucifix. The 11th Inniskillings joined them. Both battalions had suffered heavy casualties from the machine-guns of Thiepval, but they had arrived.

Unfortunately the Corps Commander was unaware of their success. No representative of Brigade Headquarters, nor any commanding officers, seconds-in-command nor adjutants of the four battalions were permitted to leave their battle headquarters until their respective units had captured their objectives. In fact two lieutenant-colonels disobeyed that order: one was killed as soon as he started into No Man's Land. General Morland had only himself to blame that his battalions had disappeared into the smoke and the confusion of the battle and he had no precise news of their doings; there was no co-ordination of com-munications on his front.

At 8:32 Major-General Nugent, 36th Division Com-mander, asked whether or no he should commit his reserve brigade, 107 — waiting in Thiepval Wood, to pass through the leading troops of the 109th Brigade and take the German second line. The Corps Com-mander, with ill tidings from VIII Corps on his left and III Corps on his right, decided against committing them. His order to hold them back was transmitted at 9:10. It was too late. They had already moved off. Some of them arrived for the attack on the second line. Six hundred yards away lay the Grandcourt Line with Stuff and Goat Redoubts. As they set off, the opposing trenches seemed to be deserted — no fire was coming from them. The attacking Irishmen were scarcely a hundred paces from their objective when Fate, in the shape of the British artillery, intervened. The Ulstermen had been too successful, too quick. The artillery programme was arranged to a careful, rigid time-table. They fired right on time; the Irishmen were ten minutes early. British soldiers and British shells arrived on the same patch of ground at the same time. Two-thirds of the men involved became casualties. The remainder tumbled thankfully into Stuff Redoubt and prepared for counter-attacks.

Behind the 36th and 32nd Divisions were the reserve battalions of the 49th (West Riding) Division. General Morland did not commit these reserves to exploit the Ulster success because, it is said, he believed a British company had gained a foothold in Thiepval. For the

same reason he did not direct his heavy artillery on to
the village to silence those murderous machine-guns.
In the smoke, din and confusion of the battle it was
obviously difficult for the Corps Commander to
evaluate conditions; but the paucity of communications
was an administrative error. Anyone attempting to
cross No Man's Land knew that little in the village of
Thiepval was happening to distract the machine-
gunners — but General Morland was not in No Man's
Land nor, to be fair, would he have been of much use if
he had been there!

So the triumphant advance of the Ulstermen was
over. They had penetrated deeper into the enemy lines
than any other major unit; but their ammunition was
running out, the shell-fire on their captured positions
was intensifying, the Germans had rallied and called
up reinforcements and multiple counter-attacks were
developing, the divisions on their flanks left and right
had not come up. As darkness fell, the Ulster soldiers
were practically besieged on three sides. They had no
alternative, the few who were left, but to withdraw to
their earlier positions. It had been such a successful
day for the 36th (Ulster) Division but at its end, through
no fault of theirs — no shortcomings in effort or bravery
— their success slipped from them.

In the valley below Thiepval runs the road from
Beaucourt to Albert. It makes a gentle left-hand curve
here into the village of Hamel; there, one of the green
and white Commonwealth War Graves Commission
signboards points to the right where the road climbs
sharply upward to Hawthorn Ridge and thence to
Auchonvillers.

"I know what happened here," she said sadly,
quickening her step, "I know what happened here."

In Auchonvillers, at the cross-roads in the middle of
the village, a right-hand turn brings the traveller on to
a road leading backwards to Beaumont Hamel in a
hollow. Somewhat over half-way along the road a track
to the left leads up on to Redan Ridge. Six battalions
fought over this ground on 1st July: the 4th Division
under Major-General Hon. W. Lambton and two battalions from the 48th Division. The leading battalions of

the 11th Brigade — 1/Rifle Brigade, 1/East Lancashires and 1/8 Royal Warwickshires — after preliminary confused success in the enemy support trenches, disappeared without trace. Many German batteries in this area had orders to fire only against a general attack: so no flashes gave them away to air observation during the preparations for the assault. At least 66 guns opened up on the support companies of the assaulting battalions and smashed into the British trenches. Machine guns from Ridge Redoubt were firing in enfilade. This forced survivors further to the left of Redan Ridge and machine-guns firing from in front of Serre put paid to their efforts.

All the commanding officers, adjutants and company commanders were either killed or wounded; no runners returned with messages. All was confusion. Major-General Lambton wisely decided that the action must be halted until the situation was clarified and new plans made. The instructions to stop 10th and 12th Brigades were sent off at 8:35 a.m. The brigade commanders had then to send the orders on by runners. Some of the rear battalions were informed, but most of the runners were killed or wounded on their way to the foremost units and they went ahead, unaware of the orders to break off the assault. Some of them reinforced a mixture of units who had captured the Heidenkopf strong-point; others pressed on for 1,000 yards to Munich Trench. Some khaki figures were observed by a British aircraft 2,000 yards to the north-east near Pendant Copse. Odd survivors eventually crawled back and reported that the force had been taken in the rear by Germans coming down the fire-trenches from the north — Serre — and from the south. Nothing more was heard of them. There are three British cemeteries on Redan Ridge, one further to the east named Munich Trench and a very large cemetery indeed called Serre Road No. 2, just north of Redan Ridge. One looks for the vanished units in there.

To the north is the battle-ground of the 31st Division. They were the flanking formation, designed to take Serre and then wheel to protect the advance of 4th and 29th Divisions. On the left of the sector 94th Brigade was attacking with two battalions — the 12th York and Lancaster and the 11th East Lancashire. On their right were the 93rd Brigade, consisting of three battalions of the West Yorkshires (15th, 16th and 18th) and 18th Battalion of the Durham Light Infantry.

After the first quarter of an hour there was no sign of 93 Brigade. Leeds and Bradford were to mourn their dead in numbers horrifying even by the standards of 1st July. It was later learned that a detachment of the Durhams had penetrated as far as Pendant Copse: possibly they were among the khaki figures spotted by the aeroplane searching desperately for information about 4th Division, their neighbours to the south. But enemy counter-attacks swallowed up the Durhams too.

On the left the York and Lancasters and the East Lancashires began their advance across the knee-high grass. Their progress was supposed to be screened by smoke, but for some reason the smoke-screen was not laid down. There were some cheering gaps in the barbed-wire entanglements ahead, but few of the soldiers reached the wire — enfilade machine-gun fire, especially from the far left, scythed them down. Those who did survive fought their way into the front trenches and some parties made their way into Serre village itself. Behind them a concentrated German barrage pounded No Man's Land, the British front and support trenches, and the reserve battalions coming up to support. Confused fighting went on until darkness, but pitifully few of the leading battalions came back to provide even the sketchiest picture of what really happened. Some apparently reached their objective because, months later when Serre was finally captured, a dozen or so graves of men of the York and Lancasters were found.

To the left of 31st Division was the 48th (South Midland) Division, minus two battalions who were engaged with General Lambton's 4th Division to the south. There was no attack on this sector: it formed a mile-long gap between the extreme left flank of Fourth Army and Third Army's diversionary attack at Gommecourt. No dummy assembly trenches were dug, no attempts at wire-cutting were made here. Brigadier-

General Rees of 94th Infantry Brigade complained to General Hunter-Weston, Corps Commander, several days before the battle: "A child could see where the flank of our attack lay, to within ten yards...." The opposing Germans were by no means children in the ways of war: obviously nothing was going to happen on that sector. On July 1st the German artillery ignored that mile-long stretch and concentrated their fire on the 36th Division attacking Serre on their left and 56th Division attacking below Gommecourt on their right.

This quiescent sector marked the boundary between General Rawlinson's Fourth Army and two divisions of General Allenby's Third Army. The VII Corps of Third Army had been detailed for what was described as a diversionary attack upon the Gommecourt Salient. The German front line here formed a sort of right-angled bulge to the west: the bulge included the strongly-fortified village of Gommecourt and, in front of it, part of the grounds of a chateau called Gommecourt Park. The German front-line ran round the edge of this park. The tactical purpose of the British attack here was not primarily to chop off the salient but to divert German troops and gun-fire from the activities further south: not an enviable task!

It was rendered even less palatable by instructions that preparations for the attack were to be deliberately advertised to the enemy beforehand as part of the diversionary plan. General von Below did, in fact, reinforce the sector with his 2nd Guard Reserve in the middle of June. General Snow, VII Corps Commander, reported (rather ruefully, one imagines) to General Haig on 27th June: "They know we're coming all right!" The resources allotted to this sector were not over-generous — only two divisions were to be employed and no extra troops were available as reserves. In addition the right flank was "in the air", pivoting on that mile-long gap between Fourth Army and Third Army. A head-on attack on one of the most strongly fortified positions on the whole front was, especially under the circumstances prevailing, unthinkable. General Snow planned to attack north and south of the village and then link up the two divisions behind

117

Gommecourt, thus cutting off the salient — a sort of pincer movement.

The 56th (London) Division began well. By nine o'clock the London Scottish, Rangers, Queen Victoria's Rifles and London Rifle Brigade had captured all their objectives. The Queen's Westminster Rifle Battalion then passed through them to attempt the proposed link-up with the 46th (North Midland) Division east of the village. The Westminsters bombed their way up about 400 yards of German trench northwards but just at the point where they expected to meet units of the North Midland Division they met instead a strong force of Germans.

The 46th had not been doing so well. There were few gaps in the wire and obviously they were bunching together at these gaps where German small-arms fire took a terrible toll of them. A smoke-screen had been laid, but a change in the wind blew it about, confusing the advancing soldiers it had been intended to protect. Fragments of assault companies got into the German trenches, but by the end of the morning they had been hunted down and got rid of.

So the London Division was in a dangerous position because of its success: they were clawing in vain towards the northern arm of the pincer movement which just was not there. They were losing men and running short of grenades. Several attempts were made to reach them, but the German artillery had put down a ferocious barrage behind them on No Man's Land and this had made forward movements all but impossible. Gradually the tide turned against the Londoners.

It all sounds like failure again; but, in fact, VII Corps had duly performed the task set them, which was to divert upon themselves troops and fire which might otherwise have been directed upon the divisions to the south of them. And General Hunter-Weston's men were having a bad enough time of it as it was!

We had walked through Hebuterne and were well on our way back to Serre before she spoke again.

"What a story!" she said. "What a dreadful story! But what in the name of —", she looked down the hill towards Redan Ridge, "in the name of all that's unimaginably horrible," she went on, "was it all for?"

I referred her hastily to acknowledged authorities. John Harris, who wrote *The Somme, Death of a Generation* says:

> July 1st, however, was not just a wanton pointless carnage. It was also an epic of heroism that proved the moral quality of Kitchener's men. In spite of everything, these untried battalions remained un-broken — even with casualties not believed possible in inexperienced units. They carried on for almost five more months and, notwithstanding their inexperience, actually came within measurable distance of breaking the German line. [7]

Sir Basil Liddell-Hart in *History of the First World War*:

> ...For the French...July 1st may be counted a victory. But the major attack was that of the British, and here the Germans could justly claim success, for with only six divisions available and roughly a regiment holding each British division's sector of attack, they had yielded only 1,983 prisoners and a small tract of ground to the assault of thirteen British divisions. The high hopes built up beforehand had fallen to the ground, and the months of preparation and sowing had only garnered a bitter fruit. Yet although a military failure, July 1st was an epic of heroism, and, better still, the proof of the moral quality of the new armies of Britain, who, in making their supreme sacrifice of the war, passed through the most fiery and bloody of ordeals with their courage un-shaken and their fortitude established.
>
> All along the attacking line these

quondam civilians bore a percentage of losses such as no professional army of past wars had ever been deemed capable of suffering — without being broken as an effective instrument. And they carried on the struggle, equally bitter, for another five months. Experience would improve their tactical action, still more their handling by the Higher Command, but no subsequent feats could surpass the moral standard of July 1st, 'a day of an intense blue summer beauty, full of roaring violence, and confusion of death, agony and triumph. And from dawn till dark all through that day little rushes of the men of our race went towards that No-man's-land from the bloody shelter of our trenches. Some hardly left our trenches, many never crossed the green space, many died in the enemy wire, many had to fall back. Others won across, and went farther and drove the enemy back from line to line till the Battle of the Somme ended in the falling back of the enemy. [8]

Colonel A. H. Farrar-Hockley in *The Somme* (British Battles Series) has this to say, with particular reference to the casualty figures for the whole battle:

...the approximate total British, French and German was about 600,000 on either side: 1,200,000 individuals.

Decades later, the sum of anguish which these figures represent horrifies us, as once it horrified Lloyd George. For what, we cry: Beaumont Hamel, Thiepval, Pozieres, Trones Wood, Delville Wood, Flers, Morval, the sinister ruins of Serre? When we learn that the Germans pulled back secretly through the winter to a new line in the rear, the protagonists of Haig claim this abandonment by the enemy of his forward areas as a prize of the battle. The antagonists counter that it proves the ground was not worth a battle at all. It is right that we should continue the argument, right that we should be moved to do so by the knowledge of 1,200,000 killed, wounded and captive. It may be right to attack the military leaders, they held the responsibility: Joffre, Haig, Falkenhayn. But it is difficult to avoid the suspicion that they have become whipping posts or scapegoats. The Somme Battle, as indeed the whole of the Great War, was ultimately the responsibility of the peoples of Europe and the United States who permitted conditions to come to such a pass. As Cowper tells us:

'War's a game, which, were their subjects wise, Kings would not play at.... '
(The Winter Walk at Noon). [9]

Of *The First Day on the Somme* Martin Middlebrook says: "The only good to emerge from that terrible day was the display of patriotism, courage and self-sacrifice shown by the British soldiers. Theirs is a memory that their country should always cherish.[10]

John Terraine in *The Great War* points out:

It was a long time before the grisly facts about July 1st penetrated the British consciousness. Neither Haig nor General Rawlinson, commanding the Fourth Army, which fought the battle, nor any other officer at first grasped what had happened. One war correspondent wrote in his newspaper: 'It is, on balance, a good day for England and France.' But when at last the British public learned what the loss of life had been in that short span of time, the paroxysm was tremendous. Its effects were felt all through the Second World

War, influencing British strategy; they are still felt in Britain today. One reason for this was the special nature of the army that marched into the holocaust. For this was, above all, "Kitchener's Army" — the eager, devoted, physical and spiritual elite of the British nation who had volunteered at Lord Kitchener's call. The massacre of this breed of men was the price the British paid for the voluntary principle.... [11]

We turned right in Beaumont Hamel on the track that leads up out of the hollow to the eastern edge of the Newfoundland Memorial Park where the statue of a Highlander commemorates the part played by the 51st (Highland) Division in the battle in November 1916.

At the end of his book John Harris reflects:

It is still possible to stand on the slopes of the hills and wonder how anyone in their senses could have sent men in rows to attack machine-guns across those bare plains. You can follow the routes of the regiments by the names on the gravestones, and on Thiepval Ridge there is a vast memorial which contains the names cut in stone of the 74,000 dead who have no known resting-place.

And as you stand there looking over the countryside in a stillness that is a remarkable feature of the whole area, the feeling of the place is so strong you can almost hear the tramp of feet again or the whine of mouth-organs playing 'Tipperary'. The thoughts that come are poignant, a memory of trial, torment and sacrifice.

Nothing can ever touch that frail, immortal glory. Even after fifty years, it is impossible not to be stricken silent or moved to the point of tears by the knowledge of what happened on the Somme. [12]

She looked up at the quiet, dignified statue, up the wide steps. "Hm! I'll say 'Amen' to that." She gave a sudden, involuntary shiver.

"What's the matter?" I asked. "You're not cold?"

"No", she replied, "must be a..." she caught her breath, and then, firmly, finished the silly, time-honoured rejoinder, "Must be a donkey walking over my grave."

She put her arm in mine and together we walked silently round the edge of the park, back towards the Caribou Memorial.

CHAPTER NINE

BUT WHERE IS THE CORPORAL?

A hundred thousand million mites we go
Wheeling and tacking o'er the eternal plain,
Some black with death — and some white with woe.
Who sent us forth? Who take us home again?
And there is sound of hymns of praise — to whom?
And curses — on whom curses? — snap the air.
And there is hope goes hand in hand with gloom,
And blood and indignation and despair.

And there is murmuring of the multitude
And blindness and great blindness, until some
Step forth and challenge blind Vicissitude
Who tramples on them: so that fewer come.
(Charles Sorley — "A Hundred
Thousand Million Mites")

"So there wasn't anyone left?" she enquired, "Just heaps of corpses!"

It was not that simple, of course. Nor is that precisely the correct way to view the matter.

But if one deals first with the figures of casualties alone, the terrible truth becomes plain that in less than half an hour on that sunny July morning this company of people ceased to exist — as a fighting unit, at any rate. At the end of the day, at ten past ten, it was reported to Divisional Headquarters by the commander of the 88th Brigade, Brigadier-General Cayley, that the Newfoundland Regiment's First Battalion had suffered 26 casualties among its officers and 700 in the other ranks. Only 68 Newfoundlanders answered their names when the roll was called.

Add to this frightening statistic the fact that ten per cent of any battalion was kept in reserve and that a number of men were attached to Battalion Headquarters staff, and the comparative slaughter becomes even more grim. The final figures reveal that 14 officers were killed and 12 were wounded; of the 26 officers who went forward to the attack not one was left unharmed at the day's end. Of the other ranks 219 were killed or died of wounds, 91 were missing and 374 were wounded.

But the important thing to remember about them is not that they were dead, but that up till that sunny July morning in 1916 they had been very much alive. They had friends and homes and families, people to whom they mattered very much. They had been individual people, and to consider them as merely numbers in a casualty list is crassly insulting. They had names as well as regimental numbers. They had been fishermen and farmers, chartered accountants and engineers, clerks and shop assistants, workers in paper mills. They were young — the average age was about 24. Some of their photographs are in the back pages of *The First Five Hundred*. Most of them look stiff and unnatural, unwontedly serious under the uniform caps — scarcely a smile among them.

She looked up at the caribou high above, casting its shadow over us. "Where are they all?" she said. "Did they just leave them out there?" She gestured, a distressed motion of the hand, over the ground sloping away in front of us. "Were there only bits of them left? What happened to them?"

It depends what is meant by "them". Of their souls, their spirits, the essential them, obviously no one can tell. It would surely be reasonable to assume that these took flight in the direction of that largest arrow — back home to Newfoundland. But their mortal remains stayed here. Some certainly made part of the ground at which you are looking: their names are on the bronze tablets below the caribou. Many bodies were recovered, though, in the dreadful days after the first of July and decently interred with the appropriate religious words said over them in most cases. If you really want to know where those are, we will go and find them.

Originally they were buried where they fell or near to that place: often disused trenches were utilised or hastily-dug shallow graves just behind the front line. A dead body is heavy, you understand. For obvious reasons many graves were clustered around First Aid

Posts and Advanced Dressing Stations. Rough wooden crosses marked the places.

The task of finding the Newfoundlanders' graves, or any of the dead of the Great War, would probably be impossible were it not for a little-known but very great man called Fabian Ware. He was the founder of the Imperial War Graves Commission, later known as the Commonwealth War Graves Commission. He was forty-five at the outbreak of the war and, although too old to fight, he offered his services to the Red Cross. By May 1915 his ambulance work had to be given up so that he could concentrate his considerable administrative energies on the newly-formed Graves Registration Commission attached to the Adjutant-General's branch of the Army. It was due to the devotion of this remarkable man that the British War Cemeteries of both the First and the Second World Wars are places of awe-inspiring dignity and great beauty. He devoted the rest of his life to ensuring that, at least in death, the soldiers should have respectful memorial: he was, very properly, knighted for this great work. He early on grasped an essential truth: that in death all men are equal. In January 1918 the Commission issued a very important policy statement:

> The Commission feels that it would be inadvisable to leave the provision of memorials to private initiative. If memorials were allowed to be erected in the War Cemeteries according to the preference, taste and means of relatives and friends, the result would be that costly monuments put up by the well-to-do over their dead would contrast unkindly with those humbler ones which would be all that poorer folk could afford. Thus, the inspiring memory of the common sacrifice made by all ranks would lose the regularity and orderliness most becoming to the resting-places of soldiers, who fought and fell side by side, and would, in the end, grow to be ill-assorted collections of in-

dividual monuments. Thus the governing consideration which has influenced the Commission's decision is that those who have given their lives are members of one family, and children of one mother who owes to all an equal tribute of gratitude and affection, and that, in death, all, from General to Private, of whatever race or creed, should receive equal honour under a memorial which should be the common symbol of their comradeship and of the cause for which they died. [1]

So there arose in every theatre of war, but particularly on the Western Front, the serried battalions of uniform white head-stones, 2 ft. 6 ins. high and 1 ft. 3 ins. broad, gently curved at the top. Each bears a regimental badge or national emblem and a simple inscription — the man's name, rank and number and a few appropriate words chosen by his relatives. In every cemetery, usually inset in a bronze niche in one of the stone gate-posts and protected by a bronze door with a cross on it, is a register and also a visitors' book. The register lists the details of each man buried in the cemetery and a reference letter and number to the plot where he may be found. It also has a frontispiece photograph of the cemetery and a map of the surrounding area identifying adjoining cemeteries. There is an account of the fighting which produced the graves. These frontispiece introductions to the registers are an invaluable source of information concerning what happened over the ground surveyed by the visitor. In all, except the smaller cemeteries, there are also the Stone of Remembrance and the Cross of Sacrifice.

The Stone of Remembrance was designed by Sir Edwin Lutyens. It is a majestic eight ton monolith, twelve feet long and suggestive of an altar. It bears the inscription, ''Their Name Liveth For Evermore'' and is raised up on three steps. The Cross of Sacrifice was designed by another eminent architect, Reginald Blomfield. It is a tall stone cross with a bronze sword on the face of it. Nearly every cemetery has one of these; those cemeteries that would have been dwarfed by the Stone of Remembrance can manage to accommodate the Cross of Sacrifice without loss of proportion.

"Yes, but all that was after the War", she said impatiently. "What happened then, at the time, just after the battle?"

The Fighting Newfoundlander records:

The collection of the casualties, including the dead whose bodies could be recovered, was a long and painful process. It was physically impossible to bury each dead soldier in a separate grave. Only at night could the work go on, for in daylight enemy snipers would challenge all movement above ground in the forward trench area. It was found necessary to make use of abandoned trenches as multiple burying grounds, in the expectation (as in most instances proved to be the case) that subsequently the remains would be exhumed and reinterred in single graves. At that period of the war each soldier wore only one identity disc, which for official casualty records had to be removed upon burial. Accordingly, as far as possible, identification of the remains was achieved by placing in the tunic pocket a slip of paper bearing the man's name and number. Later in the war the authorities equipped men going into battle with two identity discs.

Four sad days the survivors spent in burying their dead and in salvaging weapons and equipment. Heavy rain on July 4 hampered the dispiriting work as the battered trenches, all their drainage destroyed, quickly filled with water. At the end of the fifth day a soldier was seen crawling in from No Man's Land. His reply to the sentry's challenge readily identified

him as a Newfoundlander. He turned out to
be one of the draft which had arrived on the
eve of battle. Knowing nothing of the lie of
the land, and not a little dazed after being
wounded, he could not decide which were
the German trenches and which his own.
Eventually, completely "fed up" with his
environment (as he later described it) he
made up his mind to try one or the other.
Fortunately luck was with him. [2]

So they buried their dead as well as they could. The
battle did not just stop; and in any event, it took several
days before the senior generals put together the jig-saw
puzzle of disaster. Then the juggernaut was put into
gear again and lurched forward. July melted into
August, August into September. September became
October. Each month produced more names that
became battle honours on regimental flags. By
November, bogged down in mud, the battle had banged
and thundered its way towards the eastern horizon,
leaving behind the dead of July 1st.

So in 1917 a certain amount of "tidying up" was done
on the old Somme battlefield. In 1918 the Germans
surged back over it and then ebbed back again and
continued to ebb back until finally it was all over and
done with.

Gradually the poor people to whom the land belonged
came back again. Probably in 1916 no one gave much
thought to the original use of the land that was being
reduced to a pulverised desert, nor to the original
inhabitants of the villages which, by 1918, were spots of
brick-dust in a muddy wasteland. There is a plaque in
the Hotel de Ville at Albert which succinctly describes
the appearance of the town when Armistice came. It
reads: "Il ne subsiste alors que le nom, la gloire et les
ruines". Nor did anything remain of Beaumont Hamel,
Gommecourt, Serre, Longueval, Gueudecourt and a
score of others except the name, the glory and ruins. In
some cases there were not even ruins.

The famous Golden Virgin on the tower of the basilica
at Albert disappeared completely. The basilica of

Notre Dame de Brebières was a place of pilgrimage, the Lourdes of the North as the modern publicity pamphlets proudly describe it. The reason for this is a very ancient statue of the Madonna said to have been found by a shepherd long ago in the neighbourhood of Albert. To house this venerated relic a massive cathedral of red-brick and white stone was built; it was a mixture of styles, Byzantine and Arabic influences predominating. It was crowned with a gilded dome which supported a huge statue of the Virgin Mary holding the Christ Child: the attitude of the figure was unusual in that it appeared as though the Madonna were presenting the Child to the world, holding it before her at arm's length. In the early part of the war the tower was an obvious place for artillery observation and, as such, received attention from enemy gunners. One shell burst had caused the statue to lean over at a ninety-degree angle, and a legend grew up that, if the figure fell, it would be an omen that the war would end in German victory. So French engineers ran a steel cable round the metal rod that went through the centre of the statue to keep it in place: illogical as such legends may be, it would have been exceedingly bad for morale if the Madonna figure had crashed into the square below. The grotesquely pathetic statue became a familiar sight to the thousands of British troops who marched, a hundred feet below, into the maelstrom of the Somme. When the Germans captured Albert in March 1918 the British heavy guns were turned on to the tower to deny it as an observation post to the Germans. The tower was destroyed and the Golden Virgin finally did fall. The statue disappeared and no one knew what became of it. Nine years later an exact replica of the old basilica was built, based on old plans of the structure. In 1929 the Golden Virgin again surveyed the area serenely. In just over a decade the Germans returned — with tanks this time. But in 1940 no one disturbed her; she remained remote from the events below and she is still there, gleaming in the sunlight against the blue sky.

In 1918 the French government surveyed the devastation and decided that it was useless to attempt to reclaim the land or to repair the devastated habitations, so the whole area would be turned into a national forest: but they reckoned without the French peasants to whom the area was home and had been for generations. They crept back again and grimly set about the business of returning to normal. Old plans found at Amiens enabled villages to be replaced exactly on their old sites. Special labour units cleared the land and filled in the old trenches. Particular areas were allotted to various salvage contractors who made capital out of the thousands of tons of scrap metal lying about. Many British towns and cities "adopted" French towns and villages whose names had particularly poignant significance and sent help for the rebuilding programmes. Albert was linked with Birmingham in this way, Serre with Sheffield, Foncquevillers with Derby, Gommecourt with Wolverhampton, and there were many other instances of this material expression of suffering shared and remembered. In the cool recesses of Amiens Cathedral there is a stone plaque which reads: "In sacred memory of six hundred thousand men of the armies of Great Britain and Ireland who fell in France and Belgium during the Great War 1914-1918. In this diocese lie their dead of the Battles of the Somme, 1916, the Defence of Amiens, 1918, and the March to Victory, 1918." Nor are the forces of the old Empire forgotten: in the south-west corner are flags and plaques in honour of the men of Australia, Canada, New Zealand, South Africa and Newfoundland. The Americans, too, have a corner. Under the flag of Newfoundland is a stone tablet: "To the glory of God, to the honour of the Island, and to the enduring memory of those of the Newfoundland Contingent, who fell in the first battle of the Somme.

'Behold this stone shall be a witness unto us'
Joshua 24-27

The quotation is interesting. It occurs right at the end of the Book of Joshua: this great military leader of the Hebrews was reminding his people, in his old age, that they had been neglecting their religious duties and ungratefully forgetting their debt to the Lord of Israel. Joshua reproved them sharply: "Ye cannot serve the Lord: for he is an holy God; he is a jealous God; he will not forgive your transgressions nor your sins.

"If ye forsake the Lord, and serve strange gods, then he will turn and do you hurt, and consume you, after that he hath done you good." The people, much chastened, humbly promised Joshua: "The Lord our God will we serve, and his voice will we obey." But Joshua knew the children of Israel of old: they would need reminding of their promises in the future: so "Joshua wrote these words in the book of the law of God, and took a great stone, and set it up there under an oak, that was by the sanctuary of the Lord.

"And Joshua said unto all the people, Behold, this stone shall be a witness unto us; for it hath heard all the words of the Lord which he spake unto us; it shall be therefore a witness unto you, lest you deny your God."

Out in the quiet corners of the diocese of Amiens are other stone witnesses to the peoples of Europe that service to the heathen gods of Ares and Mars brings its own punishment — the peoples hurt and consume themselves, without any divine intervention.

Perhaps one of the most distressing things about the First World War is the way in which an observer is forced to accept that people killed are numbered in thousands, in millions. There are innumerable photographs in old books of the soldiers — soldiers marching to the front, soldiers on parade being inspected by some Very Important Person, soldiers in hospital beds (looking suitably cheerful for the camera), soldiers on troop-ships, blurred figures going into action with smoke and shell-bursts. The whole effect is one of terrifying anonymity; but each one of those figures was a separate individual entity and deserves to be considered in his own right as a person, not as a drowned drop in an ocean of tragedy. If she really wanted to know where they were, those Newfoundland casualties, we would find them — man by man.

There are some fifty cemeteries near Albert where the dead of July 1st may be found, but our search for the

Newfoundlanders would not concern more than about seven of these. With the names relevant to July 1st extracted from the Roll of Honour we went to look for the appropriate white headstones with the caribou emblem.

The obvious place to begin was the Memorial Park itself. The cast bronze panels below the caribou bear the names of 591 Officers and men of the Royal Newfoundland Regiment who fell in the Great War and whose graves are not known: of these 591 individuals, 139 died on 1st July, 1916. Also commemorated on the panels are 114 men of the Newfoundland Royal Naval Reserve, and 115 of the Newfoundland Mercantile Marine.

Here we found the name of 2nd Lieutenant Gerald W. Ayre. He and three cousins of his, all grandsons of C.R. Ayre, a well-known businessman in St. John's, were all killed on that day. Three of them died within yards of each other on Hawthorn Ridge, the fourth fell at Maricourt in the southern sector of the battle. 2nd Lieutenant Clifford Henry Oliver Jupp, aged 25, son of William and Marion Jupp of Pulborough, Sussex, England, gave us momentary pause: what quirk of Fate had included this man from Sussex among the Newfoundland dead? 2nd Lieutenant Robert Bruce Reid was the son of Sir William Duff and Lady Reid of "Bartra", Circular Road, St. John's: he was just twenty-one. In 1915, in Edinburgh, Richard Shortall was commissioned from the ranks; he had enlisted as number 395, one of the original First Five Hundred "Blue Puttees"; he was wounded at Gallipoli in November 1915 and eight months later he was killed here on Hawthorn Ridge. Another promotion from the ranks was number 28, Warrant-Officer George Hayward Taylor, who also died here as a 2nd Lieutenant. There are 52 names of men from St. John's who died on Hawthorn Ridge on 1st July and whose graves are unknown. The high proportion of St. John's men is hardly surprising as it was the only considerable town on the Island; Newfoundland mainly consisted of small communities scattered around its lengthy coastline. The whole population in 1914 was barely 250,000 people. But the names of these small communities appear, heart-breakingly, in the Memorial register — Twillingate, Brigus, Harbour Grace, Bonavista, Harbour Main, Ladle Cove, Fogo, Heart's Delight, Cutwell Arm, Burges, Bell Island, Bishop's Falls. Somewhat surprisingly we find Teignmouth, Devon, among these place-names: like 2nd Lt. Jupp, Private Alfred Johnson was an Englishman who served with this largely exclusively Island contingent.

We went down from the Memorial to the south-east corner of the Park where the Y Ravine cemetery is situated. It is a small, quiet, flower-bedecked corner containing 36 Newfoundland graves, all from 1st July. Here is the body of Lance Corporal Richard Edward Hynes who won the Distinguished Conduct Medal in Gallipoli in October 1915. Near him lies Private Frank Thomas Lind. He wrote what were described as "colourful but generally fairly accurate accounts of life at the front for publication in the St. John's *Daily News.* In one of these he declared that it was impossible to get good pipe tobacco overseas: shortly afterwards donations of tobacco with the brand-name Mayo were sent to the troops, and Frank Lind was nicknamed "Mayo" Lind thereafter. This part-time war correspondent was a veteran of the Gallipoli campaign and his cheery published letters had done much for civilian morale in far-away Newfoundland. His last letter from Louvencourt, dated 29th June, had assured the people at home that they could feel proud of their regiment. Indeed they could! But — sadly — after July 1st there were no more letters from "Mayo" Lind.

We tried to pin-point the position of the cemetery in relation to the old battlefield. We took the Danger Tree and Y Ravine itself as points of reference and concluded that the cemetery must be about a third of the way between Point 60 and Point 03: in fact, just south of the right flank of the Newfoundland attack. The original skeleton of the Danger Tree, around which many Newfoundlanders were caught by enemy shrapnel on that sunny July morning so long go, has rotted away in the intervening years. The Park Warden told us that the original stump has been replaced by a concrete facsimile in precisely the same position. It is halfway down the slope, and it is very probable that Lieutenant Hubert Herder met his end near that spot. When the Commander of "B" Company, Captain Nunns, was wounded in the leg he ordered Lieutenant Herder to take charge: this he did, with considerable dash, but his span of command lasted only a few yards. His grave is in Y Ravine cemetery; he was 25 and, judging by his regimental number — 3, was one of the very earliest volunteers.

We crossed from the south-east to the north-east corner of the Park in the fold of land where part of the old German trench-line is preserved, roughly parallel to the Y Ravine itself, and came to the Hawthorn Ridge No. 2 cemetery. This gives an impression of being in deep shade though the sun does strike through the surrounding trees on to the large green oblong with its serried ranks of white headstones. There are 15 caribou badges dating from 1st July in there: only four of the men have regimental numbers indicating that they were of the First Five Hundred; among them is No. 424, Private John Allan Jeans who, at 33, was considerably above the average age.

We turned, almost with relief, from this strangely melancholy plot and followed a cart track leading away from the Park up on to the top of the ridge to Hawthorn Ridge No. 1 cemetery. It is a good half-mile away, near the crater of the Hawthorn Redoubt mine, and contains the body of No. 181, Private Joseph Wellington Evans — he is the solitary Newfoundlander in this small, wind-swept cemetery. Two French gardeners, who were clipping the surrounding hedge to military neatness, paused momentarily in their work to give us quiet greeting: "Good morning Madame, Mademoiselle". It seems sad that Private Evans is so far away from his friends, but the place itself is sunlit and clean and the pink roses round the headstones seem acutely aware of the blue sky above their heads.

Also on his own is Lance Corporal Horatio Barbour in Beaumont Hamel cemetery, another half a mile or so further to the north. We crossed two fields by the appropriate tracks to the Auchonvillers-Beaumont Hamel road at the foot of Redan Ridge. There we found the Lance Corporal surrounded by the dead of many other regiments, many other actions, and wondered briefly how he had got there: but it has to be remembered that, in all, the Somme battlefield was searched at least six times for lost bodies and isolated graves and even today bodies are still being found on the Somme. One of the gardeners told us that in the same year as our visit some workmen had been putting in new foundations to the track which leads towards Hawthorn Ridge No. 1 and had unearthed the remains of two soldiers. Obviously no personal identification was possible, but the metal regimental insignia gave them some general identity and they were reverently interred in one of the neighbouring Commission cemeteries with due honour and respect. Their headstones will read: "A Soldier of the — Regiment. Known unto God". There are many of those.

We turned right out of Beaumont Hamel cemetery and through the village of Auchonvillers on the Mailly-Maillet road. Auchonvillers was nick-named "Ocean Villas" by the troops who enjoyed the doubtful shelter of its shell-wrecked buildings in 1916: almost inevitably, Foncquevillers farther to the north behind Gommecourt, was "Funky Bleedin' Villas". Modern Auchonvillers was very quiet in the July heat; all we met on our walk through it was a tabby cat, sunning itself on the steps of the French war memorial. The entrance to the Military Cemetery is obviously a right of way at the edge of a farm; the path is divided from the farm-yard by an intermittent hedge and our progress along it was accompanied by the loud barking of a farm dog. But he fell silent as we passed through the gate into the small burial ground. There are eight Newfoundlanders here, four of whom have 1st July, 1916, as their date of death: two were 19 years of age, one 22 and one 24. Here also is Sergeant Augustus Manning, No. 177, who missed the opening of the Somme Battles. He was killed on June 1st, probably a victim of one of the forty shells a day that showed the German interest in the advanced trenches that the Newfoundland Battalion was digging about that time.

Sadly recorded is No. 1764, Private Patrick Eagan, who died of wounds on 2nd July, 1916. There are at least two dozen names on the Roll of Honour, death-dated in the first fortnight of July, who, like Private Eagan, almost certainly reflect the hidden cost of that fatal half-hour at the beginning of the month.

We emerged on the Mailly-Maillet road, pursued by the valedictory barks of the dog, who renewed his attentions the moment we replaced the cemetery register in its stone box. The barking faded away behind us as we took the right-hand turn on the road to Hamel. At the extreme edge of the village, opposite the church, is a right-hand turn to Englebelmer and, about a quarter of a mile or less along it, a left-hand turn south to Mesnil-Martinsart. Before a third of the distance to that village has been covered the familiar green sign points left up a track to the twin cemeteries of Mesnil Ridge and Knightsbridge. The rough track leads up a quiet green valley and is bordered by bushes that, about Easter-time, produce spikes of startlingly white bright blossom. The track begins to climb as the two cemeteries, one on each side, are approached, and a glance at the skyline ahead reveals the somewhat surprising fact that the evergreens surrounding the Memorial Park are not many yards distant; surprising, because it seems a long way round from Auchonvillers — the approach is from the western side, going towards the front trenches. The wry humour that produced trench nomenclature inspired Edmund Blunden to write a wistful poem with that very title: "Trench Nomenclature": but it was surely some homesick London "Tommies" who named the trenches on this sector. Names like Haymarket, Bond Street, Burlington Arcade, St. James' Street and Shaftesbury Avenue are scattered over the trench maps of June 1916. The Irish had been there too, judging by Tipperary Avenue, Limerick Junction and St. Patrick's Avenue; there were the Dublin Fusiliers of the 86th Brigade, of course, in that area. The Newfoundlanders themselves temporarily proudly imprinted a name of their own on this alien French countryside: the long support trench that ran from Auchonvillers southward was called St. John's Road — part of it is still preserved in the Memorial Park. So this cemetery most likely took its name from a communication trench. Cemeteries were often given the names that the soldiers used to designate the area — Blighty Valley, Crump Trench, Dud Corner, Lichfield Crater, Orchard Dump, Woburn Abbey and the Guards Cemetery at Windy Corner. The apparently Flemish sound of Dozinghem and Mendinghem, names given to two cemeteries behind the old Ypres salient, is misleading. Some waggish spirit in the Medical Corps had dubbed two Casualty Clearing Stations "Dosing 'Em" and "Mending 'Em", and the cemeteries contain the unsuccessful applicants to these two establishments. There was apparently another one called "Bandage 'Em" which became Bandaghem, but I never actually came across it.

However it got its name, Knightsbridge now sleeps peacefully in the sunlight on that bare green slope behind Hawthorn Ridge and there are 23 Newfoundlanders within its surrounding low stone walls. Here is 2nd Lieutenant Wilfred D. Ayre, cousin of Gerald Ayre whose name is on the bronze tablets in the Park up on the top of the hill: and Lance Corporal Matthew Greeley, aged 27, of Portugal Cove who left a widow called Sadie in Glasgow; and Private Arthur Jones, at 37 years of age considerably older than most of his comrades; and Lieutenant Frederick Courtney Mellor who came from St. Luke's Rectory, Annapolis Road, Nova Scotia. It is very quiet in this Knightsbridge, a complete contrast to the London Knightsbridge; almost too quiet — one would be grateful for the companionable din of that inquisitive farm dog in Auchonvillers! Across the rutted track in Mesnil Ridge there is only one fatality belonging to the regiment: he is Private George Robert Curnew who died on 24th April, 1916. Those were the early days of the Battalion's time in France; perhaps he "copped it" on a nocturnal working party, wiring or digging trenches, or perhaps he was the unlucky victim of an early morning German "hate" or an odd "minenwerfer" tumbling its erratic course across the sky above the trench, and poor

Private Curnew, inexperienced in such matters, would not know which way to dodge for safety.

"Whichever way he went, he's not one of ours", said my daughter firmly. "You said to look for the first of July ones." She cocked a speculative eye at the line of trees on the Auchonvillers road. "If we're going to the Ancre, couldn't we go that way? It would be much quicker, and my feet ache!" After some debate it was reluctantly agreed that we should return the way we had come. The track seemed to peter out at the cemeteries, and neither of us speak French to a standard that would enable us to conduct a meaningful dialogue with some French farmer, rightly incensed at trespass over his land. The land occupied by the cemeteries themselves was generously granted in perpetuity by the French Government in December, 1915, but because so many of the grave-yards are in the middle of fields or in other inaccessible places, many rights of way were required. That these rights still exist is a tribute to the grateful memory that the French still have, speaking generally, of the British, because these tracks must be a continuing nuisance to them in the course of their agricultural work. It is advisable not to strain their tolerance by straying from the tracks so courteously provided and maintained.

Therefore we made our way back down the silent green valley and turned left on the road to Martinsart.

"Who was to blame?" she said suddenly. "For that, I mean," indicating the gentle white dignity of the Cross of Sacrifice, still visible on the hillside to our left.

We had almost reached Martinsart before I had even begun to formulate an answer because, of course, there is no real answer.

Apportionment of blame for a given situation is a normal human reaction. The obvious targets are the high-ranking officers who were responsible for planning the battle — so obvious indeed that countless thousands of critical words have been written about them ever since. No need to add to those. But soldiers, paradoxical as it may seem, do not make wars. They fight them, but that is a different matter. Someone else has written the scenario before they step on the stage to play their parts. Politicians *make* wars: it is the statesmen, the national leaders who create the conditions, make the speeches, adopt the postures that lead finally to affairs like the Battle of the Somme. And behind the leaders are the nations themselves — an agglomeration of individuals, millions of separate human identities with hopes and fears, and loves and hates, and — above all — prejudices.

"What you're saying," cried my seventeen-year-old with sudden horror, "is that they'd only themselves to blame! That's wrong. I can't accept that. They were ordinary people, people like you and me. Are you seriously suggesting that we would do anything that could possibly contribute to something like what happened on that dreadful day?"

We were almost into Hamel by this time — where the road forks back into Albert.

"Not consciously, no. But every time we allow a preconceived notion to distort our judgement, every time we say or do something deliberately malicious or hurtful, every time we are greedy or envious, every time we adopt the attitude that a foreigner is somehow inferior just because he's foreign, then we add a drop to a tide that can roll in to produce a Somme battle."

"Nonsense!" she retorted vigorously and somewhat disrespectfully. "What you are describing, in effect, is a world of saintly characters who are not human beings at all: the interesting thing about humanity is that it's good, bad and indifferent and sometimes all three mixed up at once — mostly that, I suppose. And, anyway, are you telling me that I must stand by if I see something going on that I know is wrong? That I mustn't fight in the ultimate, for what I believe is right?"

"No, that is not what I meant," I said firmly. "I was merely pointing out that the only bit of the world you can effectually influence is yourself."

We had by this time reached the eastern edge of the village. High on the sky-line to the right gloomed the three-arched memorial at Thiepval. There are nearly 74,000 names engraved there; names of men who were killed on the Somme but who have no known graves.

This does not include the New Zealanders, Canadians, South Africans, Indians, Australians or Newfoundlanders, who have their own particular memorials to the missing. She glanced up at it with a sort of distasteful awe: I had the feeling she had not really heard.

Then, suddenly, "Ambivalent," she said triumphantly, "that's the word I want — ambivalent. You have just been cataloguing the evils of war at some length. Yet at the same time you are implying that there was something admirable in what the soldiers did."

"Thucydides, over two thousand years ago, pointed out: 'That war is an evil is something that we all know, and it would be pointless to go on cataloguing all the disadvantages involved in it.' I think I'm probably guilty of over-simplification, rather than ambivalence. The historical strands that led up to the outbreak of the First World War are exceedingly complex: if you're interested, there are a number of books that set out to explain precisely why it happened. But, allowing that it was inevitable, once it had started it acquired a sort of ghastly self-propelling mechanism of its own. Men rushed to join the colours in their thousands, and the reasons that motivated them were almost as varied as the individuals who gave up civilian jobs, and the ways of peace, and took the King's shilling to go soldiering. Some of them went because they loved their country and valued their way of life, and felt it was endangered — patriotism is the blanket word for that one. Some went because all their friends were going and they didn't want to be left out. Others saw the whole thing as an adventure; dull, monotonous civilian tasks were to be exchanged for the novelty and excitement of a new way of life. Dress Cain up in a uniform, give him a flag to wave and a trumpet to blow and he acquires a special kind of glamour — very few people saw war for what it really was: murder in mass production. But to blame them for what they did is as useless as blaming lemmings for flinging themselves over a cliff. Some terrifying racial instinct grips and drives them and that's the end of them. You have an inestimable advantage over those men of 1914; you're standing this side of the Great War in time. They still had it to come, and no one knew exactly what was coming. How could they? They were not supermen or heroes, but an unfortunate and ill-used generation. Be thankful you were born in 1954!''

We had reached the level-crossing by this time, where a right branch of the road leads over the railway and the Ancre and up the hill where the Ulster Tower stands. A goods train, which must have lumbered out of Albert some ten minutes previously, caught up with us at this point. Road and railway run side by side in this narrow part of the valley and the clanging and clattering of the wagons blocked the air with a din not to be denied. Conversation was impossible. We stood and watched the laden wagons rolling past, the width of the road away. I had a quick mental picture of a photograph I had once seen of the area near Beaumont Hamel station in 1916: there were some self-conscious looking soldiers standing about and, behind them sticking forlornly up in the air, the railway lines tossed about in despairing loops by some previous mammoth bombardment. I wished the train away; the sunlight wavered and shifted and the colour seemed to be draining out of the world. We stood together like ghostly strangers, with the grey presence of the noise battering at us. And behind the noise there was a silence, and, beyond the silence, voices and a clamorous tumult impossible to interpret. We were standing on the edge of eternity and the noise was drowning us.

Eventually the unbearable wagons rolled on their appointed way towards Beaucourt and Grandcourt and Arras. Her voice clicked the world back into sudden focus again. ''It could have been me,'' she was saying gently. ''If I'd been a boy and I'd been born in 1894, say — then it might have been me. That's what you were thinking, wasn't it? That's what you meant?''

''Yes, I suppose so,'' I agreed shakily, ''something like that.''

We are not a demonstrative family. I put back a strand of brown hair that had fallen across her forehead. ''Come on'', I said, with rather more briskness than the occasion warranted. "Let's go and see who's in here." So we climbed the left hand flight of steps into the green and gold vista of the Ancre cemetery.

Here is another of the ill-fated Ayre family — Captain Eric S. Ayre. It was his only brother, Captain Bernard P. Ayre, who was killed at Maricourt on 1st July whilst serving with the Norfolk Regiment. Here also lies No. 81, Private William Clarke: he served under the name of Private William Fowler. There are two more Britons here who served and died with their Island comrades — Lance Corporal John Hockley from Olton in Warwickshire, born in Birmingham; and Private Alexander MacDougall of St. Govan, born in Islay in Argyllshire. The Lancecorporal was 38 when he died, a year older than Private Arthur Jones in Knightsbridge. As in Knightsbridge, there are 23 of the Regiment buried in the Ancre cemetery.

"Did you count Private Clarke twice?" she enquired. "Once as Clarke and once as Fowler, I mean?"

"'No."

"Then we've finished. We've found them all." She turned over the pages of the list in front of her. "No, we haven't. Look, we've missed Corporal R. Pittman."

"Perhaps he's in one of the Serre Road cemeteries. If we go towards Béaucourt and turn left...."

"One more cemetery," she said, "and I shall collapse! Back in Albert, near the station there is a small, shady garden and a little cafe. There they sell glasses of beautiful, cool white wine."

So we postponed our search for Corporal Pittman to another day — as it turned out, to many other days. Through the long, quiet daylight hours of that July we became well-acquainted with that stretch of Picardy countryside. The search widened from the immediate environs of the battle. Perhaps he was somewhere back down the valley from the Ancre cemetery itself — in Hamel, Aveluy Wood (Lancashire (Dump), Authuille or Blighty Valley? We walked through the quiet lanes up-hill to Mesnil-Martinsart, north to Englebelmer, Mailly-Maillet and the Sucrerie and Euston Road at Colincamps. We turned east to look in Hebuterne and

Serre Road No. 1, to Ten Tree Alley at Puisieux, Munich Trench and Waggon Road and Frankfurt Trench. South to Bécourt and Bapaume Post near Albert we went. But Corporal Pittman was in none of these places.

There were many beautiful things to see: there were wild flowers in the hedgerows that one does not seem to see very often in England nowadays — red campions, pale purple vetch, yellow agrimony, scarlet pimpernels, herb robert, chickwood, blue speedwell, sorrel, scabious, deadly night-shade, pale pink wild hedge-roses and, of course, poppies. There were many of these, flaring in large scarlet patches almost everywhere. One is acutely aware of the sky in Picardy, and the cloud shadows chasing each other across the bare green hillsides; there is a quiet spaciousness about the landscape — it seems scarcely credible that it is the same place that one sees in pictures and in photographs in the Imperial War Museum. And, of course, there are the cemeteries large and small; they are, in their way, so lovely — so tidy and lovingly-tended and rose-entwined that the associated melancholy is only a groundswell of feeling beneath the overlying serenity. But we could not find Corporal Pittman in any of them.

"Isn't there a poem called 'The Poppy'?" she enquired one day as we passed one of the scarlet blurs at the roadside.

In Flanders' fields the poppies blow
Between the crosses row on row
That mark our place. And in the sky
The larks, still bravely singing, fly,
Scarce-heard above the guns below.
We are the dead. Short hours ago
We lived, saw dawn, felt sunset's glow,
Loved and were loved; and now we lie
In Flanders fields. To you, from failing hands, we
    throw
The torch: be yours to hold it high.
If ye break faith with us who die
We shall not sleep, though poppies grow
In Flanders' fields.

That's the title — 'In Flanders Fields'. It was written by a Colonel Macrae about the other famous battle area to the north — the Ypres Salient. He's buried in Wimereux, I believe.''

By this time the search had widened to include areas to the west, well to the rear of the front line — Bertrancourt, Louvencourt (where the Newfoundlanders were billeted), Acheux-en-Amienois, Varennes, Harponville, Forceville, Hedauville, Bouzincourt: there was an instinctive feeling that we were somehow out of Corporal Pittman country, we were too far over; and certainly we found no sign of him in the villages athwart the reasonably busy Doullens-Albert road.

"About that poem," she said suddenly, "what was that torch he was talking about that the dead handed on to the living?"

"It's symbolic, I suppose — torches mean light, and there is a host of associated ideas connected with the word: liberty, freedom, civilisation. The Olympic Games has a very solemn torch ceremony. It has a certain religious significance, as well.''

"But the Germans must have thought they were fighting for the right too! I remember reading somewhere that all German soldiers had "Gott Mit Uns" inscribed on their belt buckles. He couldn't have been on both sides. The Germans were described as brave and courageous soldiers; they must have thought they were fighting to defend their Fatherland or something, just as the French were fighting for France and the Russians for Holy Mother Russia and the British for...," she paused.

"Brave little Belgium?" I suggested. "But the Germans were invaders, after all. It is not considered the right thing in civilised society to go trampling all over your neighbour's back-yard, particularly when you do a lot of damage in the process.''

But before the looming argument about ends and means, military initiatives, man's free will and the involvement of the Almighty in man-made messes like war, could develop, she stopped abruptly, as the road topped a rise.

"That reminds me", she said accusingly, "where are

the German dead? I haven't seen one single German cemetery: dozens of French and British ones, but no German cemeteries."

"There is," I assured her, "an enormous one at Fricourt. It is full of black crosses instead of white headstones: there are names such as Fritz and Hans and Johann, instead of Henry and John and William: there are no flowers, as far as I remember, but the grass is clipped respectfully short. There is a 'cimitiere allemande' marked on the map at Achiet-le-Petit and another at Sapignies. Furthermore," I pointed out, "we should not find Corporal Pittman in any of those."

But this reminder of our immediate pre-occupation did not serve to turn her thoughts. "That's only three," she insisted, "and their casualties were as heavy as ours."

It was difficult to explain to her that in 1918 the French would not have considered granting land in perpetuity to an enemy who had occupied and laid waste part of their country, and killed or maimed almost five million of their men. Immediately to forgive and to forget would have been asking too much. She has friends in Germany (which I have not), and in the small town near Hanover where they live there is a beautiful memorial to the dead of 1914-1918. That is where they are commemorated — where, one assumes, they would most like to be — in their Fatherland.

So we walked down the hill towards Albert in a sort of uneasy silence. Ahead of us Notre Dame de Brebieres rose high in the sky in a glitter of light. She reverted to the poem.

"Those last three lines are familiar: 'If ye break faith with us who die'. Aren't they used on the British Legion Poppy Day Appeal posters?"

I agreed that they were used in that connection.

She glanced to the left across the landscape we had come to know so well. "I don't like to think," she said gravely, "that they should not sleep peacefully, poor ghosts! But I don't see why we still have Remembrance Sundays, all the same. We have a civic service and men in uniform lay wreaths and the trumpeters play the

Last Post — it's very moving and solemn of course. Someone recites a verse — not 'In Flanders Fields'...."

> They shall grow not old as we that are left grow old,
> Age shall not weary them, nor the years condemn;
> At the going down of the sun and in the morning
> We will remember them .

"That's right. It's got meaning for you and Dad: you've got a war to remember. So had Grand-dad. But I haven't. Nor", she added hastily, "do I want to have. But all this is in the history books now and I don't honestly feel that it's got anything to do with me."

There were times when my Young Idea used to leave me with a sense of total inadequacy. This was one of them. There is so much to be said for that argument, theoretically; but Picardy makes an instinctive appeal to the feeling that it is perilous to ignore the past: the past has threads that connect it to the present, and it is the present that shapes the future in its turn.

But before this idea became articulate she made a rather odd suggestion. "Suppose Corporal Pittman were the Unknown Soldier?"

Even if he were, his name would be recorded somewhere. It is said that to a certain place were brought the bodies of six British soldiers, expressly disinterred from the unnamed graves of the battlefields. Torn unrecognisably by the manner of their dying and therefore lost to all identity, they were closed in coffins, each draped by the flag of the country in which they were and for which they died.

Then to the place was led an officer of high rank, his eyes blind-folded, to be left alone with the dead. Moving about, his hand out-stretched, he touched the first coffin that he came upon, thus giving to the man within his everlasting name: the Unknown Warrior.

In the Abbey of Westminster, in London, these words mark his tomb:

> Beneath this stone rests the body of a
> British warrior unknown by name or rank,
> brought from France to lie among the most

illustrious of the land and buried here on Armistice Day, 11th November, 1920, in the presence of His Majesty, King George V, his Ministers of State, and the Chiefs of his Forces, and a vast concourse of the nation. Thus are commemorated the many multitudes who during the Great War of 1914-1918 gave the most that man can give, life itself, for God, for King and Country, for loved ones, home and Empire, for the sacred cause of justice, and the freedom of the world. They buried him among the Kings because he had done good toward God and toward His house.

Blind chance had picked him out to be trampled out of recognition: blind chance, guiding some General's hand, had picked him out again to be laid with the utmost honour and ceremony in the land's most venerated church. His tomb is among the great and famous of the generations, and millions have bowed a respectful head as they pass by it. But no one knows who he is: he could be the owner of any one of the 73,077 names on the arches of Thiepval, or the 54,896 engraved from floor to ceiling on the Menin Gate, or from Delville Wood or Vimy Ridge or a dozen other such places. He could have been a rogue or a saint, a back-slider or an unsung hero. He might have been a poet, a musician, a carpenter, a miner, a shop-keeper, a stock-broker. No one knows. He could have been Corporal Pittman.

But even if he were, his name would be somewhere. And still we had not found the name of Corporal Pittman.

CHAPTER TEN

I THOUGHT YOU OUGHT TO KNOW

.... Something swift and tall
Swept in and out and that was all.
Was it a bright or a dark angel? Who can know?
It left no mark upon the snow,
But suddenly it snapped the chain
Unbarred, flung wide the door
Which will not shut again;
And so we cannot sit here any more.
    We must arise and go;
The world is cold without
And dark and hedged about
With mystery and enmity and doubt,
    But we must go
Though yet we do not know
Who called, or what marks we shall leave upon the
    snow.

                    ("The Call" — Charlotte Mew)

"Why you, though?" she enquired, not ungently.
"Why should you be so interested? You're a born
pacifist! You can't stand what you describe as rows and
bothers. If anyone lets off a shot-gun within a hundred
yards, you nearly jump out of your skin. We haven't
any connections with Newfoundland, either. Grandfather was in the Royal Welsh Fusiliers. Why you?"

Why indeed — a good question: unfortunately it is not
susceptible of an answer within the terms of rational
explanation.

We stood together quietly on the top of the memorial,
gazing out towards Pozières ridge. The bronze caribou
above our heads threw a great dark shadow backwards: the noble head, topped by towering antlers, was
flung back in an attitude despairingly defiant. Basil
Gotto, the sculptor who cast the bronze image,
managed to infuse it with dignity and sorrow; it looks
as though at any moment it will move forward. It does
not move, of course, any more than the pathetic rags of
what was humanity down below the ground in the

shadow of the caribou will ever move again. Nor does any sound proceed from it despite the illusion that it is uttering some grievous, enquiring cry. There was no sound in the hot July sunshine, save for the quiet murmuring of the trees round the edge of the memorial park.

There was no sound. And there surely should have been; there should have been trumpets blowing and choirs singing and the fluttering of silken standards. There should have been a strong voice to say, "These were brave men indeed: men who did their duty as they saw it. Whether, in the long perspective of history, they were right or wrong in their beliefs is unimportant; what is important is that they believed so firmly, that they walked into the dark to prove their point. There's glory."

This is the only glory about the war that until quite recently was labelled the Great War: it proved nothing, it solved nothing, it sowed the seeds of further destruction a mere twenty-one years later. Militarily there was a victory. The Germans turned and went back whence they came. The myth, so useful to Adolf Hitler, that the German army was not defeated but betrayed by politicians was exploded long ago. Nevertheless the war, apart from military considerations, was won by no one. It ended, as it began and proceeded, in a muddle. It was hideous, bloody, filthy, clangorous, bestial, degrading, pointless. It was indescribable: even the English language runs out of adjectives to depict this particular slice of hell. It ripped a hole in the fabric of European civilisation that is not yet repaired, nor ever will be. The only great thing in that Great War was the spirit in the men who came here to Picardy and Artois and Flanders. Most of them came, never to return — thousands upon thousands of them are still here within the limited compass of our gaze.

We had moved half-way down the path that winds round the mound up to the summit topped by the caribou. There are a number of bronze arrows set in the wall that guards the path and most of them point roughly eastwards: from the top they read as follows:—

1. Englebelmer 1½ miles
2. Mailly-Maillet 1¼ miles
3. Auchonvillers
4. Hawthorn Cemetery No. 2.
5. Mine Crater 1000 yards
6. Hawthorn Cemetery No. 1.
7. Hunters Cemetery
8. Newfoundland Memorial Monchy-le-Preux 17½ miles
9. 51st Div. Memorial
10. Serre 2½ miles
11. Puisieux 3¾ miles
12. Beaumont Hamel ¾ mile
13. Danger Tree
14. Y Ravine Cemetery
15. Newfoundland Cemetery Masnieres 26 miles
16. Naval Div. Memorial 2 miles
17. New Zealand Memorial Flers 8 miles
18. Newfoundland Cemetery Gueudecourt 9½ miles
19. Canadian Memorial Courcelette 6 miles
20. South African Memorial Delville Wood 8¾ miles
21. Australian Memorial Pozieres 5 miles
22. Amiens 20 miles
23. Knightsbridge cemetery

The last two point roughly south-westward, but there is another arrow, slightly larger than the rest, and it points in the opposite direction from the majority of the others, it points due west. Even in the heat of July the raised metal letters felt cold to the touch — "Newfoundland 2500 miles." I fingered them reflectively.

"Why me?" I answered lamely. "I just thought you ought to know about them." I wish I were a professional military historian with the cool detachment and narrative skill of the best of that breed, but the tears get in my way.

She looked towards the west where the sun was slipping down the sky. Then she looked eastward towards Y Ravine and the memorial to those Scotsmen of the 51st Highland Division who finally washed over Beaumont Hamel in a tidal wave of blood in November 1916. Down there too is Hunters Cemetery, which is a huge shell-hole filled with corpses and bits of people — so they tidied it and rounded it and turfed it neatly and gave each poor dead thing at least the dignity of his name on a stone. Then she turned back to me with the sun on her face and that burning, blind anger of the very young in her eyes.

"Mad!" she said forcefully. "Stark, raving insane. The whole world gone berserk!"

A shadow passed across the sun. "All right," she went on, more quietly. "All right. Brave and — you know — touching: but *barmy!* A bad business. Best forgotten."

She wound her way down to the bottom of the monument, decorated about with ferns, shrubs and plants from Newfoundland. She stopped to look at the three bronze panels at the foot of the mount that are inscribed with the names of 820 Newfoundlanders; sailors, soldiers and merchant seamen who fell in the Great War and have no known graves. Five hundred and ninety-one of these are names of officers and men of the Regiment.

She passed along the path, dappled with sun and shade, and paused to read the epitaph carved on a bronze tablet set in stone that stands beside the path. It is so placed that appropriately one must kneel or bow the head to read it.

Tread softly here —
Go reverently and slow,
Yea, let your soul go down upon its knees,
And with bowed head and heart abased
Strive hard to grasp the future gain in this sore loss
For not one foot of this dank sod
But drank its surfeit of the blood of gallant men
Who for their Faith, their Hope, for Life and Liberty
Have made the sacrifice.
Here gave their lives, and gave right willingly for you
	and me.

From this vast altar-pile the souls of men
Sped up to God in countless multitudes:
On this grim cratered ridge they gave their all,
And, giving, won the peace of heaven and im-
    mortality.
Our hearts go out to them in boundless gratitude,
Yours — then God's; for His vast charity
All sees, all knows, all comprehends — save bounds
He has repaid their sacrifice; and we —?
God help us if we fail to pay our debt
In fullest full and all unstintingly.

                                    John Oxenham

Quite what she made of that would be difficult to say!

I followed slowly and watched her step lightly through the gate and on to the road that leads from Auchonvillers to Hamel. That sunlit road in France was leading her from the first quarter of the twentieth century towards the last quarter, in which lay her problems.

I viewed her retreating back helplessly. There in front of me was the future and behind me lay my father's generation: we did not somehow seem to be communicating.

The last quarter of the century looks like having even more problems than the first quarter: problems that also have their roots in incomprehension and hatred. Some of the difficulties are a terrifying fruit of the land behind me. Some are new — pollution and over-population and terrorism and pressures of various kinds; but all take their rise from age-old human evils such as selfishness and greed and blind stupidity.

"You could do with some of their virtues young woman", I telepathed grimly to the back of her head. "They may have been misled or mistaken in their ideas: for instance, that they were fighting for life and liberty and to save the world for democracy — how do you manage to do all that, for goodness' sake? They hated the idea of German militarism becoming predominant in Europe and they were certainly right about that! The ideals may have been a bit muddled, but they had ideals. And they had a kind of sublime

153

innocence that you, through no fault of your own, have never known. They inherited from the nineteenth century a rigid set of moral standards: they were very sure what they considered was right and what was wrong, and there were no sloppy grey areas in between. They had immense courage and stamina and a superb sense of humour. The soldierly virtues of obedience, smartness, discipline and steadiness are not to be lightly dismissed. One of the deepest fears that afflicts mankind is the fear of fear itself, and they conquered that. There was among them, as a community, a feeling that ran deeper than most human emotions: it is excessively difficult to describe unless it has been experienced — it is usually given the name of comradeship. And you think all that is best forgotten?''

"Has it occurred to you," suggested the shade of Corporal Pittman mildly, "that she could be right? You cannot mourn for a lost generation for the space of even a hundred years. New young streams run into the dark river of grief and dilute it, and that is as it should be. If Europe remembered all the slaughters of history, there would be no end to the pain. Think of the Thirty Years War alone! European air is heavy with the tramp of unquiet spirits who fought for the right as they saw it: European earth is cluttered with the bones of ordinary men who imagined a short cut to Utopia could be hewn with sword or lance, bayonet or bullet or shell. They are all about you — beneath your feet, whispering at your elbow, friend and foe alike — there are no differences between them now. Death is the great peace-maker.

"Why trouble the sunshine about her with a rehearsal of our ancient woes? She will learn nothing from those. Your generation did more for her than mine. You discovered in the microcosm of the smallest unit of creation a macrocosm of destructive power, and frightened yourselves into a fragile semblance of international order for a time. But there is more distillation of evil abroad in your world than there was in mine. How do you propose to protect her against that? Showing her the frightening results of pride and arrogant stupidity and what it did to us in a previous generation will not armour her to confront the contemporary face of the Devil.

"The long tides of time swing Empires up to a high water mark, and then ebb out to eternity and drown them: but each one leaves behind on the beach of human memory some sign. The Egyptians left some embryo ideas about life beyond life; the Greeks bequeathed to Western civilisation standards of aestheticism; the Romans left a legacy of the beauty of disciplined order and legal codes. Maybe when civilisation as you and I understand it has drowned in the tides of Time, it will leave behind a memory of us as a terrifyingly good example of the ultimate wrong way to settle arguments."

"How do you settle them then? Suppose all that you value is threatened with extinction: don't you fight for it in the last resort?"

A whisper of breeze shrugged the laurel-bushes, and rippled the tree shadows along the road towards the place where she was standing. "The sin of Cain," it murmured, "The sin of Cain?"

She was standing at the southern end of the park where a rusty old skeleton of a gun pushes its urgent snout eastward, and she turned and waved impatiently.

"Come on," said the gesture unmistakably, "Do come on. Leave the dead to care for the dead. You and I have concerns in the living world."

I turned back for a moment and looked through the gates to the raised green mound where the red triangle of the Twenty-Ninth Division still bravely glows.

I had tried to explain, really I had.

CHAPTER ELEVEN

NEWFOUNDLAND —
CORPORAL PITTMAN'S HOME

When blinding storm gusts fret thy shore,
And wild waves lash thy strand,
Thro' spindrift swirl and tempest roar
We love thee, wind-swept land....
      ('Ode to Newfoundland' - Sir Cavendish Boyle)

"What sort of a place is it?" she asked, as I caught up with her, "Newfoundland I mean — where Corporal Pittman came from."

"I was there only once and that was for a brief period. I saw less than a third of the Island. I don't really know much about it."

"What do you remember about it?"

It was high summer, round about Regatta time on the Quidi Vidi lake beside St. John's. I remember standing high on the steps of the Basilica of St. John the Baptist in brilliant sunshine, watching a white fog-bank creep through the Narrows. I remember catching my breath at the sight of an old friend in Bowring Park — Captain Basil Gotto's bronze caribou. (So there were six of them, after all). On a plaque below the mound is written: "This replica of the Newfoundland War Memorial on the battle-fields of France and Flanders was presented to the city of St. John's by Major William Howe Greene, O.B.E., in memory of old friends and comrades of the Royal Newfoundland Regiment and was unveiled by the Hon. Tasker Cook, Mayor of St. John's on 1st July, 1928." On the other side of the mound is a metal cross with the dates 1914-1919 and a list of battle-names that reads like a trumpet call: "Armentieres, Passchendaele, Ledeghem, Courtrai, Harlebeke, Suvla, Beaumont Hamel, Gueudecourt, Monchy-le-Preux, Ypres, Steenbeek, Brombeek, Masnieres". On a hill high above the caribou (about two hundred yards distant) stands Captain Gotto's other famous war sculpture — the Fighting Newfoundlander or "The Bomber" as it is sometimes called. It is a life-sized figure of a soldier in fighting array poised to throw a Mills bomb. The effect of the figure silhouetted against the sky is of almost startling movement and life. The model for "the Bomber" was a soldier of the Regiment, Sergeant Thomas Pittman. (No close relation of our Corporal Richard, as far as I could find out).

Perhaps it is to be regretted that the caribou was not positioned according to a suggestion made in an article in *The Veteran*, dated April 1921, by Captain H.A. Anderson, M.B.E. It appears that the Great War Veterans' Association Executive had an idea that the "Caribou" on a large scale, twice or four times life size, should be set up on Signal Hill in a position where it would be visible from both land and sea. Captain Anderson wrote:

> If the 'Caribou' could be so placed, and still show its length against the sky-line, that it would head towards France it would have a sentimental interest that should not be lost sight of ... (it) would be seen, as the ships were making port, by the scions of those gallant sailors who went down in the North Sea. It would be seen from the land by their soldier brothers.... It would be a superb position for a unique Monument, and no obstacle, however difficult to overcome, should be allowed to stand in the way of the scheme's fulfilment. [1]

However, sadly, the obstacles apparently were insuperable because seven years afterwards the "Caribou" was given a home in the glades of Bowring Park.

The main War Memorial on Water Street is sufficiently impressive, though conventionally so. It is a group of figures, representing the naval and military men who died in the war. The tablet, on the Duckworth Street side, says:

> To the glory of God and in perpetual remembrance to one hundred and ninety-

two men of the Newfoundland Royal Naval Reserve, thirteen hundred men of the Royal Newfoundland Regiment, one hundred and seventeen men of the Newfoundland Mercantile Marine and of all those Newfoundlanders of other units of His Majesty's or Allied Forces who gave their lives by sea and land for the defence of the British Empire in the Great War 1914-1918. For enduring witness also to the services of the men of this island who, during that war, fought, not without honour, in the navies and armies of their empire:

This monument is erected by their fellow-countrymen and was unveiled by Field Marshal Earl Haig, K.T.G.C.B. etc., First of July 1924.

'Let them give glory to the Lord and declare his praise in the islands.' Isaiah 42.10.

There is a ceremonial wreath below with the names inscribed: "Egypt, Gallipoli, the Seven Seas, France, Belgium." The whole group is surmounted by a conventional figure of Peace holding a laurel wreath.

There are only a handful of survivors of Beaumont Hamel. Even allowing for the ten per cent left in reserve there were precious few of them still alive on 2nd July, 1916. In 1920 there was a Blue Puttees Reunion and ninety-two men were present. In 1975 there were twenty present at the 55th annual reunion. I met a few of them whilst I was in St. John's. Their memories of that day in 1916 were episodic but crystal-clear. One frail old soldier I talked with blenched at the mere mention of the name Beaumont Hamel: the look in his eyes was so haunted that we moved on hastily to talk of other matters, other battles — but not that one. That corner of his memory was obviously too painful to explore at all.

Mr. J. Ryan probably did not relish the memory of that day either but he recounted it with grave courtesy.

In quiet tones he recalled his personal steps in the Regiment's path to glory from the billets in Louvencourt towards that tiny French village whose name became their proudest battle honour — Beaumont Hamel.

"It was a lovely little village, Louvencourt," he began reflectively. "At that time it was not touched by shelling although it was blasted afterwards. We were there for route-marches and exercises on the hills outside Louvencourt. The people were kind. I remember when the Battalion formed up to march off the evening before the Drive, the peasants were standing by the side of the road watching us and some of them were crying". He broke off and glanced out of the window of his pleasant living-room. "Some of them were crying," he repeated. "We didn't know why." French country people in tears at the sight of a column of uniformed men marching away was not, perhaps, surprising: they would be weeping at the sore memories of sons and brothers and husbands at Verdun. for the loss of acres of land they loved blasted and burned out of recognition. Humanity was mourning for humanity and helpless to do anything for this marching mass of men that they knew instinctively they would not see again. They offered the meed of tears.

"There was a lot of artillery," he continued. "It took a year to mass the size of artillery we had there. They used to sound off now and again but towards the end they all sounded off at once and it was like the end of the world — a terrible noise. You couldn't imagine the noise. And then there was the big mine but that didn't do much good after all. The Germans were down in deep trenches and they had those pill-boxes — we didn't know what a pill-box was at that time. There were no tanks then: they came afterwards and they smashed up the pill-boxes, but there were no tanks at that time." He sighed. "It was a lovely day, 1st July — a bright, sunny day with the sun burning down. The officer gave the signal and we started off, but we never got through the wire. Most of us never got as far as the wire. Our guns were firing: we had those heavy Stokes guns we called them. We had a little bit of knowledge about where we had to go, but the wire in front of us wasn't cut really. There was a man — Jack French, I think it was — he made a dive with his wire-cutters to cut the wire, but a bullet came along and killed him and he died on the wire. We never got through it. A shell came along and pitched right amongst us and one man — name of Jack Elliott — he was blown to pieces. It must have pitched right on his toes. We were all slammed to the ground." He paused. There were no more memories of that day. "There was one chap, I remember, he was killed 1st July — he cheered us up, before the attack it was, with a recitation about Dangerous Dan McGrew". He smiled. "I forget his name," he said apologetically. "I forget, you know — names and that. It's a long time ago."

The barbed wire jags into all their memories: the blazing sunshine and the big mine and the wire. I spent the whole of one glorious summer afternoon in the D.V.A. (Department of Veterans Affairs) Pavilion in the General Hospital listening to Mr. Walter Day, a lively seventy-five year old. Despite the fact that we were talking about destruction and death there was a vibrancy in his talk — a love of life, an embracing affection in his remembrance of those comrades of long ago. He was very young at the time of the battle. "I was the youngest on the books," he told me proudly, "The youngest that enlisted at that time. I spent my fifteenth birthday in the army, so you can't get 'em much younger than that!" Indeed you cannot, ex-Private Walter Day: but surely it is a sad comment on that long-ago world that, however tall and well-grown you were, no one apparently questioned your assertion that you were four years older than you actually were? Remembering some of the youthful faces in the pictures at the back of *The First Five Hundred* you were not the only under-age volunteer.

Although Walter Day's account is not strictly chronological — mention of a name or an incident led us into some interesting by-ways of recollection and the narrative, therefore, got itself tangled up — it is, perhaps, best to set it down as exactly as possible as I heard it. Whilst I was listening, it seemed to me that the conversation held sympathetic undertones of Shakespeare's *Henry V*: occasional echoes of that most splendid of statements about warfare kept coming into my mind.

"The sun was blazin' on us," he began. "It was a Saturday morning. I'll never forget it. Our pouches were full — we had ten in, one in the breech and nine in the magazine of the rifle. And we had the small haversack which we had the artillery disc on and a red streak of paint on it, on this tin triangle thing that was the Divisional sign. And so we went over. Oh, and we had two Mills bombs, one in each pocket. I'm tellin' the truth of it: I was actually there. I was sixteen years old at the time. Tommy Ricketts's brother, George Ricketts, he went over with me. He was killed in December 1917. And Captain Gus O'Brien, he was a fine officer. Once he took the socks off his feet to give to Shea because Shea's feet were sore: he took his long boots off and took his socks off to give to Shea. He was killed at Gueudecourt in October that year. There was only an odd one got past the wire and that's where they stayed, too. We never saw Beaumont Hamel: there was never a Newfoundlander in Beaumont Hamel unless he was taken prisoner, of course. And there weren't many of those."

He paused momentarily, his gaze on a point beyond my head, as though looking down that terrible slope of long ago.

"I didn't get no more than halfway towards our own wire. Two nights before this they'd cut gaps in our own wire — the Germans see the gaps cut in the wire and they had their guns trained on them. They had us lumbered from start to finish — see? They thought that after all this shelling and bombing the Germans' line was cut to pieces: and then when the mine went up and in any case it scarcely touched their front line, why, that was it! We'd had it, but we didn't know it." He returned bitterly to those lethal corridors in the barbed-wire. "When we went it was no use 'cos it was nearly all over — they was all jammed with all dead, all killed. It was mostly machine-guns was doin' all the damage. There wasn't all that many shells, but there was an awful lot of machine-guns. The machine-guns was going right down at your feet, chopping at your feet.

"I went over and there was a man hurt right in front of me. 'I can't stop,' I said, 'I got to keep going.'

'I know that, sonny,' he said. He was trying to bandage up hisself. We had a field-dressing under our tunics. There was no such thing as bandaging — just get in and get out the best way you could. Nothing we could do — nothing — until nightfall. Then we tried to bury what we could, and then they took us out and sent up the ten per cent to do the clearing-up in the night, and still the Germans were firing at us. Couldn't leave 'em in the open with the sun — hottest day I believe we had in France, that Saturday morning, the first of July. I'll never forget it. The sun was blazin' on us. I suppose it was one of the best days we had in France — the sun blazin' right down on us!" ("Old men forget: yet all shall be forgot, But he'll remember....")

"I was at Gueudecourt, too, but I didn't go over the top: I was put back in the ten per cent on account of being in the first of July. I wasn't at Monchy either. I was back in England. I got sick and I was taken out. I got that trench-fever and I was bad with it. It was after Monchy was over I got the message back that my brother was killed. He was Captain Murphy's orderly."

Captain Leo Murphy survived the war. He wrote a melancholy little poem which survives in *The Book of Newfoundland* (Volume 1) edited by J.R. Smallwood.

SHADOWS

There hangs a sombre curtain which divides
The present from the future. What it hides
No lore can tell save that a patient band
Of shadowy tomorrows waiting stand
To issue forth and thus become today;
And then pass on, for none of them can stay.
Many or few I know not. This I know.
With ashen brow and countenance of woe,
Dumbly, the last sad morrow of them all
Still, motionless awaits Fate's final call
To swift advance from whence she stands apart;
And write with pallid fingers o'er thy heart

Life's doom, the word inevitable, "must",
That shuts Time's book, resolving dust to dust.

Perhaps Captain Murphy was remembering his friends for whom Time's book had shut prematurely; the young men of the Island whose yesterdays had been tragically few and for whom there were no tomorrows. Among them his own young orderly, Walter Day's brother.

"He was my oldest brother — the one who was killed at Monchy. I had two other brothers back home but they were too young to go."

"So were you," I interrupted gently.

"Oh God, yes," agreed Mr. Day with feeling. "Oh! By God, yes I was. I wasn't at the Dardanelles you know. Before that we were inspected by Lord Kitchener and all them. Jack Ryan, he was at Gallipoli but I wasn't. It's a wonder I got as far as I did! But about two years after I was gone, my next brother — he was only fifteen — he tried to go. But my mother stopped him rightaway. 'No more of this,' she said, 'It's bad enough to have the others gone at fifteen and seventeen — one killed and one still over there. It's bad enough.' So she told Dr. Macpherson and so he said, 'Thomas, get dressed and go home and go to school.' ("For who is he whose chin is but enriched/With one appearing hair that will not follow/Those culled and choice-drawn cavaliers to France?" *Henry V* Act III Chorus).

"I used to go to night-school and work in the day. I was driving a horse then. I used to work at the West End store. And when I was going, Mr. Parker — old Mr. Jim Parker — he shook hands before I left." He paused for a moment to contemplate his youthful pre-Beaumont Hamel memory and then continued.

"We went down over the incline towards our own wire. There was only an odd one got past the wire. We never got over no German wire, I'd swear on a stack o' Bibles. Few got past our own wire.

"There was a raid before the Drive. Captain Bert Butler got the M.C. for that. We got a few decorations for that one. Jack Lukins was killed, and his brother George was killed two days after on First July. They had their faces blackened and all, and there was a chap there called George Phillips — he was a Jacky-tar. Now what happened, he got into the German trenches in that raid and he stayed there all that night and come back the next morning; how he got back no one knows that. But he got the message out to the Battalion: 'Never make that Drive, because every German over there has a machine-gun waiting for us.' But you know, General Headquarters — a mucky lot — they didn't want to hear anything at all about it because he was a private. He got killed 12th October. Now he had the Military Medal and the Russian Cross: he was the only one who got a Russian Cross. He was a Jack-a-Tar and he looked a real hard one. He was a real soldier. He might look rugged and tobacco-chewin' and all that, but I tell you he was a man! And he was right. But the big shots didn't want to hear that from a private, specially an overseas one. He was right, though. He stayed in them German trenches all that night: when he got back in the morning — and he was there, he was really there; he had two or three German buttons and a piece of a propeller thing off a German tunic. He got out, though. He said, 'Never make this Drive', but they wouldn't listen to him.'' (''We see yonder the beginning of the day, but I think we shall never see the end of it.'' *Henry V* Act IV, Scene 1).

''They said it was a court-martial matter, but after first July they didn't do it because they knowed he was right. 'Never make this Drive' he said.'' Mr. Day shook his head sadly over the past obtuseness of the General Staff.

''We were with the English regiments — Hampshires and Worcesters and Essex — attached to the 88th Brigade. There were some good Irish regiments, too. The Guards was there too — away on the right somewhere. The whole line was like a horse-show, see, and when they gave the signal the whole line moved forward together. There was three brigades facing Beaumont Hamel but we never got into Beaumont Hamel that day. We never see that village. There was never a Newfoundlander in Beaumont Hamel unless he was taken prisoner.

"Peter - er - what was his name? Peter ...." he corrugated his brow. "He spent years in the Sanatorium — lived down here in the East End." After a moment or two his brow cleared. "Mr. Peter Barron — that was his name," he finally declared triumphantly. "I knew I'd get it! Private Peter Barron! I'm glad I got that name for you now. He was taken prisoner, taken in the raiding party on the 29th of June — second time he went over — the only prisoner that was taken.

"Captain Ayre took us over, D Company, first July. Wes March was sent home and I asked him to call at my house — we lived at 48 Mullock Street — to tell my mother and father we were all right. At that time we were. We couldn't know we were going over the top first July. He said the boys were pretty well. But, a fortnight after, the Drive was on and the slaughter was over and Wes March was still back there." ("....take mercy on the poor souls for whom this hungry war Opens his vasty jaws...." *Henry V* Act II, Scene 4). He paused momentarily and then returned to the subject of Captain Wes. "But on the twelfth of October he was in the line and he went right to town. He won the M.C. and the Croix de Guerre and he went right to town on every German he see. 'I'll give it ye,' he used to say. 'I'll give it ye, wipin' us out!' He chuckled happily at the memory of Captain March's vengeful foray at Gueudecourt amongst the enemies of Newfoundland. "He was that sort. Now Jimmy Ledeghem, Captain Jim — he was killed 12th. October — he was first in July and came out of it, but he got it right early and he fell into the shell-hole and he got brought in by stretcher-bearers. Art Hammond was one of them, I think. He's alive now out at Corner Brook. He was in here last summer; he had some business with the doctor down there but he's still going strong. He's seventy-nine years old — seventy-nine or eighty. I'm seventy-five and I was the youngest on the books." His voice trailed away for a moment.

"There's a few of us in here. Kelly, Jimmy Kelly, he was in the Signals and a "D" Company man too; and there was another man — George Lawrence, he was wounded in the head and leg, he was a "C" Company man. And then there was Eric Robinson. Oh! and Jack Aylward — they were tailors on Water Street years ago — he was a regular "D" Company man. We were side by side in the trench before we went over, before Captain Ayre blew the whistle to go over; and George Gulliver was on my left — a good soldier and a good man. He looked after me when I was young over there and he was always with me even at home now through life, even up to now but he is aged up a bit and he is a bit on the deaf side. Jack Aylward that morning, a Roman Catholic, a good Roman Catholic, he took out his scapular and a small medal. Now at that time we had no pins so he took a piece of rusty barbed wire that was there in the trench and he wound it around over his hat, the button on his tunic, his scapular, and I asked him if he would give me the little medal, and I'd do the same.

"Yes, Walter", he said, "I will." I wish to God he was here with me now. And I wound the wire with the medal around me hat and I believe from that day to this that it brought the two of us back. He was wounded too, bad, and I had to keep going. That was it.

I never seen my brother though in that drive until I seen him after in the village after he come through it. Bill MacGillivary was another he told me he was up there. That was one thing — I didn't want to leave out them two names.

We had a lot more from Beaumont Hamel in here, but they died you know. I'd roughly guess there's not forty — I'd say about thirty men left from First July here in St. John's and the outports and all." There was a short silence. ("We few, we happy few, we band of brothers: for he today who sheds his blood with me Shall be my brother...." *Henry V* Act IV, Scene 3).

The shade of Captain March fell across the conversation again. "He won the M.C. you know, at Gueudecourt, and the Croix de Guerre — he went right to town. We collected a lot of medals one way and another. But the most we collected was in the 9th. Scottish Division when Richard Power — he died a month or so ago — he was the most decorated soldier we had. He had the D.C.M. and the Military Medal,

French Croix de Guerre and Legion d'Honneur. All that was done up in Belgium. That's where Tommy Ricketts got his V.C. Did you see along Water Street they put a plaque where his shop used to be? He kept a drug-store after the war and lately they pulled it down, but they put a plaque where it used to be.''

"Memorial to Sergeant Thomas Ricketts, V.C., Croix de Guerre, D.C.M. 1901-1967. Soldier - Pharmacist - Citizen. June 10th, 1972. And a pestle and mortar in bas-relief on the top?''

"That's right,'' he agreed. "He's buried out there,'' he nodded his head towards the tree-lined cemetery across the road from the General Hospital. "They put his Victoria Cross on his grave: that is, they chiselled it on the head-stone.''

"Blue Puttees they call us,'' he said proudly. "But really the name was given to the first five hundred that enlisted. They called them that because they didn't have the proper khaki puttees and they got some navy-blue stuff from somewhere. They didn't have caps neither. Nor rifles at first. But now they call all us old soldiers Blue Puttees. But I wasn't really a Blue Puttee — that was only the first five hundred. 1660 was my number. I came out in January 1919. 1660, Private Walter Day — buck-private.''

"They're the people who win the wars, Mr. Day,'' I reminded him with a grin, and was rewarded with a shout of delighted laughter.

"That's right,'' said Walter Day. "By God, you're right.'' For a moment he watched the pencil scurrying across the pages of my note-book. "Ye're a fast writer,'' he commented admiringly.

I glanced up and out of the second-floor windows of the hospital to where the sun was slanting across the cemetery, and the shadows were lengthening over Tommy Ricketts' grave. Then I looked back at the bright old eyes.

"I have to write quickly, Mr. Day,'' I said.

ENVOI

We found him eventually, a long time afterwards, almost by accident. We were in the neighbourhood of Auchonvillers and we had turned in at the gates of the Memorial Park to pay our respects, as it were. We always felt at home there, and the quiet peace received us graciously as ever.

I went up the winding path to the top of the Memorial, but she stayed at the bottom looking at the lists of names on the bronze panels. I could not see her: she was hidden from my sight by the outward bulge of the mound. Her voice floated upwards in the still air.

"How do you spell Pittman?"

"P, i, double t, m, a, n. Why?"

She did not answer me directly but asked another question. "Where did you get his name from in the first place?"

"The Roll of Honour in the regimental history."

"Come down here a minute."

I retraced my steps to the bottom of the mound. She pointed eagerly to a name inscribed on the middle panel. "There's a Corporal R. of that name, but it's spelt with only one t — Pitman."

We looked at each other, then made our way to the stone pillar with the bronze niche containing the cemetery register. His regimental number would settle the question. Sure enough, there was the entry:

"PITMAN, Cpl. Richard, 400. Killed in action at Beaumont-Hamel 1st July, 1916. Age 28. Son of Robert and Phyllis Pitman, of Lamaline."

"But how did we miss him?" I wondered, puzzled and somehow hurt. Then I had a swift mental picture of her brown head bent over the cemetery registers, and the questing forefinger going down the long columns of names, checking at the words "Newfoundland Regiment", moving over to the date to find out whether it was 1st July, 1916: between tm and tt there are eight letters of the alphabet and that can mean a lot of space in those tragic records. Perhaps it was not so surprising after all that we had missed his name.

"I'm glad we found him, anyway," she said, giving

me a quick hug. "It lays a ghost for both of us; and it would have hurt my heart to think of one of our Newfoundlanders without even so much as his name carved on a stone."

I watched her go up the sunlit road as I had watched her go some years before. Then I turned briefly again and looked through the gate.

"One of our Newfoundlanders! It's all right, Corporal. *She* won't forget."

No answer sounded in my mind's ear. There was no reason to expect one. He had ceased to care a long time ago. The important thing was that we should care, that we should be willing to listen to the lessons that history can teach. If we are not willing to learn from the mistakes of the past then there is no hope for us. The terrorist and the bully-boy will inherit the earth, and the battlefield they will make of it will make even the Somme and Paschaendaele pale into insignificance. "The price of freedom is eternal vigilance." Corporal Pitman had stood up for what he had been told was right, what he believed he had to do.

"And what became of him?" The query is sardonic. "Your precious history rolled right over him and flattened him in the mud. What's the good of that?"

There are times when we all have to stand up and be counted and run the risk of being flattened. But stand up we must if the time does come. If it comes and if we recognise its arrival.

There was a great peace lying like a coverlet over the land, not even a slight breeze to stir the pink heads of the roses. I put the cemetery register back in its stone container behind the small bronze door with the cross on it, and quietly closed the gate.

RICHARD PITMAN

He was twenty-eight when he died. The official record of his army service is brief. The page is dated 3/10/14: it offers the following information:

Draft No. 1
Date of Enlistment — 5 Sept. 14.
Age of Enlistment — 26
Married (Yes or No) — No.

Name: Pit/man, Richard. (Strange that the confusion about the letters in his name appears at the very beginning, on this official entry).

Regt. No. 400

Next of Kin: Walters, Mrs. Elizabeth

Relationship — Sister

Casualties:

Hospital 1/1/16 Ad. Jaundice. H.S. "Oxfordshire".
   do. 4/1/16 Ad. do. St. Paul H., Malta.
   do. 23/3/16 Dis. to duty. Base, Alexandria.

Unit 9/6/16 Joined Battalion, France

Unit 1/7/16 Killed in Action. Somme.

Promotions, Reductions, etc.

17/6/15 L/Cpl.

14/11/15 Corpl.

Services in the Field

1 Bn. Date of Embarkation	Expeditionary Force
20/8/15	B.M.E.F.
13/4/16	B.E.F

And that is all. Under the heading "Honours, Awards, etc." there is a blank. The entry headed "Discharge-Authority, Date, Where, Cause" is obviously blank too. He was discharged of his duties by a very High Authority indeed; the date was almost certainly 1st July, 1916; the exact whereabouts is unknown, but is somewhere in that forty or fifty acres of French ground that form the Memorial Park; the precise cause was a shell fragment perhaps, or a shrapnel ball or a machine-gun bullet or a rifle bullet or a shell-burst or mortar explosion. The precise cause is unimportant really: what is important is that Richard Pitman ceased to exist.

What is even more important is that for twenty-eight years and three months before that hideous, sunlit day he had been very much alive. Even after sixty years there are people who remember that life with affection and respect.

He was, apparently, a fisherman. He lived in the outport of Lamaline on the southernmost tip of the Burin Peninsula. Lamaline is a scattered community of brightly-painted wooden houses round a wide bay: in the centre of the bay is an island connected to the mainland by a raised causeway. The most notable feature of the flat landscape is a fine wooden church. In the cemetery at the front of the church is a stone stele, a sort of miniature version of Cleopatra's Needle — about seven feet high. On it are inscribed these words: "Erected by the Society of United Fishermen in memory of two brethren of the Order who fell in the Great War." One of the brethren was, almost inevitably, a sailor who lost his life at sea. The other is Richard Pitman. The monument records: "In loving memory of Wm. Richard Pitman, son of the late Robert and Phyllis Pitman. Enlisted as soldier August 25th, 1914. Killed in action at the Battle of the Somme July 1st, 1916. Aged 28 years and 3 months. 'Nobly he died while doing his duty.' "

The family consisted of Richard and two sisters, Rose and Elizabeth. After the death of their mother, Phyllis Pitman, the father married a lady called Emma who became the mother of a baby girl named Dorcas. Robert Pitman died when Dorcas was seven years old and Richard assumed responsibility for the little girl. She is an elderly lady now, but recalls "he was like a father *and* a brother to me, and we loved each other very much. His death in the Battle of the Somme in 1916 was a great shock and grief to me."

One of his young boy cousins in Lamaline, Mr. George Cake (now also advanced in years, of course) remembers him as "a tall, good-looking man. He lived with his sister Rose on the west side of Lamaline. Just before the Great War he trained with the Naval Reserve in St. John's, but when the war broke out he switched to the army. In the early August, I remember, my mother gave me a note and told me to go to the Meadow where he lived and give it to him. When I arrived he was sitting at the table in the kitchen, having a meal. When he had read the note he smiled and said to me, 'You go back and tell your mother I would sooner be going to the war than sitting here eating my dinner.' So he went and he was wounded out there the next year: when he came out of hospital he wrote to my mother and told her Jonathon Brett went overseas with him in that Five Hundred crowd. He told us that Pitman had been picked out to go in the Military Police but he would have no part of it; he wanted to go back with the boys."

This is borne out by Mr. Cake's brother, Fred. "He had a narrow escape in Gallipoli when a bullet went through his cap, wounding him slightly in the head. He went into hospital in Malta and when he came out he could have stayed as a military policeman but he wouldn't as he wanted to be with the boys of his old regiment. So he was sent to France and hence to his death."

Major Frost, a fellow "Blue Puttee", remembers him very well. "He came from Lamaline and served a term in the Newfoundland Royal Naval Reserve before the war, but chose the Army for a change. He was eight years older than I: he was tall, powerful, hardy, thoughtful, sober-minded and somewhat reserved until one got to know him. He was entirely trustworthy and an excellent soldier. He served at Gallipoli, was promoted to Corporal and was killed in the battle whilst leading his section on July 1st, 1916. His body was never found and his name is inscribed on the Beaumont Hamel Memorial. I had the utmost respect for Dick and within a short time after enlistment, I counted him as one of my best friends in the Regiment.

Richard Pitman was tall — a little over six feet, I should judge. He had black hair and heavy eyebrows, and dark, piercing eyes which often looked straight ahead, a characteristic discernible in many aspects of his life, particularly in soldiering. He would often lapse into a pensive mood, seemingly with far-away thoughts in his mind, but never with a morose or distant attitude. As mentioned, he was a few years older than the average and we respected his position as tent-leader at Stobs Camp, glad it was not any one of the rest of us! Tidiness, cleanliness and discipline were inherent in him. He knew the value of discipline, perhaps learned from his experience in the Naval Reserve. While others would spend their leisure hours in the canteen or the village, he, like myself, would often be found in the tent or in barracks writing letters. Not that he did not enjoy a pint of beer or a tot of rum. Dick was an adherent of the Church of England and, like most of us, attended Church Parade with the denominational group of one's faith or choice. I do not recall that he was particularly devout: certainly he was not narrow.

His strong constitution served him well at Gallipoli though, like so many, he eventually succumbed to fever and dysentery and was evacuated to hospital on New Year's Day, 1916. He entered hospital in Malta a few days after I was evacuated to England. Dick rejoined the Battalion in France on June 9th, 1916, and within a month was killed at Beaumont Hamel.

The photograph was taken at either Hawick or Aldershot: probably in July or August, 1915, before we embarked for the Eastern Mediterranean. The only other photo I have in which Dick appears is of our little group outside our tent in Stobs Camp in fatigue clothes. I am sitting on the ground beside Dick, whose expression shows a trace of a smile. His cap is tilted to one side, giving a glimpse of his heavy crop of hair.''

So there it is: the faint echoes down the long corridor of the years. One wonders what that direct, dark gaze would have made of the world after the Great War.

Perhaps the last faint echo is the best. In Lamaline lives a distant cousin of the Corporal's, Mr. W.T. Pitman. He is well over eighty but still has that far-ranging gaze that Major Frost speaks of as typical of Dick Pitman — perhaps it occurs most among men who have their daily business in great waters. He spoke of his own service with the Royal Navy in the First War, and that of his son with the fleet in the second round from 1939 to 1945.

''I remember the last time I saw Dick'', he said. ''It was early in August 1914 — I was going to sea and I'd heard that he'd joined the Army. He came up that road outside the house there and we had a few words together.'' He indicated the dirt road that straggles around the bay: it was a blazing hot afternoon and the sun was reflected blindingly off the sea just beyond the road. ''It was a day like this, I remember, I can almost see him now, going up the road out there with a pretty girl on his arm.''

There are worse ways to be remembered.

Footnotes

CHAPTER ONE

1 George A. Paniches, Ed. **Promise of Greatness.** Cassell & Co. Ltd., 1968. p. XV

CHAPTER TWO

1 Capt. Stair-Gillon, **The Story of the 29th Division,** Thomas Nelson & Sons Ltd., 1925. p. 78.

2 Robert Blake, ed., **The Private Papers of Douglas Haig 1914-1919,** Eyre & Spottiswoode, 1952. p. 253.

3 Cecil Lewis, **Sagittarius Rising,** Transworld Publishers Ltd., 1969. p. 78.

4 A.H. Farrar-Hockley, **The Somme.** p. 91.

Col. G.W.L. Nicholson, C.D., **The Fighting Newfoundlander,** Government of Newfoundland. p. 265.

CHAPTER THREE

1 Maj.-Gen. J.C. Latter, C.B.E., M.C., **The History of the Lancashire Fusiliers 1914-1918,** Gale and Polden Ltd. Volume 1, p. 137.

2, 3 H.C. O'Neill, O.B.E., **The Royal Fusiliers in the Great War,** Wm. Heinemann Ltd., 1922. Chapter VII.

4 C.T. Atkinson **The History of the South Wales Borderers, 1914-1918,** Cambridge University Press (1937). Chap XV.

5, 6 Sir Frank Fox, O.B.E., **The Royal Inniskilling Fusiliers in the World War,** Constable & Co. Ltd. (1928). p. 70.

CHAPTER FOUR

1 Col. H.C. Wylly, C.B., **The Royal Dublin Fusiliers (O'Neill's Blue Caps),** Gale and Polden Ltd. Volume III.

2 Col. H.C. Wylly, C.B., **The Border Regiment in the Great War,** Gale and Polden Ltd. p. 87.

3 Capt. Stair-Gillon, **The King's Own Scottish Borderers in the Great War,** Thomas Nelson & Sons Ltd. p. 187.

4, 5, 6 John Wm. Burrows **The Essex Regiment - 1st Battalion - 44th Foot. 1741 - 1919,** John H. Burrows & Sons Ltd. Vol. I, p. 98.

7 C.T. Atkinson, **The Royal Hampshire Regiment 1914-1918,** Robert Maclehose & Co. Ltd. (1952). Vol. II, p. 171.

8 Capt. H.F. Stacke, M.C. **The Worcestershire Regiment in the Great War,** G.T. Cheshire & Sons Ltd., 1928. p. 210.

CHAPTER FIVE

1 **Twenty-Ninth Div. H.Q. Papers.** W095-2306.

2, 3 **Royal Newfoundland Regiment War Diary. 1915-1918.** W095-2308.

4 **Twenty-Nine Div. H.Q. Papers.** W095-2306.

5 Capt. Stair-Gillon, **The Story of the 29th Division,** Thomas Nelson & Sons Ltd. (1925). p. 81.

6 **The Times History and Encyclopaedia of the War,** Times Publishing Co. Ltd. Vol. 14, Part 175.

7 Richard Cramm, **The First Five Hundred,** C.F. Williams & Son. Inc., New York. p. 59.

8, 9 Col. G.W.L. Nicholson, C.D., **The Fighting Newfoundlander,** Government of Newfoundland. p. 269/229.

CHAPTER SIX

1 Rt. Hon. David Lloyd-George, **War Memoirs of David Lloyd-George,** Odhams Press Ltd. Vol. II, p. 2009.

2 Col. G.W.L. Nicholson, C.D., **The Fighting Newfoundlander,** Government of Newfoundland. p. 308.

3 **Royal Newfoundland War Diary 1915-1918.** W095-2308.

4, 5 Capt. Stair-Gillon, **The Story of the 29th Division,** Thomas Nelson & Sons., 1925. pp. 112/178.

CHAPTER SEVEN

1 R.C. Sherriff, **The English Public School in the War (Promise of Greatness),** Cassell & Co. Ltd., 1968. p. 139.

CHAPTER EIGHT

1 Martin Middlebrook, **The First Day on the Somme,** Penguin Press, 1971. p. 94.

2 Robert Blake, ed., **The Private Papers of Douglas Haig 1914-1919,** Eyre & Spottiswoode, 1952. p. 151.

3 Major-General Sir Frederick Maurice, ed., **The Life of General Lord Rawlinson of Trent,** Cassell & Co. Ltd., 1928. p. 161.

4, 9 A.H. Farrar-Hockley, **The Somme,** Pan Books Ltd., 1964. pp. 155/253.

5, 10 Martin Middlebrook, **The First Day on the Somme,** Penguin Press, 1971. pp. 111/292.

6, 8 Sir Basil Liddell-Hart, **The History of the First World War,** Pan Books Ltd., 1972. pp. 241/242.

7, 12 John Harris **The Somme, Death of a Generation,** Hodder & Stoughton Ltd., 1966. pp. 94/127.

11 John Terraine, **The Great War,** Hutchinson & Co. Ltd., 1965. p. 246.

CHAPTER NINE

1 Philip Longworth, **The Unending Vigil,** Constable & Co. Ltd., 1967. p. 33.

2. Col. G.W.L. Nicholson, C.D., **The Fighting Newfoundlander,** Government of Newfoundland. p. 275.

CHAPTER ELEVEN

    1 Capt. H.A. Anderson **The War Memorial** *(The Veteran* magazine dated April 1921)

    2   Captain Leo G.Murphy, **Shadows.**

RICHARD PITMAN

    1 **Regimental Records of Royal Newfoundland Regt.**

    2 **Papers of Major C. Sydney Frost.**

Bibliography

1. Blunden, Edmund. **Undertones of War.** Cobden-Sanderson, 1930.
2. Bonham-Carter, V. **Soldier True. The Life of Sir Wm. Robertson.**
3. Boraston, Lt. Colonel J.H. ed. **Sir Douglas Haig's Despatches. December 1915 - April 1919.** J.M. Dent & Sons Ltd.
4. Brophy, John and Eric Partridge. **The Long Trail — Soldiers' Songs and Slang 1914-1918.** Sphere Books. 1969
5. Carew, Tim. **The Vanished Army.** Transworld Publishers Ltd. 1971.
6. Churchill, Sir Winston. **The World Crisis 1911-1918.** Four Square Book (New English Library Limited), 1960.
7. Cooper, Duff. **Haig.** (2 volumes). Faber & Faber, 1935.
8. Edmonds, Charles. **A Subaltern's War.** Peter Davies Ltd., 1929.
9. Forester, C.S. **The General.** Penguin, 1936.
10. Graves, Robert. **Goodbye to All That.** Jonathon Cape, 1929.
11. Hay, Ian **The First Hundred Thousand.** Wm. Blackwood and Sons, 1915.
12. Jones, David. **In Parenthesis.** Faber & Faber Ltd., 1937.
13. Lewis, C. Day, ed. **The Collected Poems of Wilfred Owen.** Chatto and Windus, 1963.
14. Magnus, P. Kitchener, **Portrait of an Imperialist.** 1958.
15. Manning, Frederic, (Private 19022). **Her Privates We.** Peter Davies Ltd., 1930.
16. Masefield, John. **The Old Front Line.** Spurbooks Ltd., 1972.
17. Mottram, R.H. **The Spanish Farm Trilogy 1914-1918.** Chatto and Windus, 1927.
18. Moynihan, Michael, ed. **A Place called Armageddon.** David and Charles, 1975.
19. Pound, Reginald. **The Lost Generation.** Constable & Co. Ltd., 1964.
20. Sassoon, Siegfried. **The Complete Memoirs of George Sherston.** World Books, 1937.
21. Terraine, John, ed. **General Jack's Diary, 1914-1918.** Eyre and Spottiswoode, 1964.
22. Terraine, John. **Mons.** B.T. Batsford Ltd., 1960.
23. Von Falkenhayn, General Erich. **General Headquarters 1914-1916 and Its Critical Decisions.** London: Hutchinson & Co., 1919.
24. Wilson, H.W. and J.A. Hammerton, eds. **The Great War. The Standard History of the All-Europe Conflict.** 13 vols. London: Amalgamated Press Ltd., 1919.

GENERAL BIBLIOGRAPHY

In addition to the sources, published and unpublished, quotations from which the author acknowledges in the Special Bibliography, there is a wealth of literature, both fictional and factual, on the 1914-1918 War and the following list is a small selection, which the reader may find useful and interesting.

The Great War. The Standard History of the All-Europe Conflict
(13 volumes)
Edited by H.W. Wilson and J.A. Hammerton, published Amalgamated Press, Ltd., London (1919)

General Headquarters 1914-1916 and its Critical Decisions
by General Erich von Falkenhayn, published Hutchinson and Co., London (1919)

The World Crisis 1911-1918
by Sir Winston Churchill, published as a Four Square Book (The New English Library Ltd.) in 1960.

Sir Douglas Haig's Despatches, December 1915 - April 1919
edited by Lt. Colonel J.H. Boraston, O.B.E., published J.M. Dent and Sons, Ltd.

The Old Front Line
by John Masefield, published by Spurbooks Ltd. in 1972.

The Long Trail - Soldiers Songs and Slang 1914 - 1918
by John Brophy and Eric Partridge, published by Sphere Books in 1969.

The Vanished Army
by Tim Carew, published by Transworld Publishers Ltd. as a Corgi book in 1971.

Mons
by John Terraine, published B.T. Batsford Ltd. (1960)

The Lost Generation
by Reginald Pound, published Constable and Co. Ltd. (1964)

Undertones of War
by Edmund Blunden, published Cobden-Sanderson (1930)

The Collected Poems of Wilfred Owen
　　ed. by C. Day Lewis, published Chatto and Windus (1963)

In Parenthesis
　　by David Jones, published Faber & Faber Ltd. (1937)

Her Privates We
　　by Frederic Manning (Private 19022), published Peter Davies
　　Ltd. (1930)

Goodby To All That
　　by Robert Graves, published Jonathon Cape (1929)

The Spanish Farm Trilogy 1914-1918
　　by R.H. Mottram, published Chatto and Windus (1927)

The Complete Memoirs of George Sherston
　　by Siegfried Sassoon, published World Books (1934)

The General
　　by C.S. Forester, published as a Penguin Book in 1936.

The First Hundred Thousand
　　by Ian Hay, published Wm. Blackwood and Sons (1915) .

Soldier True. The Life of Sir Wm. Robertson
　　by V. Bonhan-Carter (1963)

Kitchener, Portrait of an Imperialist
　　by P. Magnus (1958)

Haig　(2 Volumes)
　　by Duff Cooper, published Faber & Faber (1935)

A Subaltern's War
　　by Charles Edmonds, published Peter Davies Ltd. (1929)

General Jack's Diary 1916-1918
　　ed. by John Terraine, published Eyre and Spottiswoode (1964)

A Place Called Armageddon　(Letters from the Front)
　　ed. by Michael Moynihan, published David and Charles (1975)

APPENDICES

The author would like to make it clear that the first four Nominal Rolls are completely the work of Mr. V.H.B. Snow, District Director of Veterans Welfare, and Miss Wheeler, of the Department of Veterans Affairs in St. John's.

Appendix 5, the Roll of Honour containing details of the resting-places of those killed on 1st. July, 1916 (as in Mr. Snow's Nominal Roll No. 1) was compiled by the author, by kind permission of the Commonwealth War Graves Commission.

Appendix 6, containing the details of the graves of those men who died later of wounds received at Beaumont Hamel, or who died in actions just previous to the attack, was compiled from information supplied by Major C. Sydney Frost of Toronto.

I gratefully acknowledge the help given by Mr. Snow, Miss Wheeler and Major Frost, and would point out that no part of these lists may be reproduced unless permission is sought from the Department of Veterans Affairs in St. John's.

J.B.C.

APPENDIX 1

ROLL No. 1 — KILLED

NOMINAL ROLL OF THOSE MEMBERS OF THE ROYAL NEW-FOUNDLAND REGIMENT WHO LOST THEIR LIVES AS A RESULT OF THE ATTACK AT BEAUMONT HAMEL 1 JULY 1916

The following is a Nominal Roll of those officers and men of the Royal Newfoundland Regiment who are shown in the records of the District Office of the Department of Veterans Affairs, St. John's, Newfoundland, to have been killed, to have been missing and presumed dead or to have died of wounds as a result of the Regiment's participation in the attack at Beaumont Hamel, 1 July 1916.

In some cases, lives were lost in the preparation for the attack and those casualties have been shown. Similarly, where death occurred shortly after the battle, as a result of follow-up action, or wounds, these names have also been included.

OFFICERS

RANK	NAME
Captain	AYRE, Eric S.
2nd Lt.	AYRE, Gerald W.
2nd Lt.	AYRE, Wilfred D.
2nd Lt.	FERGUSON, J. Roy
2nd Lt.	GRANT, William Hayes
Lt.	HERDER, Hubert C.
2nd Lt.	JUPP, Clifford H.O.
Lt.	MELLOR, Fred C.
2nd Lt.	REID, Robert Bruce
2nd Lt.	RENDELL, Clifford
2nd Lt.	ROSS, R. Wallace
2nd Lt.	ROWSELL, H.J.R.
2nd Lt.	RYALL, William Thomas
Lt.	SHORTALL, Richard A.
Lt.	STEELE, Owen, W.
Captain	SUMMERS, Michael Francis
2nd Lt.	TAYLOR, George Hayward

MEN

SERIAL NO.	HIGHEST RANK ATTAINED	NAME
1242	Pte.	ABBOTT, George
283	Pte.	ABBOTT, Stanley
1504	L/Cpl.	ALEXANDER, Walter Ernest
1069	Pte.	ANDERSON, Israel
1119	Pte.	ANDREWS, Joseph
1899	Pte.	ANTLE, Gilbert
1914	Pte.	ATWILL, James
1009	L/Cpl.	AYRE, Edward Alphonsus
1419	L/Cpl.	BARBOUR, Horatio
1576	Pte.	BARNES, Maxwell
372	Pte.	BARRETT, Leonard Josiah
629	Pte.	BARTLETT, Joseph Patrick
1485	Pte.	BARTON, John
700	Pte.	BASTOW, Frederick Donald
1229	Pte.	BENNETT, William
1597	Pte.	BISHOP, Wilson
1219	Pte.	BOONE, Stewart Malcolm

938	Pte.	BOWMAN, Charles
67	Pte.	BREEN, John
1794	Pte.	BRENT, David
808	Pte.	BRODERICK, Michael
1382	Sgt.	BROWN, Bertram
545	Pte.	BROWN, Edward John
624	Pte.	BURGE, Allen
1023	Pte.	BURKE, Garrett
1170	Pte.	BURKE, Leo Michael
1044	Sgt.	BURRY, Sidney George
1567	Pte.	BUTLER, Edward William
1897	Pte.	BUTLER, Harry
1442	Pte.	BUTLER, Ignatius Joseph
966	Pte.	CAHILL, John Joseph, M.I.D.
258	Pte.	CAHILL, Martin Joseph
344	Pte.	CALLAHAN, Rodger
651	Pte.	CAREW, John Joseph
1028	Pte.	CAREW, John Joseph
993	Pte.	CARRIGAN, Edward
274	Sgt.	CARROLL, Thomas
1192	Pte.	CARSONS, John
198	L/Cpl.	CARTER, Llewelyn James
709	Pte.	CHAFE, Ernest Leslie
1359	Pte.	CLEARY, Bernard
679	CQMS	CLEARY, Charles Allen
288	Pte.	CLEARY, John
1400	Pte.	COISH, Harold Gordon
195	Pte.	COLE, Edward Louis
209	Pte.	CONNORS, James Patrick
393	Pte.	COOMBS, Harry
1635	Pte.	CORCORAN, Laurence Joseph
1142	Cpl.	COSTELLO, William Patrick
1058	Pte.	COULTAS, Norman
1249	Pte.	COURAGE, Harrison
1405	Pte.	CRANE, Henry Charles
1663	Pte.	CRANFORD, Llewelyn C.
1264	Pte.	CRITCH, Kenneth
1186	Pte.	CROCKER, Harrison
1447	Pte.	CROSBIE, George Graham
1495	Pte.	CROUCHER, Nathaniel
1435	Pte.	CURLEY, John Thomas
589	Pte.	DAWE, Henry Charles

924	Sgt.	DICK, George
496	Pte.	DOHANEY, William Patrick
1014	L/Cpl.	DOYLE, John Thomas
1056	Pte.	DRISCOLL, Arthur
1964	Pte.	DUKE, John
1480	L/Cpl.	DUNPHY, John Joseph
15	Pte.	DUNPHY, William
1764	Pte.	EAGAN, Patrick
737	Pte.	EDGAR, Edwin Jr.
1251	Pte.	EDGECOMBE, Silas
450	Pte.	EDWARDS, John Charles
22	Pte.	ELLIOTT, John
1073	Sgt.	ELLIOTT, William Skeffington
443	L/Cpl.	ELLIS, John Joseph
1858	Pte.	ETHERIDGE, Gordon
1245	Pte.	EVANS, Henry
181	Pte.	EVANS, Joseph Wellington
1767	Pte.	EVANS, Nicholas
1191	Pte.	FALLON, Stephen
1798	Pte.	FARRELL, Martin Patrick
95	Sgt.	FERGUSON, Stewart Small
1268	Pte.	FEWER, Laurence Joseph
1377	Pte.	FILLIER, Frank
1559	Pte.	FORD, Gerald
81	Pte.	FOWLER, William
626	Pte.	FRAMPTON, John
1611	L/Cpl.	FREAKE, James
63	Pte.	FRENCH, John Joseph
1550	Pte.	FRY, William
892	Pte.	GALGAY, Francis Joseph
1247	L/Cpl.	GARDNER, Edward James
1580	Pte.	GARDNER, Theophilus
125	Pte.	GARF, Fred
454	L/Cpl.	GILLAM, Arthur Wilfred
335	Sgt.	GLADNEY, Edward Francis
1574	L/Cpl.	GREELEY, Matthew
1475	Cpl.	GUY, Chester Cameron
1110	Pte.	HAINES, Albert
946	Pte.	HANCOCK, John
953	Cpl.	HARBIN, Wilfred T.
1612	L/Cpl.	HARNETT, Frank
1321	Pte.	HARRIS, George William

1114	Pte.	HARRIS, Harvey Newman
65	Pte.	HATFIELD, George Bernard
1606	Pte.	HAWKINS, George
1239	Pte.	HAYES, Patrick Joseph
1648	Pte.	HAYWARD, Arthur S.
843	Pte.	HEALE, Robert William
476	Pte.	HEANEY, James Patrick
1532	Pte.	HEFFORD, Thomas Berkley
756	Sgt.	HIGGINS, Edmund James
216	L/Cpl.	HOCKLEY, John Herbert
329	Pte.	HOLDEN, Luke
1133	Pte.	HOLLAHAN, Joseph
1634	Pte.	HOLLAND, Michael John
560	Pte.	HOWARD, James John
1689	Pte.	HUDSON, Peter J.
1533	Pte.	HUSSEY, Francis Joseph
602	Pte.	HUTCHINS, Harold
1621	Pte.	HYNES, Harry
807	L/Cpl.	HYNES, Richard Edward, D.C.M.
1476	Pte.	IVANY, William Garland
697	Pte.	JACKMAN, Bert
733	Pte.	JACKMAN, Michael Joseph
1275	L/Cpl.	JANES, Frederick
1642	Pte.	JANES, George Robert
982	Pte.	JANES, Maxwell
424	Pte.	JEANS, John Allan
292	Pte.	JEFFERS, Silas
1571	Pte.	JOHNSON, Alfred
135	Pte.	JOHNSON, John Joseph
1806	Pte.	JONES, Arthur
1450	Pte.	KEARLEY, Eber
148	Sgt.	KELLY, Michael Francis
178	Pte.	KELLY, Thomas Joseph
255	Pte.	KENNEDY, Michael Francis
1881	Pte.	KING, Alexander
1356	Pte.	KING, Joseph Andrew
373	Pte.	KNIGHT, William
290	Sgt.	KNIGHT, William Blackler
254	Pte.	LAHEY, Robert Joseph
1124	Pte.	LANNIGAN, James Joseph
967	Pte.	LANNON, Michael Francis
1519	Pte.	LANNON, William Joseph
1620	Pte.	LEARNING, Samuel John

1362	Cpl.	LEBUFF, Robert
799	Pte.	LESHANA, William Edward
194	L/Cpl.	LILLY, Augustus
541	Pte.	LIND, Francis Thomas
1468	Pte.	LINEHAN, David
1725	Pte.	LUFF, Samuel
544	Pte.	LUKINS, George
547	Pte.	LUKINS, John
1222	Pte.	LYONS, Allan
900	Pte.	MACDOUGALL, Alexander
572	Pte.	MACKAY, Andrew Joseph
826	Pte.	MADDIGAN, Richard Joseph
951	Pte.	MAHER, James J.
955	Pte.	MAHONEY, Malcolm Cyril
177	Sgt.	MANNING, Augustus J.
616	Pte.	MARTIN, Eric Shannon
1599	Pte.	MARTRET, Joseph
1396	Pte.	MASTERS, William
411	Pte.	MCNEILL, Donald Frazer
279	Pte.	MCNIVEN, William Robert
1013	Pte.	MEADUS, Robert
1877	Pte.	MELEE, Thomas
1446	Pte.	MERCER, Maxwell James
1928	Pte.	MERCER, Robert
214	CSM	MILES, Victor William
587	Pte.	MILLER, George
920	Pte.	MOONEY, James Raymond
1530	Pte.	MOORE, Eric
865	Pte.	MORGAN, William
1624	Pte.	MORRIS, James R.
412	Pte.	MORRIS, Kenneth
1074	Pte.	MORRISSEY, John Thomas
1791	Pte.	MORTON, Joseph
546	Pte.	MOYES, Allan
112	Pte.	MURPHY, Edward Joseph
196	Pte.	MURPHY, Lawrence
1592	Pte.	NELSON, Charles
1391	Pte.	NEWHOOK, George Fred
487	Pte.	NEWMAN, Archibald Mark
810	Pte.	NICHOLS, Campbell Withycombe
354	Pte.	NOSEWORTHY, Herman
1068	Pte.	O'BRIEN, William Vincent
551	Pte	O'DRISCOLL, Albert
727	Pte.	O'FLYNN, Michael Joseph

521	Pte.	O'KEEFE, William Joseph
391	Pte.	O'LEARY, James Joseph
746	Sgt.	OLLERHEAD, William
763	Pte.	O'NEILL, Michael Joseph
306	L/Cpl.	OSMOND, Douglas McNeil
1586	Pte.	PARMITER, Cecil
1664	Pte.	PARSONS, Aubrey L.
1471	Pte.	PARSONS, Charles Albert
731	Pte.	PAUL, Reginald J.
1656	Pte.	PECKFORD, Edward
1546	Pte.	PENNELL, William
1399	Pte.	PENNEY, Augustus
665	Pte.	PENNEY, Josiah H.
1690	Pte.	PERRAN, William G.
1535	Pte.	PIERCEY, John Charles
898	L/Cpl.	PIKE, George Edward
1220	Pte.	PIKE, James Joseph
1235	L/Cpl.	PIKE, Stanley Gordon
1589	Pte.	PINSENT, Stanley Stewart
1158	Pte.	PINSENT, Stewart
400	Cpl.	PITMAN, Richard
1534	Pte.	PORTER, Archibald Harold
896	CSM	PORTER, Robert Branfitt
1150	Pte.	POWER, James Matthew
925	Pte.	PROWSE, William Patrick
861	Pte.	QUIGLEY, Michael Joseph
671	Sgt.	REID, Charles
1486	Pte.	REID, William Joseph
204	L/Cpl.	RENDELL, Arthur James
1062	Pte.	RICE, John Joseph
1234	Pte.	RICHARDSON, Patrick
1258	Pte.	RIDEOUT, Sydney
355	Pte.	ROGERS, Edward Joseph
250	Pte.	ROSS, Michael Joseph
1538	Pte.	ROSSITER, Matthew
571	L/Cpl.	ROWSELL, Edward Clayton
1137	Pte.	RUSSELL, William
133	Cpl.	RYAN, William Joseph
1392	Pte.	SEYMOUR, Thomas
1699	L/Cpl.	SHAVE, Edwin L.
1202	Pte.	SHORT, Richard M.
1217	Pte.	SIMMS, George Percival
576	Pte.	SIMMS, Robert Ronald
1626	Pte.	SMALL, George Stewart

1677	Pte.	SMITH, Josiah
1467	Pte.	SMITH, Zachariah
895	Pte.	SNELGROVE, John Charles
1021	Pte.	SNOW, Douglas K.
685	L/Cpl.	SNOW, Frederick E., M.M.
1923	Pte.	SNOW, John S.
253	Pte.	SPARKES, George
979	L/Cpl.	SPURRELL, Frank J.
494	Pte.	STRATHIE, Harry Groves
1326	Pte.	STRIDE, Ambrose William
1522	L/Cpl.	STRONG, Norman Wheatley
1669	Pte.	STUCKLESS, Silas
897	Pte.	TAYLOR, Alfred Penny
293	Pte.	TAYLOR, Charles F.
1018	Cpl.	TAYLOR, Herbert
1236	Pte.	TEMPLEMAN, Donald
722	Pte.	THOMAS, Walter
399	Pte.	WALSH, Michael Francis
964	Pte.	WARFORD, Garland
1426	Pte.	WATKINS, Robert James
1588	Pte.	WEST, Edward
1460	Pte.	WEST, Stanley
1805	L/Cpl.	WESTCOTT, Harry T.
1395	Pte.	WHALEN Augustin
1680	Pte.	WHEELER, Frederick
1481	Pte.	WHITE, Frederick
345	Pte.	WHITE, William
1632	Pte.	WHITE, William Arthur
739	Pte.	WHITE, Willis
1117	Pte.	WHITTEN, Edgar Charles
944	Pte.	WIGHT, Arthur
707	Pte.	WILCOX, Frederick
1115	Pte.	WILLIAMS, Robert John
1845	Pte.	WINSOR, George
675	Pte.	WINTER, Edward Rozier
908	L/Cpl.	WINTER, Randolph Milligan
364	Pte.	WOODFORD, Frank
1627	Pte.	WOODMAN, Kenneth
1035	Pte.	YOUNG, Arthur Harold .

APPENDIX 2

ROLL No. 2 — WOUNDED
NOMINAL ROLL OF THOSE MEMBERS OF THE ROYAL NEW-
FOUNDLAND REGIMENT WHO WERE WOUNDED AS A RESULT
OF THE ATTACK AT BEAUMONT HAMEL 1 JULY 1916

The following is a Nominal Roll of those Officers and men of the Royal
Newfoundland Regiment as shown in the records of the District Office of
the Department of Veterans Affairs at St. John's, Newfoundland, who were
wounded during, just prior to, or subsequent to the action at Beaumont
Hamel on 1 July 1916.

It is important to realize that this list does not take into account those who
were wounded or killed as a result of engagements other than at Beaumont
Hamel.

Those who served in this action and who are shown on the list who lost
their lives or who died of wounds or injuries after Beaumont Hamel have
been shown with an asterisk against their names.

These records show details during the period of service only and do not
take into account deaths attributable to service following the end of World
War I.

OFFICERS

RANK	NAME
2nd Lt.	BAIRD, Henry
*2nd Lt.	BARRETT, Harold G., M.M.
Major	BUTLER, Bertram, D.S.O., M.C. & Bar, M.I.D.
Capt.	BYRNE, Gerald Guy, M.C.
Capt.	DICKS, Christopher B.
2nd Lt.	DUNCAN, George Templeton
2nd Lt.	DUNPHY, Thomas Joseph, D.C.M., C de G. (Belg.)
Lt.	FORSEY, Bernard
Col.	FRANKLIN, Will Hodgson, D.S.O., M.I.D.
	(while serving with Royal Warwickshire Regt.)
2nd Lt.	FRASER, Nutting S.
*2nd Lt.	GARDNER, Cyril, D.C.M. & Bar
Lt.	GARLAND, Charles F.
Lt.	GOODYEAR, Harold Kenneth
*Lt.	GREENE, Walter M., D.C.M.
*2nd Lt.	HERDER, Arthur John
Lt.	HERDER, Ralph Barnes
Capt.	HICKS, Henry George, M.C. & Bar
Lt.	KNIGHT, Francis Herbert

*Lt.	LANGMEAD, George
*Capt.	LEDINGHAM, James Allan
Capt.	MADDICK Henry M.
2nd Lt.	MELVILLE, Charles Andrew
2nd Lt.	MURCELL, Chesley Gordon
Capt.	NUNNS, Joseph, M.C.
Capt.	PATERSON, R. Grant, M.C. & Bar
Major	ROBERTSON, Stanley
*Lt.	ROWSELL, Reginald, M.C.
Lt.	SEYMOUR, Frederick
Lt.	SMALL, Harvey Haynes
Capt.	SMITH, Stephen Kevin
Lt.	STEELE, James Robert
Capt.	STICK, J. Robins, M.C.
Capt.	STICK, Leonard Tretheway
*Capt.	STRONG, Charles St. C.
Lt.	TRESISE, George Leach
Capt.	WARREN, William V.
Capt.	WATERMAN, Frederick W., M.C., M.I.D.

MEN

SERIAL NO.	HIGHEST RANK ATTAINED	NAME
1332	Pte.	ADAMS, James
1668	Pte.	ADEY, Frank
1618	L/Cpl.	ALLAN, Michael Joseph
1541	Pte.	ALLEN, James Frederick
777	Pte.	ANDREWS, Harold James
1811	Pte.	ASH, John
795	Pte.	ATKINS, Thomas Joseph
*1525	Pte.	ATTWOOD, George
1107	Pte.	AYLWARD, John Joseph
1294	S/Sgt.	BAGGS, James Robert
1440	Pte.	BALLAM, Samuel Robert
1184	L/Cpl.	BARNES, John Thomas
* 528	Pte.	BARNES, Lawrence
945	Pte.	BARRON, Peter
568	Pte.	BARRON, Thomas Frank
1563	Pte.	BARTER, Alexander
678	Pte.	BASTOW, Ralph
1070	Pte.	BELLMORE, Robert

903	Sgt.	BELLOWS, Levi
*1470	Pte.	BENNETT, Edward
* 770	Pte.	BENNETT, Peter Francis
688	Pte.	BENSON, Eleazor
* 42	Cpl.	BEST, Frank Gordon, M.M.
970	Pte.	BISHOP, Cyril Washington
241	Pte.	BIXBY, Samson
765	Cpl.	BOLAND, James Francis
1898	Pte.	BOONE, Walter
1762	Cpl.	BRAKE, Alphonsus
1368	Cpl.	BRAZIL, Matthew, D.C.M., M.M.
80	Sgt.	BRIEN, Patrick
1781	Pte.	BROWN, Bertram Field
752	Cpl.	BUCKLEY, William
718	Pte.	BURKE, James Joseph
191	Cpl.	BURRIDGE, Hubert F.
*1152	Pte.	BURT, Eric
205	Sgt.	BUTLER, Charles Oakley
457	Cpl.	BUTLER, George
1434	Pte.	BUTLER, John Joseph
1180	Pte.	BUTLER, Kenneth Augustine
*1623	Pte.	BUTT, Edward
667	Pte.	BYRNE, Alexander
636	Sgt.	CALDWELL, Edward Charles
151	Pte.	CALDWELL, John
469	Sgt.	CAREW, William Patrick
269	Pte.	CARTER, James
1814	Pte.	CARTER, Kenneth
*1031	L/Cpl.	CARTER, Thomas
1835	Pte.	CASTELLA, Reuben
374	Sgt.	CAUL, John Joseph
1320	Pte.	CHIPMAN, Robert
1518	Pte.	CHURCHILL, Daniel
210	Cpl.	CLARE, Robert
1655	Pte.	CLARKE, Allan
1455	L/Cpl.	CLARK, Howard Samuel, M.M.
239	Pte.	CLARK, Selby
1679	L/Cpl.	CLEARY, David Robert
131	Sgt.	CLEARY, John Sullivan
384	L/Cpl.	CLEARY, William
775	Pte.	COADY, Andrew
1422	Cpl.	COLLINS, Duncan
* 567	Pte.	COLLINS, James

710	Sgt.	COLLINS, Matthew, M.M.
492	Pte.	COOMBS, Archibald
1472	Pte.	COOMBS, Leinus
98	Cpl.	COOPER, James
1507	Pte.	CORBIN, Archibald
1407	Pte.	CORMEY, George
429	Pte.	CORNECT, Eugene
860	Pte.	COSTELLO, Daniel Stephen
1157	Pte.	COSTELLO, Michael Francis
1304	Pte.	COXWORTHY, Fred Pierre
* 363	L/Cpl.	CRANE, Nathaniel
*1585	Pte.	CRON, James Matthew
459	Pte.	CROTTY, Stan F.
* 630	Pte.	CUFF, George Little
524	Cpl.	CUFF, Heber
* 815	Pte.	CUMMINGS, Arthur
1022	Pte.	CURRAN, Daniel
1552	Pte.	CURTIS, Doyle, M.M.
899	Pte.	CUTLER, Howard Frank
1079	Pte.	DALTON, William Francis
842	Pte.	DALTON, William Patrick
915	Cpl.	DAWE, Frank Gilbert
328	Cpl.	DAWE, Joseph
97	Pte.	DAWE, William Gordon
1340	Pte.	DAWSON, Augustus
607	Sgt.	DAYMOND, Joseph
1477	Pte.	DEAN, Norman Kenneth
1474	Pte.	DELANEY, Nicholas
755	Pte.	DEMPSTER, James
1402	Pte.	DICKS, George
1027	Pte.	DODD, William
818	Cpl.	DOOLEY, Francis Joseph
*1551	Pte.	DORAN, Joseph
1299	Pte.	DOYLE, Edward
717	Pte.	DRISCOLL, Michael
*1096	Pte.	DULLANTY, George
1088	Pte.	DUNN, Ronald
980	Pte.	DWYER, George Ralph
811	CQMS	EATON, Duncan MacKinnon
1225	L/Cpl.	EDDY, George Roland
1503	Pte.	ELGAR, William
936	Sgt.	ELLIS, Charles Herbert
*1336	L/Cpl.	EZEKIEL, Joseph

1075	Pte.	FAOUR, Edward
694	Cpl.	FARRINGTON, William
1087	Pte.	FENNELL, Leo
1165	Pte.	FIFIELD, Mark
507	Pte.	FILLIER, Maximillian William
357	L/Cpl.	FLEMING, Richard Francis
1890	Pte.	FOLEY, Patrick W.
1983	Pte.	FORAN, Patrick J.
*1194	Pte.	FORTUNE, William
* 919	L/Cpl.	FURLONG, David J.
338	RSM	GALGAY, Nicholas Augustus
144	CSM	GARDINER, John
695	Sgt.	GEAR, James Joseph
100	Pte.	GELLATELY, William Thomas
*1445	Pte.	GILLINGHAM, Charles
1253	Pte.	GILLINGHAM, George
1487	Pte.	GOLDING, Sylvester
1884	Sgt.	GOOBIE, Andrew
1085	Sgt.	GOODYEAR, Arthur Colin
1041	Pte.	GORE, Eliol Pike
1081	L/Cpl.	GOSSE, Alfred Joseph
1411	L/Cpl.	GOSSE, Solomon
*1051	L/Cpl.	GOSSE, Thomas Joseph
132	Pte.	GOUGH, Frank George
984	S/Sgt. M	GREEN, Cecil, S.S.M.
1055	Pte.	GREEN, Patrick
251	Pte.	GREENE, Augustus Peter
1506	Pte.	GREENING, Garland
13	Pte.	GRIEVE, Robert Cecil
785	Sgt.	GUSHUE, George W.
937	Sgt.	GULLIVER, George McFarrell
1271	Pte.	GUY, Mark
1097	Cpl.	HACKETT, David Manuel
1505	Pte.	HAINES, Edward G.
1000	Pte.	HALEY, Leonard
1197	L/Cpl.	HAMPTON, George Edgar
1255	L/Cpl.	HANN, Bertram Gordon
*1830	Pte.	HANN, William S.
792	L/Cpl.	HANNAFORD, John Joseph
341	Sgt.	HARSANT, Lawrence George
1406	L/Cpl.	HARTERY, John
1497	Pte.	HARVEY, Leslie
1672	Cpl.	HAWKE, Michael

627	Pte.	HAYWARD John
743	Sgt.	HEAD, Louis
*1024	Pte.	HEARN, Augustine
1666	Pte.	HEATH, Thomas
1575	Pte.	HEFFORD, William John
1577	Cpl.	HEPDITCH, Otto Cecil
*1496	Pte.	HIBBS, John Leslie
252	Pte.	HICKEY, John Joseph
586	Pte.	HICKEY, John Joseph
1886	Pte.	HICKEY, Lawrence
119	Pte.	HICKEY, William Francis
1163	L/Cpl.	HICKS, John Benjamin
940	Pte.	HICKS, Mark Brown
1670	L/Cpl.	HIGGINS, Thomas
1558	Pte.	HILLIER, Robert
237	Pte.	HOGAN, Aiden Joseph
1539	Sgt.	HOLLETT, Levi, D.C.M., C. de G
248	Pte.	HOOPER, Albert Norman
212	Pte.	HORAN, Thomas Anthony
500	Cpl.	HOULAHAN, James Patrick
1172	L/Cpl.	HOUSE, Ronald Herbert
1463	Cpl.	HYNES, Alfred Lacey
118	Pte.	JACKMAN, George Arthur
854	Cpl.	JACKMAN, Thomas Joseph
* 702	CSM	JANES, Albert Evelyn, D.C.M.
1704	Pte.	JANES, Edward L.
* 113	L/Cpl.	JANES, Stephen
1501	Pte.	JANES, Stephen Francis
136	Pte.	JANES, Thomas Patrick
1515	L/Cpl.	JENNINGS, Keyward
1808	Pte.	JESSO, Edward
1630	Pte.	JOE, James Patrick
1583	Sgt.	JOHNSON, Dudley
1039	Pte.	JUDGE, Joseph
* 203	L/Cpl.	KEATS, William
490	Pte.	KEEL, Fred
1779	L/Cpl.	KEHOE, Lawrence
27	Cpl.	KELLY, Ernest
1011	Pte.	KELLY, James J.
1548	Pte.	KENNELL, Ebenezer
1365	Cpl.	KEOUGH, Edward Nicholas
1713	Pte.	KILFOY, Leo J.
*1572	Pte.	KING, Ephraim
1829	Pte.	KING, Samuel

242	Pte.	KIRBY, Stanley S.
1659	Pte.	KNIGHT, Frank Scott
77	L/Cpl.	LACEY, Roland Stephen
387	SQMS	LAMBERT, James, M.S.M.
*1482	Pte.	LANE, Gideon Harland
1010	Pte.	LARNER, George Thomas
1280	Pte.	LAWRENCE, George
1686	Pte.	LAWRENCE, Stephen
764	Pte.	LEARNING, George
*1284	L/Cpl.	LEARY, Charley
1837	Pte.	LEDREW, Bertram
911	Cpl.	LEMEE, Michael Francis
853	Sgt.	LEMESSURIER, Francis Ernest
632	Pte.	LESLIE, Clarence Vivian
950	Cpl.	LEWIS, Frederick A.
1640	Pte.	LEWIS, Frederick J.
189	Pte.	LEWIS, John
1828	Cadet	LILLY, Raymond R.W.
1347	Pte.	LUFF, Elias
350	Sgt.	LUFF, John
1598	Pte.	LUFF, William Andrew
*1355	Cpl.	LYNCH, Thomas
*1458	Pte.	MADORE, George Albert
114	Pte.	MAHON, James Thomas
971	Sgt.	MAHONEY, Thomas Gregory
749	Cpl.	MANSFIELD, Edward
867	Pte.	MANUEL, Arthur W.
272	L/Cpl.	MANUEL, Willis
1100	Pte.	MARTIN, George Francis
1093	Pte.	MARTRET, Auguste
1366	Pte.	MASTERS, Reginald
1206	L/Cpl.	MAY, Ernest
1030	Pte.	MCBAY, John Field
1817	Sgt.	MCDONALD, Hugh Joseph
1431	Pte.	MCDONALD, Ralph
*1678	Pte.	MCDONALD, Walter G.
1423	Pte.	MCFATRIDGE, James
1063	L/Cpl.	MCGORY, David
1231	Pte.	MCGRATH, James Joseph
128	Sgt.	MCGRATH, Thomas Bernard
1408	L/Cpl.	MCKAY, Isaac
278	L/Cpl.	MACKAY, John Joseph
748	CQMS	MCKINLEY, Joseph
1302	Pte.	MCNAUGHTON, John

846	Pte.	MCWHORTER, George William
1901	Pte.	MEANEY, Brian
1353	Pte.	MEANEY, Ronald Joseph
1709	Pte.	MEANEY, Thomas J. M.M. & Bar
1173	Pte.	MELEE, William
264	Pte.	MERCER, Albert
* 994	Pte.	MERCER, Allan
159	CSM	MERCER, Fred, M.I.D.
256	Pte.	METCALFE, Albert Edward
*1691	Pte.	MILES, Thomas
1500	Pte.	MITCHELL, William
1651	Cpl.	MOAKLER, Francis Stephen
*1527	Pte.	MOORE, Thomas
218	Pte.	MOORES, Harrison
* 943	L/Cpl.	MOORES, Samuel J.
*1894	L/Cpl.	MORRIS, Edward A.
1492	Pte.	MOSS, Hector
1425	Pte.	MOYLES, Edgar
*1698	Pte.	MULLINGS, Gordon A.
787	Pte.	MUNN, Robert Stewart Errol
1582	Sgt.	MURCELL, Richard Baxter
401	Pte.	MURPHY, James Edward
805	Pte.	MURPHY, Michael Patrick
822	Pte.	MUTFORD, Ward
650	Pte.	MYLER, Alexander J.
1488	Pte.	NARDINI, Raphael
*1343	Pte.	NEVILLE, Gregory Joseph
* 376	Pte.	NEVILLE, William John
1896	SQMS	NEWBURY, William
129	L/Cpl.	NICOL, Ethelbert John Burden, M.M.
1032	Pte.	NOFTALL, Chesley
1357	Pte.	NOFTALL, William Robert
1454	L/Cpl.	NORTHCOTT, Archelaus
1451	Pte.	NORTHCOTT, Lewis
1190	Pte.	NOSEWORTHY, Albert
669	CQMS	NOSEWORTHY, Chesley
1383	Pte.	NOSEWORTHY, Joseph
1570	Pte.	NOSEWORTHY, William James
1380	Pte.	O'BRIEN, Allan Francis
1375	Pte.	O'BRIEN, Andrew Joseph
186	Sgt.	O'DEA, Leo Patrick
996	Pte.	O'DRISCOLL, James William
1701	Cpl.	OLIPHANT, John J.
704	Pte.	O'NEIL, John Joseph

402	Pte.	O'NEILL, Frederick Michael, M.I.D.
804	Pte.	O'ROURKE, William J.
1131	Pte.	OSMOND, Arthur Fred
1688	Pte.	PARDY, George Richard
927	SQMS	PARDY, Norman B. Windsor
1633	L/Cpl.	PARSONS, Reuben
1911	Pte.	PATEY, Gilbert
51	RSM	PATRICK, Neil
1542	Pte.	PENNELL, John
229	Sgt.	PENNY, Arthur Nicholas
1089	Pte.	PENNY, Stephen
*1273	Pte.	PERRY, Alfred
423	L/Cpl.	PERRY, Thomas Avery
1513	Sgt.	PHELAN, William Francis
*1164	Pte.	PHILLIPS, George, M.M., Russian Order of St. George 3rd. Cl.
1161	SQMS	PIKE, Launcelot
729	L/Cpl.	PITTMAN, Corbett
1641	Pte.	POLLETT, William Arch
1569	Pte.	POND, Levi
1710	Pte.	POWER, John Francis
1200	Pte.	POWER, Michael
1281	Pte.	POWER, Pierce, M.M.
1077	Cpl.	POWER, Peter
780	Pte.	POWER, William T.
522	Cpl.	PRATT, Arthur Milligan
916	Cpl.	PURCELL, Roderick Joseph, D.C.M.
1298	Pte.	QUIRK, James
94	Pte.	RANDELL, Hubert Job
*1276	Pte.	RANDELL, Peter
801	Cpl.	RAYNES, Henry Richard, D.C.M. C de G.
1329	Sgt.	REDMOND, Richard S.
1214	L/Cpl.	REID, Dougald Stewart
513	Pte.	REID, Henry
231	Pte.	RENDELL, Leonard True
147	Cpl.	RENOUF, Charles James
991	Pte.	RICHARDS, Cyril
*1082	Pte.	RICHARDS, David
8	L/Cpl.	RICHARDS, Finley McN. Campbell
952	Pte.	RICHARDS, Harry Victor
715	Pte.	RICHARDS, John Edwin
41	Pte.	RICHARDS, William Walter
* 66	Cpl.	RICHARDSON, Frank
*1595	L/Cpl.	RIDEOUT, Garland

1043	Pte.	ROACH, Richard Joseph
440	Pte.	ROBERTS, Frederick George
497	Pte.	ROBERTSON, Eric McKenzie
480	Sgt.	ROBINSON, John Joseph
631	Pte.	ROBINSON, Reuben Thomas
* 76	L/Cpl.	ROOST, William
217	Pte.	ROSE, Wilfred John
682	Pte.	ROWE, Arthur Boyne
*1118	Pte.	ROWE, Harry
*1466	Pte.	ROWSELL, Gordon
1801	Pte.	ROWSELL, Walter
1254	Pte.	RUTH, Walter
* 123	Pte.	RYAN, Bernard
1288	Pte.	RYAN, Richard
1293	Pte.	RYDER, John
1215	Pte.	SAUNDERS, Henry James
1198	Pte.	SCEVIOUR, Cyril
543	Cpl.	SHAVE, William Burton
874	Cpl.	SHEA, Edmund Francis
1274	Pte.	SHEARS, John Robert
* 35	Sgt.	SHEEHAN, John Joseph
712	Pte.	SHEEN, Joseph
1263	Pte.	SHELLEY, Joseph
1681	Pte.	SHEPPARD, Hildyard
1420	L/Cpl.	SHEPPARD, Leonard
473	Pte.	SHEPPARD, Robert
493	Pte.	SHIRRAN, George
1683	Pte.	SHORT, John Charles
*1199	Cpl.	SHORT, Joshua
830	Pte.	SINOTT, Brendan
1040	Pte.	SINNOTT, William Joseph
1285	Pte.	SLANEY, Arthur
1516	L/Cpl.	SMALL, George
614	Pte.	SMALL, William Archibald
405	Pte.	SNELGROVE, Frank
1381	Pte.	SNOW, Francis Joseph
*1870	Pte.	SNOW, Joseph
265	Pte.	SOMERTON, William James
1052	Pte.	SPARKES, Louis
859	Pte.	SPENCER, Roy
275	L/Cpl.	SPRY, Herbert
367	Pte.	SQUIRES, Jack
1449	Pte.	STARES, Frank William
1121	Pte.	STARKES, James Baxter
1318	Pte.	STEELE, Allan George

1802	Pte.	STEVENSON, Joseph
772	Pte.	STONE, George Joseph
361	Pte.	STONE, Henry Skinner
26	Pte.	STONE, Llewelyn
1902	Pte.	STOWE, Samuel
1662	Cpl.	STRONG, Herbert
1900	Pte.	STUCKLESS, William T.
1483	Cpl.	SULLIVAN, Peter
1072	Sgt.	SWEENEY, William John
*1129	L/Cpl.	TAYLOR, Hedley
7	L/Cpl.	TAYLOR, Herbert
821	CSM	TAYLOR, James Arthur
452	Sgt.	TAYLOR, Walter Cameron
232	Sgt.	TEMPLE, John Vincent
277	Pte.	TETFORD, Robert
1661	L/Cpl.	THISTLE, Howard
1776	Pte.	THOMAS, Arthur Stanley
138	L/Cpl.	THOMPSON, Walter
1564	Pte.	THOMSON, Charles Moncrief
*1404	Pte.	TILLEY, Lawrence
21	Pte.	TILLEY, Richard
583	Pte.	TIPPLE, Austin Gerald
*1209	Sgt.	TOBIN, Patrick Francis
1556	Cpl.	TOBIN, Walter Albert
864	Pte.	TRACEY, Augustus James
18	Cpl.	TREBBLE, William
1607	Pte.	TUCKER, Michael
2	Cpl.	TUFF, George Beverley
1195	Pte.	UPWARD, Robert
973	Pte.	VATERS, John Edgar
* 800	Pte.	VAUGHAN, Joseph Patrick
873	Pte.	VAVASOUR, Charles Joseph
1171	Pte.	VIGUERS, William
*197	Pte.	WADE, Edgar
1957	Pte.	WAGG, Austin J.
161	CQMS	WALSH, Frank
693	Pte.	WALSH, John Aloysius
1609	Pte.	WALSH, Richard
942	Pte.	WALSH, Richard Joseph
683	Pte.	WALSH, William
1413	Pte.	WARREN, Alexander
1649	Pte.	WARREN, Gilbert S.
641	Sgt.	WATTS, Arthur
416	Pte.	WELLS, Alfred

*1147	L/Cpl.	WELLS, Joseph Warren
1639	Pte.	WEST, Garland
1591	Pte.	WEST, Henry
25	L/Cpl.	WEST, William Emeel
1452	Pte.	WHIFFEN, Patrick
*1374	Cpl.	WHITE, Albert Clarence
1473	Sgt.	WHITE, Richard Henry
655	Sgt.	WILCOX, Ernest
813	L/Cpl.	WILLAR, Sydney George
735	Sgt.	WILLIAMS, George Moulton
317	Sgt.	WINSLOW, George Joseph
1390	Pte.	WISEMAN, Mark
1628	Cpl.	WISEMAN, William F.
386	L/Cpl.	WYATT, Thomas Walter
570	Pte.	YATES, Gordon Bemister
43	Pte.	YETMAN, Andrew
610	Pte.	YETMAN, William
1286	Pte.	YOUNG, Allan Stephen
823	L/Cpl.	YOUNG, Arthur James

APPENDIX 3
ROLL No. 3 — ROLL CALL

NOMINAL ROLL OF THOSE MEMBERS OF THE ROYAL NEW-
FOUNDLAND REGIMENT WHO ANSWERED ROLL CALL FOLLOW-
ING THE ATTACK AT BEAUMONT HAMEL 1 JULY 1916.

The following is a nominal roll showing the names of those who answered
Roll Call, in accordance with the records of the District Office of the
Department of Veterans Affairs, St. John's, Newfoundland, following the
attack at Beaumont Hamel on 1 July 1916.

The original entry in the records is:

"4.7.16 'Roll Call following attack 1 July 1916'."

It is pointed out that 4 July is the date of the entry made in the records and
is not the date of the Roll Call. Also the rank shown is the highest rank
attained according to the records and an asterisk is used to indicate that an
officer or man lost his life at a later date during his service.

OFFICERS RANK

Lt.	GODDEN, Malcolm
Lt.	LEMEE, John M. - Awarded Royal Humane Society Testimonial for gallantry.
2nd Lt.	STANFORD, Reginald - D.C.M., Croix de Guerre with Bronze Star

SERIAL No.	HIGHEST RANK ATTAINED	NAME
879	L/Cpl.	ADAMS, William Frederick
1643	Sgt.	BLAKE, Kenneth
1650	Pte.	BLYDE, Philip Henry
1461	Pte.	BOLAND, Michael Leo
992	Pte.	BOONE, Nathaniel
1409	Cpl.	BRAKE, Harrison
851	Pte.	BUTT, Edward
1545	Cpl.	CAHILL, Alphonsus
1360	Pte.	CARTER, John
78	CSM	CHAUNCEY, George Wilbur
1128	Pte.	CONWAY, Philip James
809	Sgt.	COX, John, M.M.

736	Cpl.	CRANE, Joseph
1352	Pte.	CRUMMELL, Ronald
738	Pte.	DAVIS, John, M.M.
*1484	Pte.	DAY, James Lewis
1660	Pte.	DAY, Walter B.
1373	Sgt.	DELACEY, Leo Francis
668	Sgt.	DUDER, Charles Robert
116	Cpl.	ERLEY, Joseph
153	Sgt.	FIELD, Larry
420	Cpl.	FIFIELD, Isaac
1602	Pte.	FITZGERALD, Arthur Wilfred
*1645	Pte.	FITZGERALD, Thomas J.
1025	Pte.	FOWLOW, William, M.M.
1149	Pte.	FROST, John Albert Victor
573	Sgt.	GOODYEAR, Josiah Robert
1610	CQMS	GOSSE, Douglas
1573	Pte.	GREALEY, George
320	Pte.	GREEN, William Joseph
174	Cpl.	HARTLEY, Arthur Percy
*1166	Pte.	HEATH, Adolphus Garrett
829	Pte.	HEATH, Ernest
342	Pte.	HISCOCK, George Craniford
588	L/Cpl.	HUMPHRIES, William
1008	Pte.	IVANY, Walter Donald
*1297	Pte.	JACOBS, Frederick James
* 502	Sgt.	JOY, Edward, M.M. & Bar
613	Pte.	KEATS, Hubert John
1512	Pte.	KENNELL, John
1593	Pte.	KNOX, Peter
259	Cpl.	LAHEY, Edward
1549	Pte.	LEE, Harry Nash
* 163	Cpl.	LIDSTONE, Harold, M.M.
47	Pte.	MADDIGAN, Michael
836	CSM	MARTIN, George Chesley
1711	L/Cpl.	MCFATRIDGE, Arthur
1012	CSM	MEADUS, Allan George, C. de G. (Belgium)
1036	RQMS	MEWS, Colin McDougall
637	Pte.	MICHELIN, Joseph
* 300	Cpl.	MILLER, Benjamin
529	Pte.	MOORE, James William
689	Sgt.	MORRISSEY, John Joseph, M.M.

726	Pte.	MORRY, Howard
1037	Pte.	MURPHY, James Francis
1098	Pte.	NOSEWORTHY, Ernest Ivan
1874	Pte.	PAYNE, Bernard
1042	Sgt.	PEET, Arthur Thomas
1076	Pte.	POOLE, Stephen
* 965	Pte.	POWER, William Joseph
* 968	Pte.	PYE, Edward
72	Cpl.	REARDIGAN, John Joseph
1344	Pte.	REED, Nathaniel
1059	L/Cpl.	RIGGS, Frederick Michael
1106	Sgt.	RIGGS, Leslie Rose
*1005	Sgt.	ROBERTS, Francis
* 394	Pte.	RODGERS, Thomas Edward
260	Cpl.	RYAN, Thomas Brown
73	Pte.	SEARS, Michael Francis
1176	Pte.	SKEANS, William
838	Pte.	SNOW, Gordon
618	Cpl.	STEWART, Henry
1616	Pte.	SULEY, William A.
215	Cpl.	THISTLE, Walter Leslie
152	L/Cpl.	VOISEY, Richard Herbert
*1462	Pte.	VOISEY, Richard Patrick

APPENDIX 4
ROLL No. 4 — OTHER

NOMINAL ROLL OF OTHER MEMBERS OF THE ROYAL NEW-FOUNDLAND REGIMENT ON STRENGTH 1 JULY 1916

The following nominal roll of officers and men of the Royal Newfoundland Regiment shows those members who were on the strength of the unit in France at the time of the attack on Beaumont Hamel, as indicated by the records of the District Office of the Department of Veterans Affairs, St. John's, Newfoundland. These members of the unit were not included in the previous nominal rolls because they were not wounded or killed at the time of the attack, nor are they shown as having answered the Roll Call. They make up the following groups:

1. The ten percent reserve which were held back from the initial attack and were brought up as reinforcement on the afternoon of the first of July.

2. Stretcher bearers, personnel engaged in transportation and cooks.

3. Attachments to brigade, machine gun companies and other higher formations. These could have taken part in the action at Beaumont Hamel but because of their detachment were not included in the Roll Call.

4. One or two of the members listed on this nominal roll may have been en route to or from hospital but these numbers are minimal. Also one was taken prisoner of war and one other was believed to be the person who called the roll following the attack but who is not included on the Roll Call.

5. Personnel who were en route from the United Kingdom in Draft No. 7 left the United Kingdom on 29 June 1916 but were not actually attached to the regiment until 12 July 1916 and have consequently not been included in the nominal roll.

As in the preceding nominal rolls, decorations have been shown where the information is available, death at some later time during service has been shown with an asterisk and ranks are the highest rank attained during service. (There are one or two names which have been included where records are incomplete but according to the best information available, it is believed they were on the strength of the unit at the time of the attack).

OFFICERS

RANK	NAME
*Capt.	BARTLETT, Rupert W., M.C. & Bar, Order of Crown of Italy
Capt.	BEMISTER, John G.
Lt.	CLARE, William, M.I.D.
Lt.	CLOUSTON, Andrew, M.
*Capt.	DONNELLY, James John, M.C.
Adj.	DULEY, Cyril C., M.B.E.
*2nd Lt.	EBSARY, Samuel
*Lt.	EDENS, John F.
2nd Lt.	FORAN, Sebastian
Lt. Col.	FORBES-ROBERTSON, James, V.C., D.S.O. & Bar, M.C., M.I.D.
Capt.	FROST, Charles Sydney, M.C.
*Lt.	GOODYEAR, Stanley C., M.C.
Maj.	HADOW, A.L., C.M.G., M.I.D. (2)
Lt.	IRVINE, James
Lt.	JAMES, C. Stanley
Lt.	JANES, Harold C., M.S.M.
2nd Lt.	LANG, James Patrick
Capt.	MCNEIL, Hector, O.B.E., M.I.D.
Lt.	MUNN, William L.G.
*Lt.	NORRIS, Stephen Casimir
*Capt.	O'BRIEN, Augustus, M.I.D.
2nd Lt.	PHILLIPS, George Gordon
Lt.	POWER, Herbert J.
Maj.	RALEY, Arthur, M.C., Croix de Guerre (SS)
*Capt.	RENDELL, Herbert, M.C., M.I.D.
*2nd Lt.	SMITH, Samuel R.
Capt.	SNOW, Joseph H.
*2nd Lt.	STEPHENSON, John Sydney
*2nd Lt.	THOMSON, James E.
Maj.	WINDELER, Henry Stanton, M.C.

MEN

SERIAL NO.	HIGHEST RANK ATTAINED	NAME
*1770	Pte.	ADAMS, Otto Herbert
643	Sgt.	AITKEN, Ernest Peyton, M.M. & Bar
263	L/Cpl.	ALLEN, Thomas Wilfred

55	Sgt.	ANDREWS, Ralph Martin
663	Sgt.	ANTLE, John Aquilla
648	Pte.	BAIRD, John Joseph
*1523	Pte.	BALDWIN, Henry Herbert
* 930	CQMS	BASTOW, Gordon Clarence
*1430	Pte.	BELLOWSE, Stewart
1327	Pte.	BENOIT, Austin
1049	Pte.	BENSON, Frederick Chesley
1769	Pte.	BIRD, Silas
57	Cpl.	BISHOP, Alexander
*1578	Pte.	BLACKMORE, Edgar
1674	L/Cpl.	BOONE, Edgar
* 526	Pte.	BOWDEN, Hugh Pierson, M.M.
103	Sgt.	BRADBURY, Edward Charles
* 398	Pte.	BRADLEY, Wilfred
1319	Pte.	BROWN, David, M.M.
1565	Sgt.	BROWN, Robert Gill
1315	Pte.	BUCKLEY, John Joseph
1625	Pte.	BUCKLEY, Sydney
1856	Pte.	BUDGELL, Stanley
1139	Sgt.	BURSEY, Uriah George
*1282	Pte.	BUTLER, Robert
*1560	Pte.	CAREW, Victor
*1903	Cpl.	CARROLL, Bernard, M.M.
* 343	Cpl.	CLARE, Lawrence Edward
444	Pte.	COLBOURNE, Arthur Frederick
16	L/Cpl.	COLFORD, George
* 863	Cpl.	COLLINS, John Joseph, M.M.
* 483	Pte.	COOK, Henry Whitten
747	Pte.	COOMBS, Thomas
* 649	Pte.	CONNORS, Daniel Francis
1579	Cpl.	CRANFORD, Moses
1335	CSM	CURNEW, Charles, M.M.
20	CSM	DEWLING, Stewart, M.M.
1916	Pte.	DOWNTON, Frederick T.
*1363	Pte.	DRUKEN, Thomas
173	Sgt.	DUNN, John
44	Pte.	DUNPHY, John
137	SSM	EATON, William John
*1714	Pte.	EDNEY, Samuel R.
* 658	Pte.	EVANS, Leonard
1418	Pte.	EVANS, Sidney Wilfred
642	Pte.	EVANS, Thomas Bowring

1092	S/Sgt.	FALLON, Luke Anthony
1555	Pte.	FITZGERALD, Sylvester
1397	Sgt.	FLYNN, Thomas Joseph
311	L/Cpl.	FOWLER, James Francis
1441	Pte.	FREAKE, Frederick
*1526	Pte.	GALPIN, John
* 901	CQMS	GEAR, George
771	Pte.	GLADNEY, James Joseph
1250	Pte.	GLEESON, Richard
154	CSM	GOOBY, Archibald, M.M.
219	Pte.	GOOD, Robert Joseph
1421	Sgt.	GOSSE, Nathan
1918	Pte.	GOUGH, Newman, M.M.
*1272	Sgt.	GRACE, Martin Joseph
1322	Cpl.	GUY, Frederick
489	Pte.	HALEY, Robert
1986	Sgt.	HALFYARD, Wallace
* 352	Sgt.	HALL, William
844	L/Cpl.	HALLETT, Frederick
79	CSM	HAMMOND, Arthur, M.M.
360	S/Sgt.	HAMMOND, Thomas, M.S.M.
90	Pte.	HANN, Jacob
* 353	L/Cpl.	HARDING, Herbert
* 677	Pte.	HARDY, Edward
458	Pte.	HARNETT, Walter Joseph
1517	Pte.	HAWCO, John
875	L/Cpl.	HEALE, Arthur
461	Sgt.	HENNEBURY, Alexander, M.M.
19	Cpl.	HENNEBURY, Ewan
1257	Pte.	HENNESSEY, James John
299	Pte.	HIBBS, James Francis
113	Pte.	HICKEY, James Joseph
1929	L/Cpl.	HISCOCK, William J.
1706	Pte.	HOLLETT, Allan
*1799	Pte.	HOLLETT, George
887	CQMS	HOPKINS, Thomas Roland
449	Pte.	HOSKINS, Lawrence Amour
564	Pte.	HUNT, James
1267	L/Cpl.	HUSSEY, James Harwood
* 356	Sgt.	HUSSEY, William Thomas
820	Sgt.	INNES, Robert Elrich
1310	SSM	IVANY, Alfred James
*1201	L/Cpl.	IVANY, William Cox

* 533	Cpl.	JACKMAN, Arthur Joseph
56	Sgt.	JANES, Walter Harold
*1932	Pte.	JONES, Nathaniel
1376	Cpl.	JOY, William, M.M.
106	Pte.	KAVANAGH, Joseph Arthur
1301	Pte.	KENNEDY, Samuel
1178	Pte.	KENNY, Richard
*1270	L/Cpl.	KENT, Martin Patrick
1168	Pte.	KING, Albert Victor
929	Pte.	LAWLOR, Richard Joseph
1882	Pte.	LEE, William
1972	Pte.	LEGROW, Reuben
1323	Sgt.	LILLY, Paul U.
1292	Pte.	LITTLE, Theophilus
1226	L/Cpl.	LYONS, James Vincent
* 841	L/Cpl.	MACLEOD, Neil Charles
1557	Pte.	MADDEN, John Joseph
183	Sgt.	MADDIGAN, Michael J.
1216	Pte.	MALEY, Denis Francis
687	Pte.	MANNING, Peter Joseph
85	Cpl.	MANSFIELD, Peter
* 721	Cpl.	MANUEL, Alfred, M.M.
86	Cpl.	MARCH, Charles Llewelyn
1401	L/Cpl.	MCCARTHY, John Francis
1490	Pte.	MCDOUGALD, Patrick
976	Pte.	MCGILLVARY, William Douglas
* 856	Pte.	MCGRATH, Thomas White, M.M.
1631	Pte.	MCKAY, William
24	Pte.	MCLEOD, Ernest Frederick
1317	Pte.	MILLS, Edgar
997	L/Cpl.	MILLS, Robert
741	Pte.	MOORE, Daniel Joseph
* 719	Cpl.	MORGAN, Robert Stanley
*1581	Pte.	MORRIS, William
446	Pte.	MOTTY, Edgar Page
1211	Pte.	MUGFORD, Walter
1429	Pte.	MUISE, Moses
437	Pte.	MULLETT, Abraham Thomas
1412	Pte.	MURRIN, Walter
1367	Pte.	MYERS, Albert
*1080	Sgt.	NEVILLE, Richard, M.M.
520	L/Cpl.	NEWELL, William Thomas
336	Pte.	NICHOL, John Francis
664	CQMS	NICHOLLE, Edward Henry, M.I.D.

* 812	Pte.	NOONAN, Robert Anthony
527	Pte.	NOSEWORTHY, Francis Thomas
1167	Pte.	NOSEWORTHY, Heber
*1378	Pte.	O'BRIEN, James John
654	Pte.	O'BRIEN, John Joseph
1775	Cpl.	O'DONNELL, Edward V.
1658	Pe.	O'KEEFE, Charles Patrick
783	Sgt.	PARSONS, Charles, M.M. & Bar
438	L/Cpl.	PARSONS, William John
987	L/Cpl.	PENNY, Esau
1448	Pte.	PENNEY, James
757	Pte.	PIERCEY, Samuel C.
609	Pte.	PIKE, Ernest
310	L/Cpl.	POWER, David
1103	Pte.	PRICE, John Joseph
1246	Pte.	PROWSE, John Leo
1237	Pte.	PUMPHREY, John Louis
1145	Sgt.	QUICK, Ernest Chesley
1305	Pte.	QUIRK, Daniel Joseph
2016	Pte.	READ, John H.
1135	Pte.	READER, Alexander
* 790	Pte.	REID, Carl
* 228	Pte.	RIDEOUT, Pierce
*1494	L/Cpl.	ROLLS, Walter
1547	Pte.	ROSS, William Leslie
* 611	Sgt.	ROWE, Harry Mott
917	Pte.	RUSSELL, John
38	L/Cpl.	RYAN, John Joseph
884	Pte.	RYAN, Samuel Patrick
*1540	Pte.	SARGENT, John
1314	Pte.	SAUNDERS, James Joseph
* 88	Pte.	SIMMS, John Henry, M.M.
*1243	Pte.	SIMMS, Leaten
59	L/Cpl.	SKEFFINGTON, Sydney Bemister
273	Pte.	SLADE, Albert Ernest
1389	Cpl.	SMALL, Titus
1737	Pte.	SMITH, Peter Galloway
512	Cpl.	SMYTH, Michael Frank
*1140	Pte.	SNELGROVE, Isaac John
640	Sgt.	SNOOK, William Ed
* 750	Pte.	SNOW, William
378	Sgt.	SPURRELL, Charles Patrick, D.C.M.
466	Sgt.	STACEY, Anthony James
656	L/Cpl.	STAMP, Patrick D.

1638	Pte.	STRIDE, Albert
1453	Pte.	STYLES, Alfred
1108	Sgt.	SYMONDS, Joseph
990	Pte.	TAYLOR, Charles
111	CQMS	TAYLOR, Victor G.
711	Pte.	TAYLOR, William Bernard
139	Pte.	THOMPSON, John
* 753	Pte.	TIZZARD, Gordon
234	Cpl.	TULK, Ralph Wellon
*1694	Pte.	TUFF, Frank Payne
* 23	Cpl.	TUFF, James Roy
1185	Pte.	VOISEY, Edward Joseph
1566	Pte.	VOISEY, Herbert Lawrence
* 959	Pte.	VOISEY, Leo Michael
506	Pte.	WALSH, George Edward
1562	Pte.	WALSH, James
* 789	Provost Sgt.	WATERFIELD, Joseph Ross, M.M.
* 397	Pte.	WATTS, James Pittman
236	Sgt.	WEBBER, Arthur, M.M., Bronze Medal (Italian Dec.)
1734	Pte.	WELLS, Isaac
475	Pte.	WHEELER, Heber
*1432	L/Cpl.	WHEELER, James
1154	Pte.	WHITE, Arthur Joseph
652	Pte.	WILLIAMS, Richard
1262	Pte.	WISEMAN, Stephen
29	Pte.	WOOD, Ernest
371	Pte.	WYATT, Edward
1700	Pte.	YETMAN, Nathan, M.M.

APPENDIX 5

Details and resting-places of men of the Newfoundland Regiment who died on 1st. July, 1916

ROLL OF HONOUR

No. Name	Age	
1242 Pte George Abbott	22	Son of Henry and Emily Abbott of Battery Road, St. John's; Memorial Park.
283 Pte Stanley Abbott	21	Son of Henry and Emily Abbott of Battery Road, St. John's; Memorial Park.
1069 Pte Israel Anderson	20	Son of Joseph and Jessie Anderson, Mouse Island, Newfoundland; Y Ravine (Sp. Mem. C. 31)
1119 Pte Joseph Andrews	27	Son of Mrs. Catherine Andrews of St. John's; Memorial Park.
1899 Pte Gilbert Antle	21	Son of Thomas and Mary Antle of Botwood, Twillingate; Memorial Park.
1914 Pte James Atwill	26	Son of Samuel and Charlotte Atwill; Ancre (Sp. Mem. 37)
1009 L/Cpl. Edward Alphonsus Ayre	19	Son of Edward and Selena Ayre of Isle aux Morts; Y Ravine.

Capt. Eric S. Ayre	27	Son of Robert Chesley and Lydia Gertrude Ayre of St. John's. Husband of Janet of St. John's; Ancre.
869 2nd Lt. Gerald W. Ayre	25	Son of Frederick William and Mary Julia of St. John's; Memorial Park.
164 2nd Lt. Wilfred D. Ayre	21	Son of Charles P. and Diana Ayre of St. John's; Knightsbridge.
1419 L/Cpl. Horatio Barbour	26	Son of William and Amy H. Barbour of Port Rexton; Beaumont Hamel 1.
1576 Pte Maxwell Barnes	22	Son of Mrs. Sarah Ann Barnes; Memorial Park.
372 Pte Leonard Josiah Barrett	21	Son of Mrs. Maud Barrett; Memorial Park.
629 Pte Joseph Patrick Bartlett	22	Son of John Bartlett of Marysvale, Brigus; Memorial Park.
1485 Pte John Barton	29	Son of William and Annie Barton of The Goulds (Bay Bulls Road), St. John's West; Memorial Park.
1229 Pte William Bennett	31	Son of William and Agnes Bennett of St. John's; Memorial Park.

1597 Pte Wilson Bishop	22	Son of John and Annie Bishop of 10 Second Avenue, Grand Falls; Ancre.
1219 Pte Stewart Malcolm Boone	20	Son of William Thomas and Sarah Jane Boone of South River, Clarke's Beach; Ancre.
938 Pte Charles Bowman	26	Son of Frigaz Bowman, St. John's, Nfld.; Memorial Park.
67 Pte John Breen		Son of Mrs. Breen, Alexander St., St. John's, Nfld.; Memorial Park.
1794 Pte David Brent	23	Son of Mr. and Mrs. John Brent of Botwood, Twillingate; Memorial Park.
1382 Sgt. Bertram Brown	21	Son of Amos and Selina Brown of Grand Falls; Memorial Park.
545 Pte Edward John Brown	28	Son of Eli and Annie Brown of Harbour Grace; Memorial Park.
624 Pte Allen Burge	20	Son of George and Mary Jane Burge of Bonavista; Memorial Park.
1023 Pte Garrett Burke	25	Son of Silvester and Mary Ellen Burke of Tor's Cove, Ferryland; Knightsbridge.

1170 Pte Leo Michael Burke	18	Son of Martin and Annie Burke of St. John's West; Ancre.
1044 Sgt. Sidney George Burry	31	Son of Job and Matilda Burry of Greenspond, Bonavista; Memorial Park.
1567 Pte Edward William Butler	25	Son of John and Phoebe Butler of Fogo; Y Ravine
1897 Pte Harry Butler	20	Son of Henry Stephen and Laura May Butler of "Hillcrest" LeMarchant Road, St. John's; Y Ravine.
1442 Pte Ignatius Joseph Butler	20	Son of Mrs. Mary C. Butler of St. Georges; Memorial Park.
258 Pte Martin Joseph Cahill	24	Son of Mary E. Sweeney (formerly Cahill) of Bell Island, Conception Bay and the late John Cahill; Memorial Park.
344 Pte Rodger John Callahan	26	Son of Rodger Callahan of St. John's; Memorial Park.
651 Pte John Joseph Carew	26	Son of David and Carrie Carew of 2 Brien Street, St. John's; Y Ravine.
1028 Pte John Joseph Carew	24	Son of John Michael and Elizabeth Carew of 13 Simms Street, St. John's; Memorial Park.

993 Pte Edward Carrigan — 21 — Son of James and Isabel Carrigan of Placentia; Y Ravine.

274 Sgt. Thomas Carroll — 46 — Son of Thomas and Ellen Carroll of Harbour Grace; Hawthorn Ridge 2.

1192 Pte John Carsons — 20 — Lorenzo Carsons, brother, Bear's Cove, Harbour Grace; Hawthorn Ridge 2.

709 Pte Ernest Leslie Chafe — 25 — Son of Jacob W. and Jane D. Chafe of 140 Casey Street, St. John's; Y Ravine.

81 Pte William Clarke (served as Fowler) — 24 — Son of Richard Clarke of Alexander Street, St. John's and Mary Teresa Clarke (now Mrs. Hawco) of Roaches Line, Brigus; Ancre.

1359 Pte Bernard Cleary — 19 — Son of Edward and Ellen Cleary of Harbour Main; Memorial Park.

679 C.Q.M.S. Allan C. Cleary — 21 — Son of Philip J. and Katherine Cleary of 3 Monkstown Road, St. John's; Knightsbridge.

288 Pte John Cleary — 21 — Son of John Cleary of 63 Compton Street, Boston, Mass: U.S.A.; Ancre.

1400 Pte Harold Gordon Coish	21	Son of William and Maud Coish of Ladle Cove, Fogo; Memorial Park.
209 Pte James Patrick Connors	23	Son of Patrick and Mary Ann Connors of St. John's; Memorial Park.
393 Pte Harry Coombs	21	Son of Harry and Mary Coombs of Upper Island Cove, C.B.; Ancre.
1635 Pte Laurence Joseph Corcoran	33	Son of Laurence Joseph and Julia Corcoran of 29 Central Street, St. John's; Memorial Park.
1142 Cpl. William Patrick Costello	29	Son of Mrs. W.P. Costello of 619 Aylmer Street, Montreal, Canada; Knightsbridge.
1058 Pte Norman Coultas	17	Son of Myles and Maria Coultas of 80 Patrick Street, St. John's; Memorial Park.
1663 Pte Llewellyn C. Cranford	24	Son of John and Flora Cranford of New Harbour, Trinity Bay; Memorial Park.
1264 Pte Kenneth Critch	25	Son of William and Mary Ann Critch of LaScie, St. Barbe; Knightsbridge.
1186 Pte Harrison Crocker	25	Son of Samuel and Emily Crocker of Heart's Delight, Trinity Bay; Memorial Park.

1495 Pte Nathaniel Croucher	19	Son of Elias and Hagar Croucher, Cutwell Arm, Notre Dame Bay; Memorial Park.
1435 Pte John Thomas Curley	35	Son of Phillip and Ann Curley, husband of J.T. Curley of Woods Island, Bay of Islands; Memorial Park.
589 Pte Henry Charles Dawe	25	Son of John and Dorcas Dawe of Topsail; Ancre.
496 Pte William Patrick Dohaney	24	Son of Thomas and Elizabeth Dohaney of 21 Prospect Street, St. John's; Knightsbridge.
1014 Cpl. John Thomas Doyle	25	Son of Edward and Lucy Doyle of King's Cove, Bonavista; Memorial Park.
1056 Pte Arthur Driscoll	20	Son of Absalom and Virtue Driscoll of St. John's; Memorial Park (also headstone in Serre Road No. 2).
1964 Pte John J. Duke	24	Son of the late Michael Duke and Mary Carrigan (formerly Duke) of Iona, Placentia Bay; Ancre.
1480 L/Cpl. John Joseph Dunphy	20	Son of Michael Dunphy; Y Ravine.
15 Pte William Dunphy	23	Son of Martin Dunphy of 23 Princes Street, St. John's; Hawthorn Ridge 2.

737 Pte Edwin Edgar	19	Son of Edwin and Helen Edgar of Greenspond, Bonavista Bay; Memorial Park.
22 Pte John Elliott	20	Son of John and Elizabeth Elliott of St. John's; Memorial Park.
1073 Sgt. William Skeffington Elliott	22	Son of Albert and Annie Elliott of Newmans Cove, Bonavista Bay; Memorial Park.
443 L/Cpl. John Joseph Ellis	22	Son of John Joseph and Annie Ellis of 359 South Side Road, St. John's; Memorial Park.
1858 Pte Gordon Etheridge	24	Son of John and Priscilla Etheridge of Champneys, Trinity Bay; Memorial Park.
1245 Pte Henry Evans	22	Next of kin: Mrs. Edward Murray, mother, Adams Cove, Bay de Verde; Memorial Park.
181 Pte Joseph Wellington Evans	22	Son of Jethro and Lydia Evans of St. John's; Hawthorn Ridge 1.
1767 Pte Nicholas J. Evans	20	Son of Luke and Mary Evans of St. John's; Memorial Park.
1191 Pte Stephen Fallon	17	Son of John and Susie Fallon of Harbour Grace; Memorial Park.

1798 Pte Martin Patrick Farrell — 19 — Son of John and Mary Farrell of Marystown, Burin; Memorial Park (also headstone in Serre Road No. 2).

882 2nd Lt. J. Roy Ferguson — 27 — Son of David and Isabella Ferguson of 273 Southside Road, St. John's. Husband of Jeanette Ferguson of Grand Falls; Memorial Park.

95 Sgt. Stewart Small Ferguson — 26 — Son of David and Isabella Ferguson of 273 Southside Road, St. John's; Memorial Park.

1268 Pte Laurence Joseph Fewer — 23 — Son of William and Ellen Fewer of Placentia; Knightsbridge.

1377 Pte Frank Fillier — 19 — Son of Thomas Fillier of Petty Harbour, St. John's West; Memorial Park.

1559 Pte Gerald Ford — 22 — Son of Thomas G. and Sarah Ford of Amherst Cove, Bonavista Bay; Memorial Park.

81 Pte William Fowler — — real name Clarke, which see.

626 Pte John Frampton — 21 — Son of Robert and Emma Jane Frampton of Bay Bulls, Ferryland; Knightsbridge.

1611 L/Cpl. James Freake — 22 — Son of Henry Freake; Knightsbridge.

63 Pte John Joseph French 25

Son of Benjamin and Bridget French of Brigus; Memorial Park.

1550 Pte William Fry 24

Son of John and Elizabeth Fry of Charleston, Newfoundland; Auchonvillers Military Cem.

892 Pte Francis Joseph Galgay 21

Son of Francis Galgay of 235 Water Street West, St. John's, and the late Mary Galgay; Memorial Park.

1247 L/Cpl. Edward James Gardner 25

Son of Arthur and Mary Gardner of British Harbour, Trinity; Memorial Park.

125 Pte Fred Garf 22

Son of Charles and Laura Garf of St. John's; Ancre.

454 L/Cpl. Arthur Wilfred Gillam 21

Son of Charles Gillam of Robinson's Head, St. George's; Memorial Park.

335 Sgt. Edward Francis Gladney 22

Son of John and Margaret Gladney, Lumber Factory, Colinet, Placentia; Y Ravine.

1574 L/Cpl. Matthew Greeley 27

Son of Jabez and Sarah Greeley of Portugal Cove, Conception Bay. Husband of Sadie of 46 Carmtyne Terrace, Shettleston, Glasgow, Scotland; Knightsbridge.

1475 Cpl. Chester Cameron Guy	20	Son of John Robert Guy; Memorial Park.
1110 Pte Albert Haines	22	Son of Robert John and Rosanna Haines of Jamestown, Bonavista; Memorial Park.
946 Pte John Hancock	18	Son of Joseph and Amelia Hancock, Goose Cove, Treaty Shore; Y Ravine.
953 Cpl. Wilfred T. Harbin	18	Son of Henry and Elizabeth Harbin of Twillingate; Memorial Park.
1612 L/Cpl. Frank Harnett	32	Son of Mark and Mary Harnett of Wild Cove, Seldom; Knightsbridge.
1321 Pte George William Harris	24	Son of John Harris of Humbermouth; Memorial Park.
1114 Pte Harvey Newman Harris	20	Son of William Henry and Evelina Harris of Burgeo; Memorial Park.
65 Pte George Bernard Hatfield	22	Son of Stephen and Margaret Hatfield of Coronation Street, St. John's; Memorial Park.
1606 Pte George Hawkins	26	Son of John and Matilda Hawkins of Durrall's Arm, Twillingate; Ancre.
1239 Pte Patrick Joseph Hayes	19	Son of John and Mary Hayes of 6 Brennan Street, St. John's; Memorial Park.

1648 Pte Arthur S. Hayward   20   Son of Thomas Hayward of St. John's and Dorcas (now Mrs. Andrews) of 110 Casey Street, St. John's; Ancre.

476 Pte James Patrick Heaney   22   Son of James and Anastatia Heaney of St. John's; Memorial Park.

1532 Pte Thomas Burkley Hefford   27   Son of James and Lydia Hefford of New Harbour, Trinity Bay; Ancre.

3 Lieut. Hubert Clinton Herder   25   Son of William James and Elizabeth Herder of St. John's; Y Ravine.

216 L/Cpl. John Herbert Hockley   38   Son of William and Jane Hockley of 13 Richmond Road, Olton, Warwickshire. Born at Birmingham; Ancre.

329 Pte Luke Holden   21   Son of William V. and Alice Holden of Harbour Main; Memorial Park (also headstone in Serre Road No. 2).

1133 Pte Joseph Hollahan   26   Son of Samuel and Julia Hollahan, husband of Isabel Hollahan of 89 Southside Road, St. John's; Memorial Park.

1634 Pte Michael John Holland   19   Son of Richard and Jane Holland of 37 Freshwater Road, St. John's; Y Ravine.

560 Pte James John Howard — 22 — Only son of Patrick and Joan Howard of 52 Colonial Street, St. John's; Memorial Park.

1533 Pte Francis Joseph Hussey — 18 — Son of John and Sarah Hussey of Kenmount Road, Freshwater, St. John's; Memorial Park.

602 Pte Harold Hutchins — 19 — Son of Philip Henry and Louise Hutchins of Greenspond, Bonavista Bay; Ancre.

1621 Pte Harry Hynes — 21 — Son of Esau and Mary Hynes of Norris' Arm, Twillingate; Memorial Park.

807 L/Cpl. Richard Edward Hynes D.C.M. — 25 — Son of George and Annie Hynes of Indian Islands, Fogo; Y Ravine.

1476 Pte William Garland Ivany — 21 — Son of George and Caroline Jane Ivany of Gambo, Bonavista; Ancre.

733 Pte Michael Joseph Jackman — 19 — Son of David J. and Catherine Jackman of Bell Island. Educated at St. Bonaventure's College, St. John's. Member of Catholic Cadet Corps, Bell Island; Memorial Park.

1275 L/Cpl. Frederick Janes — 23 — Son of Alexander and Bertha Janes of St. John's; Y Ravine.

1642 Pte George Robert Janes — 29 — Son of James and Harriet Janes of Bishops Falls; Memorial Park.

982 Pte Maxwell Janes — 20 — Son of Harry and Emma Janes of 13 Barters Hill, St. John's; Knightsbridge.

424 Pte John Allan Jeans — 33 — Son of William and Martha Jeans of Catalina, Trinity; Hawthorn Ridge 2.

292 Pte Silas Jeffers — 23 — Son of Francis and Sarah Jeffers of Freshwater, Bay de Verde; Y Ravine.

1571 Pte Alfred Johnson — 23 — Son of Madeline Rebecca Naiss of 31 Bilton Avenue, Teignmouth, Devon. Adopted by the late Alfred and Mary Johnson of Teignmouth, Devon; Memorial Park.

135 Pte John Joseph Johnson — 23 — Son of Andrew & Mary Johnson of 45 LeMarchant Road, St. John's; Memorial Park.

1806 Pte Arthur Jones — 37 — Son of John and Susannah Jones of St. Philip's, St. John's West; Knightsbridge.

157 2nd Lt. Clifford Henry Oliver Jupp — 25 — Son of William and Marion Jupp of Pulborough, Sussex, England; Memorial Park.

1450 Pte Eber Kearley — 21 — Son of Charles Kearley of Blaketown, Trinity Bay; Memorial Park.

148 Sgt. Michael Francis Kelly — 26 — Son of Henry and Elizabeth Kelly of 37 Cabot Street, St. John's, husband of Gertrude; Memorial Park.

178 Pte Thomas Joseph Kelly — 26 — Son of James and Mary Ann Kelly of Jersey Side, Placentia; Memorial Park.

255 Pte Michael Francis Kennedy — 22 — Son of Nicholas and Margaret Kennedy of 187 LeMarchant Road, St. John's; Memorial Park.

1356 Pte Joseph Andrew King — 22 — Son of Silas and Dinah King of Broad Cove, Bay De Verde; Memorial Park.

373 Pte William Knight — 22 — Son of Stephen and Ellen Knight of St. John's. Husband of K. Knight of 284 Pacific Street, Brooklyn, New York, U.S.A.; Auchonvillers Military Cem.

290 Sgt. William Blackler Knight — 23 — Son of Frederick W. and Emilie Florence Knight of 355 Southside Rd., St. John's; Memorial Park.

254 Pte Robert Joseph Lahey — 28 — Son of Richard and Margaret Lahey of Bell Island, Conception Bay; Knightsbridge.

967 Pte Michael Francis Lannon — 23 — Son of James and Esther Lannon of South East Placentia; Memorial Park.

799 Pte William Edward LeShana — 24 — Son of William and Mabel LeShana, Husband of Jeanette of 654, 12th Avenue, East Vancouver, British Columbia, Canada; Memorial Park.

194 L/Cpl. Augustus Lilly — 33 — Son of George A. and Olivia Lilly of Quidi Vidi Lake, St. John's; Y Ravine.

541 Pte Francis Thomas Lind — 37 — Son of Henry and Elizabeth Lind of Little Bay, Notre Dame Bay; Y Ravine.

1468 Pte David Linehan — 21 — Son of John and Margaret Linehan of Johns Pond, St. Mary's Bay; Hawthorn Ridge 2.

1725 Pte Samuel Luff — 20 — Son of William and Lydia Luff of Campbellton; Knightsbridge.

544 Pte George Lukins — 23 — Son of Frederick and Johanna Lukins of St. John's, husband of Alice of 21 Tessier Place, Carter's Hill, St. John's; Hawthorn Ridge 2.

1222 Pte Allan Lyons — 24 — Son of James and Margaret Lyons of Avondale, Conception Bay; Memorial Park.

900 Pte Alexander MacDougall — 23 — Son of John and Marion MacDougall of 105 Elderpark St., Govan. Born in Islay Argyllshire; Ancre.

826 Pte Richard Joseph Maddigan — 19 — Son of Richard and Ellen Maddigan of 259 Water Street West, St. John's; Y Ravine.

951 Pte John James Maher — 20 — Son of William and Clara Maher of Quidi Vidi Road, St. John's; Memorial Park.

955 Pte Malcolm Cyril Mahoney — 23 — Son of Mrs. Elizabeth Mahoney of Carbonear; Y Ravine.

616 Pte Eric Shannon Martin — 23 — Son of Alfred and Jessie Martin of St. John's; Hawthorn Ridge 2.

1599 Pte Joseph Martret — 20 — Son of Augustus and Mary Ellen Martret of 254 New Gower St., St. John's; Memorial Park.

1396 Pte William Masters — 23 — Son of George and Mary Masters of Harbour Buffett, Placentia Bay; Hawthorn Ridge 2.

279 Pte William Robert McNiven — 21 — Son of Frederick and Rosann McNiven of Portugal Cove Road, St. John's; Memorial Park.

1013 Pte Robert Meadus — 20 — Son of Henry and Susanna Meadus of St. John's; Memorial Park.

1877 Pte Thomas Melee — 19 — Son of Thomas and Mary Melee of South Side Road, St. John's; Memorial Park.

91 Lieut. Frederick Courtney Mellor	28	Son of Thomas C. and Mary L. Mellor of St. Luke's Rectory, Annapolis Royal, Nova Scotia, Canada; Knightsbridge.
1446 Pte Maxwell James Mercer	19	Son of Isaac and Anastatia of Bay Roberts, Harbour Grace; Memorial Park.
1928 Pte Robert Mercer	25	Son of Eliel Mercer of Blaketown, Trinity Bay; Memorial Park.
214 C.S.M. Victor William Miles	31	Son of Henry and Selina Miles; Memorial Park.
587 Pte George Miller	26	Son of Bertha Summerton (formerly Miller) of 26 Ryde Street, Montreal Canada, and the late William James Miller; Memorial Park.
920 Pte James Raymond Mooney	23	Son of Alfred and Agnes Mooney of Placentia; Memorial Park.
1530 Pte Eric Moore	21	Son of Alexander and Janet Moore of 16 Waldegrave Street, St. John's; Hawthorn Ridge 2.
865 Pte William Morgan	16	Son of John A. and Sarah Morgan of Alexander Street, St. John's; Memorial Park.

1624 Pte James R. Morris — 24 — Son of Joseph and Rebecca Morris of Robinson's, St. George's Bay; Y Ravine.

412 Pte Kenneth Morris — 27 — Son of Joseph and Jane Morris of Lower Island Cove, Bay de Verde; Memorial Park.

1074 Pte John Thomas Morrissey — 25 — Son of Lawrence and Catherine Morrissey of 46 Wickford Street, St. John's; Memorial Park.

1791 Pte Joseph Morton — 25 — Son of George Morton of Burin North; Memorial Park.

546 Pte Allan Moyes — 24 — Son of Mrs. Annie Maria Moyes of Topsail, Conception Bay; Memorial Park.

112 Pte Edward Joseph Murphy — 24 — Son of Matthew and Mary F. Murphy of Pleasant Street, St. John's; Memorial Park.

196 Pte Lawrence J. Murphy — 21 — Son of Thomas and Mary Murphy of Petty Harbour, St. John's West; Y Ravine.

1592 Pte Charles Joseph Nelson — 24 — Son of Charles and Bridget Nelson of 26 Lime Street, St. John's; Memorial Park.

1391 Pte George Frederick Newhook — 22 — Son of John and Lizzie Newhook of Dildo, Trinity Bay; Memorial Park.

810 Pte Campbell Withycombe Nichols — 20 — Son of John H.A. and M. Elizabeth Nichols of Deer Lake; Memorial Park.

354 Pte Herman Noseworthy — 21 — Son of John and Julia Emma Noseworthy of 160 Casey Street, St. John's; Memorial Park.

1068 Pte William Vincent O'Brien — 21 — Son of John and Mary O'Brien of Avondale District, Harbour Main; Y Ravine.

551 Pte Albert O'Driscoll — 27 — Son of James and Sarah O'Driscoll of Tor's Cove, Ferryland; Y Ravine.

727 Pte Michael Joseph O'Flynn — 22 — Son of David A. and Annie O'Flynn of Grand Falls; Memorial Park.

521 Pte William Joseph O'Keefe — 21 — Son of Peter and Mary O'Keefe of 28 Fleming Street, St. John's; Memorial Park.

391 Pte James Joseph O'Leary — 37 — Son of Philip and Catherine O'Leary of 21 Scott Street, St. John's; Memorial Park.

746 Sgt. William Ollerhead — 25 — Son of James and Susannah Ollerhead of Heart's Content, Trinity Bay, Memorial Park.

763 Pte Michael Joseph O'Neill — Brother of A. O'Neill of Mount Cashel, St. John's; Memorial Park.

1586 Pte Cecil Parmiter	19	Son of John and Sarah Parmiter of Topsail, Conception Bay; Y Ravine.
1664 Pte Aubrey L. Parsons	19	Son of John and Martha Parsons of Lumsden North, Fogo; Memorial Park.
1471 Pte Charles Albert Parsons	25	Son of Mrs. Matilda Parsons of Stephenville Crossing, St. Georges; Memorial Park.
731 Pte Reginald J. Paul	21	Son of William John and Maria Veil Paul of Burin; Hawthorn Ridge 2.
1546 Pte William C. Pennell	25	Son of Joseph and Martha Pennell of Stephenville Crossing, Bay St. George; Y Ravine.
1399 Pte Augustus Penney	22	Son of Patrick and Helen Penney of Holyrood, Harbour Main; Y Ravine.
665 Pte Josiah H. Penney	26	Son of Josiah and Anna Penney of Carbonear; Memorial Park.
1690 Pte William G. Perran	19	Son of Thomas and Elizabeth Perran of St. John's; Auchonvillers Military Cem.
1535 Pte John Charles Piercey	19	Son of Robert and Patience Piercey of Bay Bull's Arm, Trinity Bay; Y Ravine.

898 L/Cpl. George Edward Pike	33	Son of Nathaniel and Emma Pike of Grand Falls; Y Ravine.
1220 Pte James Joseph Pike	19	Son of Joseph and Winifred Pike of Avondale, Harbour Main, Newfoundland; Memorial Park.
1589 Pte Stanley Stewart Pinsent	21	Son of James and Selena Pinsent of Musgrave Harbour; Knightsbridge.
1158 Pte Stewart Pinsent	28	Son of Samuel and Emma Pinsent of Dildo, Trinity Bay; Memorial Park.
400 Corporal Richard Pitman	28	Son of Robert and Phyllis Pitman of Lamaline; Memorial Park.
1534 Pte Archibald Harold Porter	21	Son of Aaron and Lucy Ann Porter of Change Islands, Fogo; Y Ravine.
896 C.S.M. Robert Branfitt Porter	29	Son of John and Mary Grace Porter of Grand Falls; Memorial Park.
1150 Pte James Matthew Power	19	Son of Martin and Johanna Power of Boston, U.S.A.; Y Ravine.
861 Pte Michael Joseph Quigley	27	Son of Timothy and Margaret Quigley of St. John's; Y Ravine.

671 Sgt. Charles Reid — 30 — Son of George and Jessie Reid of 17 Cook Street, St. John's; Hawthorn Ridge 2.

593 2nd Lieut. Robert Bruce Reid — 21 — Son of Sir William Duff and Lady Reid of "Bartra", Circular Road, St. John's; Memorial Park.

1486 Pte William Joseph Reid — 21 — Son of Arthur and Sarah Elizabeth Reid of 125 New Gower Street, St. John's; Knightsbridge.

204 L/Cpl. Arthur James Rendell — 20 — Son of James and Rebecca Rendell of 16 Kings Road, St. John's; Hawthorn Ridge 2.

1062 Pte John Joseph Rice — 27 — Son of Patrick and Agnes Rice. Husband of Bridget of 17 Fleming Street, St. John's; Memorial Park.

1234 Pte Patrick Richardson — 21 — Son of John and Jane Richardson of St. John's; Memorial Park.

1258 Pte Sydney Rideout — 21 — Son of Ambrose and Elizabeth Rideout of Cottle's Island, Moreton's Harbour; Memorial Park.

355 Pte Edward Joseph Rogers — 19 — Son of Stephen and Katherine Rogers of 34 Flower Hill, St. John's; Memorial Park.

250 Pte Michael Joseph Ross — 19 — Native of Colchester England. Son of James and Margaret Ross of Portugal Cove, St. John's East, Newfoundland; Auchonvillers Military Cem.

1182 2nd Lieut. Robert Wallace Ross — 22 — Son of Hector and Elizabeth Ross of Toronto, Ontario, Canada; Hawthorn Ridge 2.

1538 Pte Matthew Rossiter — 20 — Son of Joseph and Ellen Rossiter of Fermeuse, Ferryland; Memorial Park.

571 L/Cpl. Edward Clayton Rowsell — 24 — Son of Uriah and Sarah Rowsell of 49 Hayward Avenue, St. John's; Memorial Park.

1137 Pte William Russell — 19 — Son of Samuel and Edith Russell of Brooklyn, Bonavista Bay; Knightsbridge.

53 2nd Lieut. William Thomas Ryall — 28 — Son of Robert and Elizabeth Ann Ryall of 40 Hayward Avenue, St. John's; Memorial Park.

133 Cpl. William Joseph Ryan — 25 — Son of William and Catherine Ryan of Southside West, St. John's; Memorial Park.

1392 Pte Thomas Seymour	27	Son of George and Lucy Seymour of Gooseberry Island, Bonavista Bay; Knightsbridge.
1699 L/Cpl. Edwin L. Shave	19	Son of Constable William Henry and Isobel Shave of Fogo; Memorial Park.
1202 Pte Richard M. Short	20	Son of William Miller and Annie Short of New Bonaventure; Memorial Park.
395 Lieut. Richard A. Shortall	25	Son of Richard and Catherine Shortall of Cross Roads, St. John's; Y Ravine.
1217 Pte George Percival Simms	25	Son of Ezriah and Lucy Simms of St. Anthony, St. Barbe; Ancre.
576 Pte Robert Ronald Simms	19	Son of Adam and Mary Ann Simms of St. Anthony, St. Barbe; Memorial Park.
1626 Pte George Stewart Small	19	Son of Robert Jabez and Amelia M. Small of Lewisporte, Notre Dame Bay; Hawthorn Ridge 2.
1677 Pte Josiah Smith	19	Foster son of Matthew Smith of Hopeall, Trinity Bay; Ancre.
1467 Pte Zachariah Smith	23	Son of John Peddle and Mary Ann Smith of Snooks Harbour, Trinity Bay; Memorial Park.

895 Pte John Charles Snelgrove	24	Son of Samuel and Annie Snelgrove of St. John's; Memorial Park.
1021 Pte Douglas K. Snow	19	Son of Charles and Patience Snow of 6 Mullock Street, St. John's; Y Ravine.
685 L/Cpl. Frederick E. Snow, M.M.	21	Son of George and Dinah Snow of 116 Pleasant Street, St. John's; Memorial Park.
1923 Pte John S. Snow	20	Son of Robert and Margaret Snow of Harbour Grace, Conception Bay; Hawthorn Ridge 2.
253 Pte George Joseph Sparkes	19	Son of George and Annie Sparkes of Bell Island; Memorial Park.
979 L/Cpl. Frank J. Spurrell	21	Son of Mr. and Mrs. John Spurrell of Wickford Street, St. John's; Memorial Park.
494 Pte Harry Groves Strathie	23	Son of Ronald and Mary Strathie of Bonavista; Memorial Park.
1522 L/Cpl. Norman Wheatley Strong	20	Son of James and Lydia Strong of Little Bay Islands, Twillingate; Memorial Park.
897 Pte Alfred Penny Taylor	22	Son of G. Hedley and Dorcas Gay Taylor of St. John's; Memorial Park.

293 Pte Charles F. Taylor	23	Son of Leonard I. and Susan M. Taylor of South Side, St. John's; Y Ravine.
28 2nd Lieut. George Hayward Taylor	24	Son of Eugene F. and Mary Taylor of 5 Maxse Street, St. John's; Memorial Park.
1018 Cpl. Herbert Taylor	20	Son of Herbert and Margaret Taylor of 152 Casey Street, St. John's; Knightsbridge.
1236 Pte Donald Templeman	23	Son of Philip and Catherine Templeman of Water Street, St. John's; Ancre.
399 Pte Michael Francis Walsh	25	Son of Patrick and Catherine Walsh of Placentia; Memorial Park.
964 Pte Garland Warford	22	Son of William and Susannah Warford of Upper Gullies, Conception Bay; Y Ravine.
1426 Pte Robert James Watkins	26	Son of Ephraim J. and Jane Watkins of Botwood, Twillingate; Memorial Park.
1460 Pte Stanley West	23	Son of Joseph and Sarah West of 4 John Street, Halifax, Nova Scotia; Memorial Park.
1805 L/Cpl. Harry T. Westcott	23	Son of Henry and Margaret Westcott of Catalina, Trinity Bay; Memorial Park.

1395 Pte Augustus Patrick Whalen — 22 — Son of John and Hanna Whalen of 18 Boncloddy Street, St. John's; Ancre.

1481 Pte Frederick White — 24 — Son of Edward and Sarah White of Durrell's Arm, Twillingate; Memorial Park.

345 Pte William White — 26 — Son of Levi and Alice White of Loon Bay, Notre Dame Bay; Y Ravine.

1632 Pte William Arthur White — 21 — Son of Mr. and Mrs. John White of Rattling Brook, Notre Dame Bay; Memorial Park.

739 Pte Willis White — 20 — Son of C.S. and Sarah White; Memorial Park.

707 Pte Frederick Wilcox — 27 — Son of John M. and Mary Wilcox of 823 St. Catherine Street West, Montreal, Canada. (Native of Brigus, Newfoundland); Knightsbridge.

1115 Pte Robert John Williams — 21 — Son of Harry and Emma Williams of 50 Cabot Street, St. John's; Knightsbridge.

1845 Pte George Winsor — 18 — Son of David and Annie Louisa Winsor of Wesleyville, Bonavista Bay; Memorial Park (also headstone in Serre Road No. 2)

675 Pte Edward Rozier Winter	18	Son of Thomas and Florence Winter of St. John's (Served at Gallipoli and in Egypt); Ancre.
908 L/Cpl. Randolph Milligan Winter	29	Son of John and Adelaide Winter of Burin North; Memorial Park.
364 Pte Francis Patrick Woodford	24	Son of Joseph and Sarah Woodford of 7 Convent Square, St. John's; Ancre.
1627 Pte Kenneth Berkley Woodman	22	Son of Edward and Susanna Woodman of New Harbour, Trinity Bay; Memorial Park.

APPENDIX 6

ROLL OF HONOUR

Details and resting-places of men of the Newfoundland Regiment who were wounded on the 1st July, 1916, and who died later of these wounds. The actual date of death is in brackets.

1504 Alexander, L/Cpl. Walter Ernest 24 (5th July 1916) Son of Robert & Annie Alexander of Hollyhill, Norwich, England; Beauval Communal Cemetery.

808 Broderick, Pte. Michael 27 (3rd July 1916) Son of Patrick & Catherine Broderick of St. Brendan's, Newfoundland; Gezaincourt Communal Cemetery Extension.

966 Cahill, Pte. John Joseph 36 (5th July 1916) Son of Joseph & Mary Cahill of St. John's, Newfoundland; Achiet-le-Grand Communal Cemetery Extension.

198 Carter, L/Cpl. Llewelyn James 21 (2nd July 1916) Son of William & Martha Carter of Channel, Newfoundland; Doullens Communal Cemetery Extension No. 1.

1249 Courage, Pte. Harrison 23 (12th July 1916) Son of George & Eliza Courage of Catalina, Newfoundland; Ste Marie Cemetery, Le Havre.

1405 Crane, Pte. Henry Charles   29   (2nd July 1916) Son of John & Susanna Crane of Island Cove Rd., Harbour Grace, Newfoundland; Doullens Communal Cemetery Extension No. 1.

1447 Crosbie, Pte. George Graham   17   (3rd July 1916) Son of Walter & Mary Crosbie of Bay Roberts, Newfoundland; St. Sever Cemetery, Rouen.

924 Dick, Sgt. G.   27   (12th July 1916) Son of John & Anna Dick of Netherall, Largs; Largs Cemetery, Ayrshire, Scotland.

1764 Eagan, Pte. Patrick   28   (2nd July 1916) Son of Patrick & Brigid Eagan of Keels, Bonavista Bay, Newfoundland; Auchonvillers Military Cemetery.

1251 Edgecombe, Pte. Silas   (11th July 1916) Son of Edward & Janet Edgecombe of Ochre Pit Cove, Bay de Verde, Newfoundland; Wandsworth Cemetery, London.

450 Edwards, Pte. John Charles   24   (21st July 1916) Son of Joseph & Clara Edwards of Grand Falls, Newfoundland; Wandsworth Cemetery, London.

1580 Gardner, Pte. Theophilus

22

(11th July 1916) Son of Thomas William & Eugenie Gardner of British Harbour, Trinity Bay, Newfoundland; Gezaincourt Communal Cemetery Extension.

Grant, 2nd Lt. William Hayes

25

(16th July 1916) Son of Jas. William & Julia Hayes McMillan of Bridgeville, Nova Scotia, Canada; Auchonvillers Military Cemetery.

843 Heale, Pte R.W.

(3rd July 1916) Son of Wm. Heale, 41 Forest Road, St. John's, Nfld.; Louvencourt Military Cemetery.

756 Higgins, Sgt. Edmund James

(2nd July 1916) Son of James & Margaret Higgins of Military Rd., St. John's, Newfoundland; Beauval Communal Cemetery.

1689 Hudson, Pte. Peter

18

(4th July 1916) Son of James & Bride Hudson of Mullock St., St. John's, Newfoundland; Gezaincourt Communal Cemetery Extension.

697 Jackman, Pte. Bert

27

(5th July 1916) Son of Capt. Francis Jackman & Ellen Jackman of 33 Angel Place, St. John's, Newfoundland; Etretat Churchyard.

1881 King, Pte. Alexander — 24 — (4th September 1916) Son of Willis P. & Sarah Jane King of Western Bay, Newfoundland; Etaples Military Cemetery.

1124 Lannigan, Pte. James Joseph — 20 — (8th August 1916) Son of John & Minnie Lannigan of 38 Codner's Lane, St. John's, Newfoundland; Ste Marie Cemetery, Le Havre.

1620 Learning, Pte. Samuel John — 20 — (4th July 1916) Son of Absalom Joseph & Carrie Learning of St. John's, Newfoundland; Doullens Communal Cemetery Extension No. 1.

1362 LeBuff, Cpl. Robert — 25 — (11th August 1916) Son of Richard & Eliza LeBuff of Restigouche, Quebec, Canada; Wandsworth Cemetery, London.

572 Mackay, Pte. Andrew Joseph — 18 — (13th July 1916) Son of John & Mary Mackay of St. John's, Newfoundland; Wimereux Communal Cemetery.

411 McNeill, Pte. Donald Fraser — 20 — (6th July 1916) Son of James & Fannie McNeill of St. John's, Newfoundland; Doullens Communal Cemetery Extension No. 1.

487 Newman, Pte. Archibald Mark 26 (3rd July 1916) Son of Henry & Edith Newman of Twillingate, Newfoundland; Gezaincourt Communal Cemetery Extension.

306 Osmond, L/Cpl. Douglas McNeill 26 (8th July 1916) Son of J.B. & Margaret A. Osmond of Moreton's Harbour, Notre Dame Bay, Newfoundland; Gezaincourt Communal Cemetery Extension.

1656 Peckford, Pte. Edward 20 (29th August 1916) Son of Eli & Elizabeth Peckford of Change Islands, Newfoundland; Wandsworth Cemetery, London.

1235 Pike, L/Cpl. Stanley Gordon 25 (10 August 1916) Son of Mr. & Mrs. William S. Pike of 61 Hayward Avenue, St. John's, Newfoundland; Wandsworth Cemetery, London.

925 Prowse, Pte. William Patrick 23 (18th July 1916) Son of Charles & Catherine Prowse of St. John's, Newfoundland; Etretat Churchyard.

Rendell, 2nd Lt. Clifford 21 (22nd July 1916) Son of Herbert & Lizzie Rendell of St. John's, Newfoundland; Etaples Military Cemetery.

Rowsell, 2nd Lt. H. John R. — 21 — (8th July 1916) Son of John & Lydia Rowsell of Bonavista, Newfoundland; Abbeville Communal Cemetery.

Steele, Lt. Owen William — 29 — (8th July 1916) Eldest son of Samuel Owen & Sarah Blanche Steele of "Avalonia", Kingskerswell, Newton Abbott, England; Mailly-Maillet Communal Cemetery Extension.

1669 Stuckless, Pte. Silas — 26 — (18th July 1916) Son of Isaac & Caroline Stuckless of Norris Arm, Lewisporte, Newfoundland; Bristol (Arno's Vale) Cemetery, England.

Summers, Capt. Michael Francis — 26 — (19th July 1916) Son of Michael & Catherine Summers of 330 Water Street, St. John's, Newfoundland; Gezaincourt Communal Cemetery Extension.

722 Thomas Pte. Walter — 27 — (15th July 1916) Son of Charles Henry & Isabel Thomas of New Glasgow, Nova Scotia, Canada; Birmingham (Lodge Hill) Cemetery, England.

1680 Wheeler, Pte. Frederick — 19 — (10th July 1916) Son of Aaron & Mrs. M. Wheeler of Tizzard's Harbour, Newfoundland; St. Sever Cemetery, Rouen.

1117 Whitten, Pte. Edgar Charles 23 (16th July 1916) Son of George Charles & Margaret Jane Whitten of St. John's, Newfoundland; Auchonvillers Military Cemetery.

1035 Young, Pte. Arthur Harold 23 (6th July 1916) Son of Archibald & Cordelia Young of Twillingate, Newfoundland; Beauval Communal Cemetery.

ROLL OF HONOUR

Men of the Newfoundland Regiment who died just previous to 1st July, 1916, or who were killed or died of wounds in the French raid on 28th June. Date of actual death is in brackets.

700 Bastow, Pte. Frederick Donald
(12th October 1916)* Son of Augustus & Margaret Bastow of Barters Hill, St. John's, Newfoundland; Wandsworth Cemetery, London.

195 Cole, Pte. Edward Louis
18
(28th June 1916) Son of Edward James & Fanny Jane Cole of Gilbert Street, St. John's, Newfoundland; Beaumont Hamel (Newfoundland) Memorial.

1519 Lannon, Pte. William Joseph
23
(18th June 1916) Son of Patrick & Johanna Lannon of St. John's, Newfoundland; Beauval Communal Cemetery.

547 Lukins, Pte. John
(28th June 1916) Son of Frederick & Joanna Lukins. Husband of Mary Campbell (formerly Lukins) of 99 New Gower Street, St. John's, Newfoundland; Beaumont Hamel (Newfoundland) Memorial.

177 Manning, Sgt. Augustus J.   22   (1st June 1916) Son of James & Elizabeth Manning of St. John's, Newfoundland; Auchonvillers Military Cemetery.

1326 Stride, Pte. Ambrose William   24   (19th June 1916) Son of James & Philapina Stride of Moreton's Harbour, Notre Dame Bay, Newfoundland; Beauval Communal Cemetery.

1588 West, Pte. Edward   28th June 1916) Son of Mrs. Rose Shelley of Aspey Cove, Fogo, Newfoundland; Beaumont Hamel (Newfoundland) Memorial.

944 Wight, Pte. Arthur   26   (28th June 1916) Son of Samuel & Annie Wight of Shoal Brook, Bonne Bay, Newfoundland; Beaumont Hamel (Newfoundland) Memorial.

* Died of wounds received before 1st July 1916.

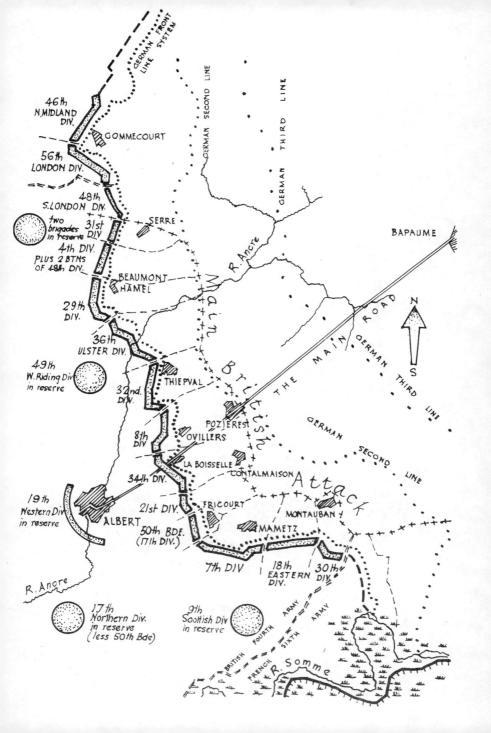

GERMAN FRONT LINE SYSTEM

46th N.MIDLAND DIV.

GOMMECOURT

56th LONDON DIV.

GERMAN SECOND LINE

GERMAN THIRD LINE

48th S.LONDON DIV.

two brigades in reserve

31st DIV.

SERRE

4th DIV. PLUS 2 BTNS OF 48th DIV.

BEAUMONT HAMEL

R. Ancre

BAPAUME

N
S

29th DIV.

36th ULSTER DIV.

49th W.Riding Div. in reserve

THIEPVAL

32nd. DIV.

Main British

POZIERES

THE MAIN ROAD

GERMAN THIRD LINE

8th DIV.

OVILLERS

LA BOISSELLE

CONTALMAISON

GERMAN SECOND LINE

34th DIV.

19th Western Div. in reserve

ALBERT

21st DIV.

50th BDE. (17th DIV.)

FRICOURT

MAMETZ

Attack

MONTAUBAN

R. Ancre

17th Northern Div. in reserve (less 50th Bde)

7th DIV

18th EASTERN DIV.

30th DIV.

9th Scottish Div. in reserve

BRITISH FOURTH ARMY

FRENCH SIXTH ARMY

R. Somme

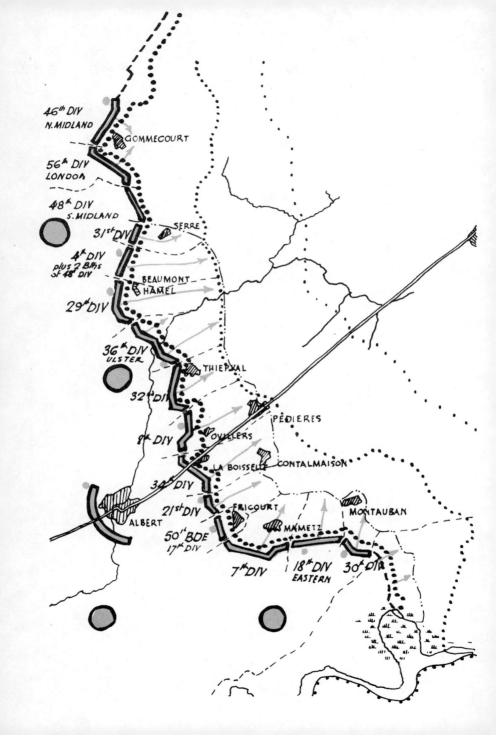

46th DIV
N. MIDLAND

GOMMECOURT

56th DIV
LONDON

48th DIV
S. MIDLAND

31st DIV

SERRE

4th DIV
plus 2 Bns
of 48 DIV

BEAUMONT
HAMEL

29th DIV

36th DIV
ULSTER

THIEPVAL

32nd DIV

PÉDIERES

8th DIV

OVILLERS

LA BOISSELLE

CONTALMAISON

3rd DIV

ALBERT

21st DIV

FRICOURT

MONTAUBAN

50th BDE
17th DIV

MAMETZ

30th DIV

7th DIV

18th DIV
EASTERN

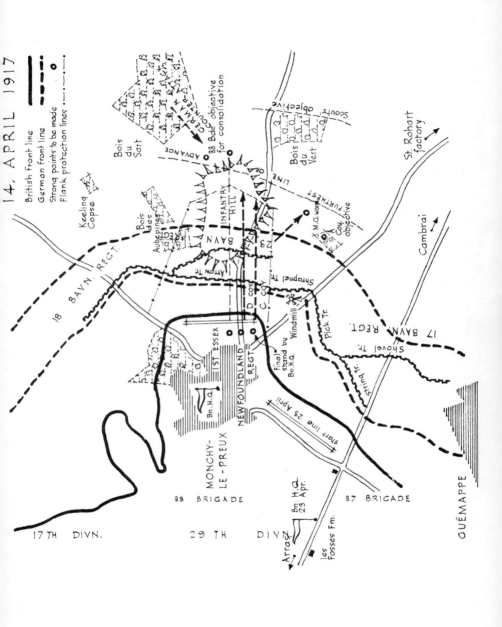

14. APRIL 1917

British front line
German front line
Strong points to be made
Flank protection lines

Bois du Sart

Keeling Copse

88 Bde objective for consolidation

Bois des Aubépines

Scouts' objective

GERMAN COUNTER-ADVANCE

Bois du Vert

St. Rohart factory

INFANTRY HILL

LINE OF FURTHEST ADVANCE

1ST ESSEX REGT.

BAVN.

23 BAVN.

Arrow Tr.

Cav. objective

M.G. nest

18 BAVN. REGT.

Sharpnel Tr.

Windmill

D coy

C coy

Pick Tr.

Cambrai

Bn.H.Q.

NEWFOUNDLAND REGT.

Final stand by Bn.H.Q.

String Tr.

Shovel Tr.

17 BAVN. REGT.

MONCHY-LE-PREUX

Start line 23 April

88 BRIGADE

Bn. H.Q. 23 Apr.

87 BRIGADE

GUÉMAPPE

17TH DIVN.

29TH DIVN.

Arras

les Fosses Fm.